The authors examine the crucial period of second-century Christianity from the death of St. John to the earliest Apologists. They describe the propagation of Christianity, the persecutions under the Flavians and the Antonines, the Apostolic Fathers and their times, ecclesiastical organizations, and the various churches of the East and West. An excellent survey of Christian life is provided through discussions of Christian practices and social life, martyrdom, pagan hostility, and the origin and development of the catacombs and their works of art.

This is the second volume in *A History of the Early Church*. It is a complete work in itself, and may be read independently of the others in the series. Although primarily written for the Catholic reader and scholar, it will prove equally valuable for others interested in the early history and theology of the Church.

Other Volumes in This Collier Series

The Church in the New Testament (BS77V)
Heresy and Orthodoxy (BS79V)
The Triumph of Christianity (BS80V

JULES LEBRETON, S.J.
AND JACQUES ZEILLER

Translated from the French by
ERNEST C. MESSENGER, Ph.D.

THE

OF THE

EMERGENCE CHURCH IN THE ROMAN WORLD

Book II of
A History of the Early Church

With a Foreword by
AUGUSTIN FLICHE AND
MGR. VICTOR MARTIN

COLLIER BOOKS
NEW YORK, N.Y.

This volume originally appeared, under the section title of *From the Death of St. John to the End of the Second Century,* as Book II, Volume I of *The History of the Primitive Church,* which general title has here been changed to *A History of the Early Church*

This Collier Books edition is published by arrangement with The Macmillan Company

Collier Books is a division of The Crowell-Collier Publishing Company

First Collier Books Edition 1962

NIHIL OBSTAT:
REGINALDUS PHILLIPS, S.T.L.
 Censor deputatus
IMPRIMATUR
E. MORROGH BERNARD
 Vic. Gen.
WESTMONASTERII
die 28a Juli, 1944

9-86

Library of Congress Catalog Card Number: A62–8270

gift
S.H.

Foreword

By the General Editors

OF ALL THE BRANCHES of history, there is scarcely one which has made so much progress in the last half century as ecclesiastical history. Its growth has been favoured by a combination of favourable circumstances: the opening of the Vatican archives to all students by Pope Leo XIII, the creation at Rome, by various nations, of institutes for the study of archives or inscriptions, the founding almost everywhere of scientific societies dealing more especially with religious history, the development of auxiliary sciences, the publication of collections and catalogues which make easier the utilising of texts, the extension of historical studies in theology and canon law. Though much still remains to be done, it cannot be denied that important results have been obtained. In addition, besides the manifold works of scholarship which have elucidated or at least thrown light on so many obscure problems, great syntheses have been attempted, dealing with some special period, or the religious activity in a particular country in the East or West, or again a group of ecclesiastical institutions at a particular time. Lastly, some writers have endeavoured to give a general survey of the chief results obtained by contemporary scholarship, and to trace out, with more or less detail, the general history of the Church.

Among the last mentioned works, there are some which are deserving of all praise, and which have rendered real service. At the same time they have been criticised as being too condensed, or as not giving sufficiently numerous references, or more often, as not possessing the same scientific value in their various parts. Those who wrote them were qualified, by their personal researches, to deal with one period of ecclesiastical history; they could not be equally competent in others, and in spite of praiseworthy efforts, they have sometimes encountered obstacles which it was very difficult for them to overcome.

In fact, it seems clear at the present time that, in view of the ever increasing number of books and articles appearing in all languages, one can cannot himself write a history of the Church from its most remote beginnings to the present day.

5

In contrast to what has happened in the domain of ecclesiastical history, the recent universal histories in course of publication, such as the *Histoire Générale* of G. Glotz, *Peuples et civilisations* by L. Halphen and C. Sagnac, *Histoire du monde* by E. Cavaignac, are collective works produced by groups of specialists who have been entrusted with one or two volumes at most, and hence they are of high scientific value.

We have decided to adopt a similar method here. The present work differs from the general histories of the Church which have preceded it, first in its size, for it will consist of no less than twenty-four double volumes, but still more because it will not be the work of one single historian or of a few collaborators.

More than thirty writers from various parts of Europe have agreed to take part in its production. Whether they belong to the laity or to the clergy, secular or regular, whether they be professors at Universities or State schools, in Catholic faculties, in seminaries, or Universities outside France, they are all men of learning and competence: some have already produced works which do honour to French scholarship; others who are younger have shown on many occasions that they are quite worthy of our hopes, and that it would not be rash to confide to them, along with their elders, a task for which they are certainly well prepared.

Thus we have been able, as in the already mentioned general histories, to entrust the various periods of Church history to specialists possessing a deep personal knowledge of the matters in question, and very capable of drawing from the works of scholarship which have already appeared the conclusions which must be accepted, and also of filling up, if necessary, the gaps which still exist.

This History of the Church from its origins to our own time, which begins with the present four books, aims above all at bringing fully to the light the general results acquired by the various researches in ecclesiastical history during recent years, and to put them at the disposition of all those who for various reasons desire to attain them in a speedy and easy way.

It is intended more particularly for students who, for purposes of their studies, require certain knowledge drawn from the best sources; for general readers desirous of instruction or of enlightenment, or to correct false statements; and lastly for workers of all kinds who, before specialising in the study of one subject, desire to envisage this in the framework of general history, in order not to go astray, and to avoid dangerous misinterpretations.

To all it will present an accurate statement, based on a critical knowledge of earlier works, or, where such do not exist, of the original sources, and it will, according to the case, be capable of satisfying all legitimate curiosity, or of giving direction for personal research.

From this general idea of the work there follow its distinctive characteristics.

Since it is a matter above all of initiation and of accurate statement, the various readers of this History of the Church should not only have at their disposition an accurate account of events, but should also be able constantly to refer to the works which have inspired it. Hence, besides the General Bibliography at the end of the different volumes, each chapter will be preceded by a list of articles and works indispensable for anyone who wants to study more deeply the matters there treated. From these bibliographies we have deliberately eliminated works which are not altogether scientific in character, and retained exclusively those which may rightly be regarded as definitive, or at least as making an important contribution to the subject. Moreover, we have thus avoided recommending undeservedly those books and articles which so heavily encumber the literature of ecclesiastical history, and which for reasons which are not at all scientific, only too often give a wrong idea of the true character of the facts.

The text itself will be always accompanied by indispensable references. Original sources will be indicated wherever this seems necessary, but generally the reader will be referred to the most recent scientific works in which he will find these sources indicated. When dealing with questions which have given rise to diverse or contradictory opinions, we shall indicate briefly the reasons why one view has been adopted rather than another; at the same time, when the arguments in favour of the thesis enunciated have been set forth in a conclusive form in some book or article, we shall content ourselves with a reference to this. In every case, in one form or another, every affirmation, of whatsoever nature, will be justified, and the means of controlling it will be freely put at the disposition of all.

The same scientific preoccupations will inspire the utilisation of the materials thus tested and presented to the reader. We shall endeavour to banish personal considerations which prove nothing, and to give a picture as exact and complete as possible of the different forms of ecclesiastical activity through the ages, leaving aside no essential aspect. The fault of some publications similar to the present one is the almost exclusive consideration of what we may call the *external* history of the Church, that is to say, of its relations with States and with organised societies. Without wishing to sacrifice this aspect, we think it would be regrettable to relegate to the background, as is too often done, the *internal* activity of Catholicism which has enabled it to radiate its light, and to spread its influence through all the spheres of the lives of nations as well as of individuals. Everything is interconnected in the life of the Church through the ages, and if we want to discover its deep significance, we must endeavour to grasp the bond which exists at all times between the dogmatic conceptions and canonical rules on the one hand, and the social, political and economic structure on the other.

Accordingly, no source of information will be neglected. At the present time, scholars who are dealing with the history of the Church are not content to utilise literary and diplomatic documents, but direct their investigations more and more towards theology, canon law, and works of controversy, in which can often be found the explanation of events and of the direction these have taken. General history should profit by this orientation: it will thus be able to view facts from the correct angle, to grasp their real causes, establish the relations which unite them to the theological or canonical conceptions of a particular epoch, and thereby give them a wide and exact interpretation.

We may be allowed to hope that in this way there will appear in its full light the extraordinary universality of the Church's influence through the ages. Need we add that in order to arrive at a more complete and more solidly established historical truth, those who are collaborating in this work have decided to fulfil all the requirements of modern methods? Thirty-five years ago, the Chanoine Cauchie wrote in the first number of the *Revue d'histoire ecclésiastique*[1]: "Every Christian who is loyal to his faith accepts the government of the world by Providence, but this does not prevent

[1] *Revue d'histoire ecclésiastique*, Vol. I, 1900, p. 141.

him from studying scientifically the action of second causes."
The distinguished Louvain professor in writing these lines
was but echoing the desire often expressed by Pope Leo
XIII, who wanted to see a universal Church History brought
into line with the progress of modern critical research.

The present work has no object other than that set forth
by the Pontiff who did so much for the development of historical studies. Aiming as it does at being really scientific and
synthetic, dealing equally with all the periods and all the
forms of ecclesiastical activity, we trust that it will, thanks
to the collaboration of historians all inspired by the same
ideal, realise the programme laid down, to the greatest possible satisfaction of all.

Translator's Preface

THE VOLUME here presented to the English reader constitutes the second of a massive series of twenty-four volumes designed to cover the whole History of the Church from its beginning down to our own time. The General Editors, Monsieur Augustin Fliche, the Dean of the Faculty of Letters at Montpellier, and Mgr. Victor Martin, Dean of the Faculty of Catholic Theology at Strasburg, have entrusted each volume in the series to one or more specialists, thus ensuring that the whole work will have the highest scientific value. The present volumes, on the Early Church, are from the pen of Père Lebreton, Dean of the Faculty of Theology at the Institut Catholique in Paris, and Monsieur Jacques Zeiller, Director of Studies at the Ecole des Hautes Etudes (Sorbonne). Their work needs no further commendation than the mention of their names.

As to the work of translation, I have adhered to the original as faithfully as possible. Here and there I have added to the footnotes, or substituted references to English translations in the case of certain well-known works. Citations from Scripture are in the main quoted according to the version in common use amongst English Catholics, but I have not hesitated to modify this where the quotation is intended to express a sense not well brought out in the current text. For quotations from the Fathers and other ecclesiastical writers, I have followed the excellent versions given in the French, with an occasional glance at the original, or standard English translations.

I owe a debt of gratitude to my friend and former colleague, the Very Rev. Mgr. John M. Barton, D.D., Consultor to the Pontifical Biblical Commission, for so kindly reading through my translation, and for making many valuable suggestions, especially in matters of bibliographical detail.

It only remains for me to express the honour I feel it to be associated with a work of this kind, and my hope that it will be found possible to present the whole work to English readers as the several volumes appear.

ERNEST C. MESSENGER

Contents

**The Emergence of the Church
in the Roman World**

Chapter 1

Christian Life at the End of
The First Century[1]

§1. CHRISTIAN LIFE AND WORSHIP

REJECTED BY THE SYNAGOGUE and persecuted by the Roman Empire, the Church nevertheless developed an intense interior life. From the first, this life calls for the admiration of the historian by reason of its overflowing plenitude, but precisely because of its richness it seems to defy all description. Attempts have been made to grasp this exuberance by describing successively the various aspects of the new-born Christianity. In this way, Harnack, in his *Mission and Expansion of Christianity,* has studied, in a series of chapters, the Gospel of Love and Charity, the religion of the Spirit and of Power, of Moral Earnestness and Holiness, the Religion of Authority and of Reason, of the Mysteries and of Transcendentalism, the Tidings of the New People, the Religion of a Book and a Historical Realisation, the Conflict with Polytheism and Idolatry.[2] All these developments are of interest, and bring into the light some characteristics of primitive Christianity. However, as we are not able here to enter into detail, we would prefer to study the principle of unity from which all the rest proceeds. We know that Harnack, in his *Essence of Christianity,* thought he could trace everything back to the religion of God the Father. It seems to us that, during the apostolic period, Christianity is above all the religion of the Christ.[3] This may seem a truism, but nevertheless

[1] Bibliography. P. Batiffol, *L'Eglise naissante et le catholicisme,* 9th edn., Paris 1927 (English tr.: *Primitive Catholicism,* London, 1911); J. Lebreton, *La vie chrétienne au premier siècle de l'Eglise,* Paris, 1927; E. Amann, *L'Eglise des premiers siècles,* Paris, 1927; Dom Cabrol, *La prière des premiers chrétiens,* Paris, 1929; G. Bardy, *L'Eglise à la fin du premier siècle,* Paris, 1932.

[2] All these chapters form Book II of *Mission und Ausbreitung,* pp. 111-331.

[3] This does not mean that the emphasis on Christ caused the Father to be forgotten; quite the contrary. Hence we are entirely opposed to the extreme thesis of A. C. MacGiffert, *The God of the Early Christians,* New York, 1924.

it deserves to be considered attentively: it is indeed the distinctive character of this religion, and the secret of its power.

The Religion of the Christ

Already in the early days at Jerusalem, the conflict centred round this point. The Sanhedrin forbade the apostles to preach in the name of Jesus; Peter replied that there was no other saving name. Later on, when the procurator Festus wished to inform King Agrippa as to the case against St. Paul, he told him that it concerned "one Jesus deceased, whom Paul affirmed to be alive" (*Acts* xxv, 19). Tacitus himself, whose information is limited, nevertheless speaks correctly when he thus defines Christianity: "He who gave His name to this sect, the Christ, was put to death. . . ."; and Suetonius in turn, speaking of the Edict of Claudius, expresses himself thus: "The Jews caused disturbances, under the impulse of a certain Chrestus."

And what the earliest adversaries perceived appears clearly in the first Christian preaching: "God has made him Lord and Christ"; "He raised him up": that is what Peter affirmed from the first days at Jerusalem, Paul at Antioch in Pisidia, at Athens and everywhere else. Doubtless, when he was preaching to pagans, the apostle had first of all to preach to them the One God and to draw them away from their idols; but he at once went on to Christ, to His resurrection, and to His second coming, even at the risk of being abandoned by his sceptical hearers.

At the same time that Christ is the central object of faith, He is also the Saviour in whom every man must hope. The prize which the apostles set forth constantly to those they wish to win is the forgiveness of sins and salvation through Christ. Such is the theme of St. Peter's sermon on Pentecost day (*Acts* ii, 38), and in his speeches on his two appearances before the Sanhedrin (*ibid.*, iv, 12; v, 31); it is also the theme of St. Paul's homily at Antioch in Pisidia (xiii, 38). This is the echo of the appeal which Jesus himself made to his hearers, and through them, to all men: "Come to me, all you that labour, and are burdened, and I will refresh you" (*Matt.* xi, 28). Later on Celsus will write with indignation: "Those who endeavour to win followers for the other mysteries, say: 'Let him whose hands are pure . . . enter here!' . . . But we hear these people on the contrary cry: 'Whosoever is a sinner, foolish, simple or miserable, will receive the kingdom of God.' " [4]

Those who have thus been won and redeemed belong no longer to themselves; they belong to the Lord:

> "None of us liveth to himself, and no man dieth to himself. For whether we live, we live unto the Lord; or whether we die, we die unto the Lord. Therefore, whether we live or whether we die, we are the Lord's. For to this end Christ died and rose again; that he might be Lord both of the dead and of the living" (*Rom.* xiv, 7-9).
>
> "You are not your own, for you are bought with a great price" (*I Cor.* vi, 19-20).[5]

Christianity is not only a new condition of life: it is a new life. By baptism, Christians are buried with Christ in death, and raised again with him to life.[6] And they do not rise again as isolated individuals, but as members of the body of Christ, the Church: "We were all baptised into one body, whether Jews or Gentiles, whether bond or free." [7] And this life-giving primacy of Christ extends not only to the Church which He sanctifies, but also to the whole world of which He is the Ruler and the Head:

> "All things were created by him and in him. And he is before all, and by him all things consist. And he is the head of the body, the Church, who is the beginning, the first-born from the dead; that in all things he may hold the primacy, because in him, it hath well pleased the Father that all fulness should dwell, and through him to reconcile all things unto himself, making peace through the blood of

[4] Quoted by Origen, III, 59.
[5] To make his thought better understood, St. Paul employs the very terms used to signify sacred manumissions: just as the slaves who wished to put their newly acquired liberty under the patronage of a god had to be purchased by him by a fictitious sale, so also, but this time in reality, the Christian has been redeemed by Christ to be free: *I Cor.* vii, 23; *Gal.* v, 1-19. Cf. *Histoire du Dogme de la Trinité,* I, p. 406.
[6] *Rom.* vi, 3-11; *Col.* ii, 12; 111, 4.
[7] *I Cor.* xii, 13; cf. xii, 27; *Rom.* xii, 5; *Col.* i, 18; iii, 15; *Ephes.* iv, 4.

his cross, both as to the things that are on earth, and the
things that are in heaven" (*Col.* i, 16-20).

All this is not mere speculation, for it governs the whole
of the Christian life. The Church is the body of Christ; all
its functions are produced in it by the action of the Head
who dispenses its life (*Ephes.* iv, 11-16). The sacraments are
set forth only in this light: baptism is the burial and resurrection with Christ; marriage is a union representing that of
Christ and the Church (*Ephes.* v, 25-32); the Eucharist
above all, which is the centre of all worship and the indispensable food of the Christian, is the representation of the
death of the Lord, the participation of his body, the communion in his blood.[8]

Moral exhortations are inspired by this ever-present
thought: we must flee fornication because our bodies are the
members of Christ (*I Cor.* vi, 15); we must be generous,
after the example of Christ, who being rich became poor (*II
Cor.* viii, 9); we must forget ourselves in order to imitate
Jesus Christ, who being in the form of God humbled himself
and took the form of a slave (*Phil.* ii, 6-7); husbands must
love their wives as Christ loved the Church (*Ephes.* v, 25);
servants must be obedient to their masters as to Christ (*ibid.*,
vi, 5). This constant reference to the highest mysteries in
order to inculcate upon Christians fidelity to their duties, even
the most humble ones, fills the whole of life with the memory of Christ and of His love.

These are a few of the very numerous features in which
St. Paul's theology reveals the ineffaceable impress with which
Christ had marked the apostle's life: "for me, to live is
Christ" (*Phil.* i, 21).

The same impress is found in the other apostles, as for instance in this text of St. Peter, quoted already in the early
years of the second century by St. Polycarp:[9] "Jesus Christ,
whom having not seen, you love; in whom also now, though
you see him not, you believe: and believing shall rejoice with
joy unspeakable and glorified, receiving the end of your faith,
even the salvation of your souls" (*I Pet.* i, 8-9). And further
on: "Desire the rational milk without guile, that thereby you
may grow unto salvation: if so be you have tasted that the

---

[8] *I Cor.* x, 16-17; xi, 26-27.
[9] Letter to the Philippians, i, 3.

Lord is sweet. Unto whom coming, as to a living stone, rejected indeed by men, but chosen and made honourable by God" (ii, 2-4). And yet again: "Christ suffered for us, leaving you an example that you should follow his steps." [10]

We find the same note in the Johannine literature, the epistles [11] and the *Apocalypse;* Christians are the servants of Jesus (i, 1; xii, 20); the martyrs are the witnesses of Jesus (ii, 13); the closing sentence is the suppliant cry of the Church: "Amen. Come, Lord Jesus!" (xxii, 20).

This last prayer brings home to us what it was that the Christians desired when they awaited the Second Coming with such impatience: admittedly it was the triumph and coming of the Kingdom, but above all it was the coming and the definitive presence of the Son of God. Thus we read in the first letter to the Thessalonians (iv, 16): "So shall we be always with the Lord." Later on, when this perspective of the Second Coming was less prominent in the apostle's mind, the desire to be with Christ remained as active as ever (*Phil.* i, 23).

All this is clear, and yet too often it is overlooked. Thus, in the question of virginity, the apostle's counsels are manifestly inspired by the desire to belong wholly to the Lord without other cares: "He that is without a wife, is solicitous for the things that belong to the Lord, how he may please God. But he that is with a wife, is solicitous for the things of the world, how he may please his wife, and he is divided" (*I Cor.* vii, 32-33). Accordingly numerous Protestant critics are wrong when they explain this counsel of the apostle as due solely to the expectation of an imminent Second Coming.[12]

[10] ii, 21; cf. iii, 18; iv, 1, 13, 14.
[11] It is sufficient to recall the commencement of the first epistle, i, 1-4.
[12] Thus Sabatier, *L'apôtre Paul,* p. 160: "On one single point the judgment of the apostle seems still narrow: I refer to celibacy. This narrowness, for which he has been so much reproached, does not at all arise from a dualistic asceticism. . . . What narrows and confines the apostle's judgment here are his eschatological opinions. The Second Coming is imminent; the time is short; all other interests disappear before this immediate future. But very soon there is a progress in this respect in Paul's thought. He succeeds in freeing himself from the narrow bonds of Jewish eschatology; in the epistles of the Captivity we shall see that he arrives at a

The Sacraments

The spiritual life is not purely individual; it is the life of members of the Body of Christ which is the Church. The latter is likewise not purely spiritual: it is maintained and expressed by material symbols. The old Protestant thesis which rejected the sacraments as late corruptions has been definitely condemned by history.[13] It is true that sacramental theology has escaped the attacks of the Reformed theologians only to be a prey to the hypotheses of the historians of Comparative Religion. These new opponents recognise that the apostolic theology is wholly penetrated with the sacramental idea, but they see in this penetration a pagan influence which in their view dominated the Church from the beginning.

Catholic historians have continued the fight on this new ground, and nowadays scientific opinion agrees with them, even that of those who do not accept the Catholic faith: these recognise that the sacraments, and in particular, baptism and the Eucharist, which have been specially attacked, cannot, as

---

wider and juster view of marriage and of domestic life." Certainly "the time is short," "the figure of this world passes away," and it is foolish to be too much attached to it; but the decisive motive is the desire to belong exclusively to the Lord.
[13] Let us recall, for instance, what Harnack wrote in *Mission und Ausbreitung*, p. 247: "To regard water, bread, and wine, as holy elements, to plunge into water in order that the soul may be washed and purified, to regard bread and wine as the Body and Blood of Christ, and as a food which confers immortality upon men's souls—this is a language which was well understood at that time. The dull-minded realist understood it, but the most sublime spiritualist did so equally. The two most sublime spiritualists in the Church, John and Origen, became the most powerful exponents of the mysteries, and the great Gnostic theologians linked their most abstract theological theorems to realist mysteries; they were all theologians of sacraments. . . . The phrase of the later scholastics, 'sacramenta continent gratiam,' is as old as the Church of the Gentiles; it is even older than that; it existed long before her." Again, p. 252: "Read the stories concerning the Supper told by Dionysius of Alexandria, a disciple of Origen, or what Cyprian narrates concerning the miracles of the Host. . . . It is objected *Ab initio sic non erat.* That may be so, but one would have to go back very far—so far, in fact, that this very brief period cannot be discovered by us."

was supposed, be explained by the influence of the pagan mysteries, and still less by the Mandæan liturgy.[14]

Baptism

What we have said above concerning the life and teaching of Christ has enabled us to attain to the real origin of the sacraments, and in particular, of baptism and the Eucharist.[15] We saw how Jesus received the baptism of John (*Matt.* iii, 13-17), and that, when He began His public life, baptism was administered by His own disciples,[16] and that after the

[14] On this question, consult L. de Grandmaison, *Les mystères paiens et le Mystère chrétien; Jésus Christ,* Vol. II, pp. 535-561; E. Jacquier, *Les mystères paiens et saint Paul,* in *Dictionnaire apologétique,* Vol. III, col. 964-1014 (on baptism, col. 1004-1008; on the Eucharist, col. 1008-1010); F. Prat, *Saint Paul et le paulinisme,* Vol. III, *Le paulinisme et les religions orientales hellénisées, ibid.,* Vol. III, col. 1047-1051.

The question of baptism has been specially dealt with from this point of view by J. Coppens' article, *Baptême,* in *Supplément* to *Dictionnaire de la Bible, Le baptême et les religions à mystères,* Vol. I, p. 883-886; *Mystères paiens et baptême chrétien,* p. 903-924. This question of the Eucharist is dealt with by W. Goossens in *Les Origines de l'Eucharistie,* Gembloux, 1931, pp. 252-323.

The Mandæan hypothesis has been specially pressed by R. Reitzenstein, *Die Vorgeschichte der christlichen Taufe,* Leipzig, 1929, especially pp. 152-292. This hypothesis has been generally rejected even by the independent critics: cf. H. Lietzmann, *Ein Beitrag zur Mandäerfrage,* in *Sitzungsberichte der Akad. Berlin,* 1930, pp. 596-608; A. Loisy, *Le Mandéisme et les origines chrétiennes,* 1934, especially pp. 104-141; Erich Fascher, art. *Taufe,* in Pauly-Wissowa, *Real-Encyclopädie,* Vol. IV, A[2], 1932, p. 2507; the influence of the pagan mysteries is similarly rejected, *ibid.,* pp 2511-2512. On this last question see also A. von Stromberg, *Studien zur Theorie und Praxis der Taufe in der christlichen Kirche der ersten zwei Jahr hunderte,* Berlin, 1913, pp. 36-45, cf. pp. 125-126, and A. Schweitzer, *Die Mystik des Apostels Paulus,* Tübingen, 1930, pp. 27-41.

[15] The other sacraments appear already in the apostolic period, but we cannot give them a special treatment here; what we have to say later on concerning the primitive hierarchy will deal with Order and its chief degrees, the episcopate, priesthood and diaconate; Confirmation appears in the laying on of hands which completes the graces of baptism (*Acts* vii, 24); cf. J. Coppens, *L'imposition des mains,* pp. 174-248.

[16] *John* iii, 22; iv, 2. On the nature of this baptism, two different opinions have been held by the Fathers and theologians: some

Resurrection He commanded his apostles to baptise all nations in the name of the Father, Son, and Holy Spirit (*Matt.* xxviii, 19). This baptism was not a ritual ablution, like those to which the Jews were accustomed,[17] nor a baptism of penitence, like the baptism of John; [18] it was a new birth, by which the person baptised was regenerated "by water and the Holy Ghost." [19] It was thus that Jesus explained to Nicodemus the nature and effect of baptism, and this conception will remain familiar to the apostles and to the Church.[20] The mysteries of the death and resurrection of Christ put this transformation in a new light: by baptism the neophytes were incorporated into Christ, died with Him and rose again with Him; they died to the flesh, they rose again in the spirit; being members of Christ, living with His life, they were freed from the servitude of the old Adam. Doubtless the old man still lived in them, but he had been mortally wounded by baptism, and would be constantly mortified by faithful Christians until death was swallowed up in life, and Christ was all in all.[21]

Baptism was indispensable for salvation. On Pentecost Day, the Jews, touched by the preaching of Peter, asked him: "What must we do?" "Do penance, and be baptised every one of you in the name of Jesus Christ," replied the apostle, and at the same time he promised them the fruits of baptism: the

---

see in it only the baptism of John the Baptist; others regard it as Christian baptism. This second view is the more common. Cf. A. d'Alès, *De Baptismo*, Paris, 1927, p. 19, and art. *Baptême* in *Supplément* to *Dictionnaire de la Bible*, Vol. I, p. 858.

[17] On the baptism of proselytes and the other Jewish ablutions, cf. J. Coppens, art. *Baptême*, col. 892-894.

[18] John himself expressly recognised this: "I have baptized you with water; but he shall baptize you with the Holy Ghost" (*Mark* i, 8); "I indeed baptize you in water unto penance . . . he shall baptize you in the Holy Ghost and fire" (*Matt.* iii, 11); cf. *Luke* iii, 16.

[19] *John* iii, 5; cf. iii, 3, 7-8.

[20] *Tit.* iii, 5; *I Pet.* i, 3. Often again the new birth is set forth as a divine adoption; *John* i, 12-13; *Rom.* viii, 15-16; *Gal.* iii. 26-27; *I John* iii, 1-2; v. 18; or as a new creation: *Gal.* vi, 15; *Ephes.* ii, 10. On all these ideas cf. A. d'Alès, art. *Baptême, col.* 863-866.

[21] Cf. Lebreton and Zeiller, Bk. I, p. 262; D'Alès, art. *Baptême*, col. 866-868; Schweitzer, *Die Mystik des Apostels Paulus,* pp. 119-158; in this book this idea is developed with great force, but the author wrongly contrasts it with the conception of regeneration, which he thinks foreign to St. Paul, pp. 13-15 and 120-211.

forgiveness of sins, and the gift of the Holy Spirit (*Acts* ii, 38). The converts of Samaria were baptised in the same way (viii, 12), also the Ethiopian eunuch (viii, 38), Saul (ix, 18), Cornelius the centurion and his household (x, 48), and indeed all the neophytes who appear in the apostolic history.

All were called to baptism: it was the Lord's command (*Matt.* xxviii, 19), and in the case of the centurion Cornelius, the Holy Ghost himself dispelled all hesitation. This principle was never questioned, even by the Judaisers.[22] In all candidates for baptism, faith was required; hence the custom, witnessed to already in apostolic times, of requiring from the candidates for baptism a profession of faith; this was the origin of the baptismal creed.[23] Every Christian, in order to be saved, had to confess with his mouth that Jesus was Lord, and believe with his heart that God had raised him from amongst the dead (*Rom.* x, 9); this profession of faith showed the adhesion of the neophyte to the traditional catechesis, such as that we find referred to, for instance, in the epistle to the Corinthians (*I Cor.* xv, 3 *et seq.*).

As to the rite of baptism in the apostolic age, the most explicit account we possess is the sixth chapter in the *Didache:*

"Baptize in the following manner: After saying all which precedes, baptize into the name of the Father, and of the Son, and of the Holy Ghost, in running water. If you have not running water, baptize in other water; and if you cannot baptize in cold water, baptize in warm. If both are lacking, pour some water thrice upon the head, in the name of the Father and of the Son and of the Holy Ghost. Before baptism, let the baptizer and the baptized fast, and other persons who are able; enjoin the baptized person to fast one or two days before." [24]

---

[22] What they desired was not to keep the pagans from baptism, but to impose circumcision on them.

[23] Cf. *Histoire du dogme de la Trinité,* Vol. II, pp. 146 *et seq.*; P. Feine, *Die Gestalt des apost. Glaubensbekenntnisses in der Zeit des N.T.,* Leipzig, 1925. We return to the baptismal creed later.

[24] Jacquier remarks on this passage: "This is the earliest mention we have of baptism by infusion; nevertheless it is likely that this was the most usual mode of baptism in apostolic times: the three thousand Jews who were converted by Peter's sermon on Pentecost Day and were baptized (*Acts* ii, 41) must have been baptized thus. The same applies to the five thousand converts mentioned in

The Eucharist

The origin of the Eucharist is already known to us.[25] We know that Christ instituted at the Last Supper this living representation of His sacrifice, and commanded His apostles to "do this in memory of him." Jesus was obeyed: the apostolic writings bear witness to the celebration of the Eucharist at Jerusalem and in the Pauline churches.[26]

This celebration is called in the accounts in the *Acts* (ii, 41-42; 46-47; xx, 7-11) the "breaking of bread." [27] In the

---

Acts iv, 4, and to the Philippian jailor and his family baptized by St. Paul in the prison (*ibid.*, xvi, 33). It would also appear that the baptism of the Ethiopian eunuch could not have been by complete immersion (*ibid.*, viii, 38)" (p. 194). This mention of baptism by infusion was suppressed when this text passed into the *Apostolic Constitutions*, vii, 22. Cf. St. Cyprian, ep. 69, 12-16, who had to defend the validity of baptism administered by infusion to the sick; and Cornelius, letter to Fabius of Antioch (*Hist. Eccles.*, vi, 43, 17), which says that those who had been thus baptized could not be admitted into the ranks of the clergy. At the date of these various documents, the construction of the baptismal piscinas had caused baptism by infusion to fall into desuetude for a time, and it was practised only in the case of the sick.

On baptism for the dead mentioned in *I Cor.* xv, 29, cf. Prat, *Theology of St. Paul,* Vol. I, p. 136: "A curious usage existed in Corinth and probably also in other Christian communities. When a catechumen died before being far enough advanced as to be baptized, one of his relatives or friends received for him the ceremonies of the sacrament. What precise signification was attached to this act? It is difficult to say. St. Paul neither approves nor condemns it; he treats it only as a profession of faith in the resurrection of the dead." See also Père Allo, O.P., *I Ep. aux Corinthiens,* Paris, 1934, pp. 411-13.

[25] Cf. Bk. I, pp. 141-44.

[26] The apostolic texts relating to the Eucharist have been conveniently collected together by W. B. Frankland in *The Early Eucharist,* London, 1902, pp. 3-11, and less completely by G. Rauschen, *Florilegium Patristicum,* Vol. VII, *Monumenta Eucharistica et Liturgica vetustissima,* Bonn, 1909. A detailed and exact interpretation of the texts will be found in W. Goossens, *Les origines de l'Eucharistie,* Gembloux, 1931, especially pp. 147-174.

[27] Cf. Goossens, *op. cit.*, pp. 172-173. Jacquier, in his commentary, recognises the eucharistic reference in the first and third texts, but

first days of the Church at Jerusalem, the faithful were "persevering in the doctrine of the apostles, and in the communication of the breaking of bread and in prayers" (ii, 42); "continuing daily with one accord in the Temple, and breaking bread from house to house, they took their meat with gladness and simplicity of heart" (ii, 46). This brief description indicates, side by side with the Eucharist, a common meal which probably took place at the same time.[28] This meal was certainly the custom at Corinth; but there it had led to abuses which St. Paul corrected:

"When you come therefore together into one place, it is not now to eat the Lord's supper. For every one taketh before his own supper to eat. And one indeed is hungry and another is drunk." [29]

The apostle, in order to put an end to these abuses, writes:

"Wherefore, my brethren, when you come together to eat, wait for one another. If any man be hungry, let him eat at home; that you come not together unto judgment." [30]

Again, we have the Supper celebrated at Troas by St. Paul: it was the first day of the week (Sunday); the faithful were gathered together for the breaking of bread. Paul, who was to depart the next day, was speaking to the brethren; he continued his discourse until midnight. In the upper room in which the meeting was taking place, many lamps were lit; in the course of the apostle's long discourse, a young man

---

not in the second; Goossens writes, apparently more correctly: "The breaking of bread in two passages so close to one another and having the same subject must have the same meaning in the two cases."

[28] It seems to me that this is wrongly contested by Goossens, *op. cit.*, p. 134; but it does not follow that this meal was the agape. The agape is certainly attested for the end of the second century; nothing justifies us in affirming its use in the first century. Cf. Goossens, pp. 127-146.

[29] *I Cor.* xi, 20-21. Cf. Bk. I, p. 248.

[30] *Ibid.*, 33-34. It seems to follow from this text that the Christian assembly ought to be exclusively eucharistic, and that all other meals were to be banished from it (Goossens, *op. cit.*, pp. 138-141).

named Eutychius went to sleep; he fell from the third floor to the ground, and was picked up dead. Paul went down, took him in his arms, and brought him to life again; then he went back, broke bread, ate, and conversed with the brethren until daybreak (*Acts* xx, 7-11).

The vigil was exceptionally prolonged on that occasion because of the imminent departure of the apostle, but this fact did not make any change in the character of this liturgical assembly: the breaking of bread was its central feature; it took place on the Sunday, the day especially assigned for the celebration of the Eucharist.[31]

These few texts enable us to see how from the time of the apostles the command of the Lord: "Do this in memory of me" was carried out; and already we recognise here the outline of the liturgy which was very shortly to develop. Some have endeavoured to distinguish between two different types of apostolic Eucharist: they suggest that in the accounts in the Acts concerning Jerusalem and Troas, we have a brotherly meal, a symbol of the union of Christians with each other and with Jesus; in the epistle to the Corinthians we have a sacrificial meal, wholly penetrated with the memory of the death of the Lord.[32] This hypothesis is an arbitrary one, and is contradicted by the texts of St. Paul; the apostle, far from being aware of innovating in any way in this matter, appeals expressly to the tradition which he has received and transmitted;[33] he himself moreover sets forth the double aspect of the eucharistic mystery, the sacrifice (*I Cor.* x, 16-21) and the mystery of union (*ibid.*, 17; cf. *Rom.* xii, 5).

But though from the first we see only one Eucharist, we can distinguish already in the eucharistic doctrine the trace of the two great dogmas of the Incarnation and the Redemption. The Son of God present in us, uniting us to himself and to our brethren, is what St. John brings out above all in the two discourses of Christ at Capernaum and after the Last Supper; the Son of God who died for us and unites us to

[31] Cf. *I Cor.* xvi, 2; *Didache* xiv, 1; Goossens, *op. cit.*, p. 172, n. 6.
[32] This thesis has been maintained by H. Lietzmann, *Messe und Herrenmahl*, Bonn, 1926, pp. 238-263. Cf. *Recherches de science religieuse*, 1927, pp. 330-333.
[33] *I Cor.* xi, 23. On this text, cf. the article *Eucharistie* in the *Dictionnaire apologétique*, col. 1552 *et seq.* Also Allo, *op. cit.*, 302-16.

His sacrifice is what St. Paul chiefly dwells upon. And from that time onwards in the whole history of eucharistic theology, we can follow these two doctrinal currents; they will never be isolated from each other, but they will lead theologians to contemplate by preference either our life-giving union with the "bread which has come down from heaven," or else our participation in His death, in the communion of the "blood of the testament." [34]

§2. THE PRIMITIVE HIERARCHY [1]

Peter and the Twelve

In our account of the life of Jesus, we found around him a group of twelve apostles.[2] These were chosen by Him, formed by Him, sent by Him, and invested with the powers of teaching and government which constituted them the heads of the Church here below,[3] and in heaven the judges of mankind.[4] After His Resurrection, the Lord confirmed these privileges to the apostles, gave them the Holy Spirit, and sent them forth to convert and baptize all nations.[5]

Amongst these twelve apostles, we saw that Peter was the first (*Matt.* x, 2). It was on him in the first place that the Church rested as on an unshakable rock; it was he who, before the other apostles, received the power of binding and loosing (*Matt.* xvi, 16-19); it was he who, after the Resurrection, was once more singled out by Jesus from the apostolic group, and charged with the feeding of the lambs and the sheep (*John* xxi, 15-19).

Thus, even before founding the Church by His death and the outpouring of the Holy Spirit, Jesus revealed the plan of the building He intended to construct: the Christian Church was to be a hierarchical society, taught and governed by the apostles, with Peter at their head.

[34] Already in the *Didache* we can recognise, in the eucharistic prayers, this double influence, Pauline and (above all) Johannine.
[1] Cf. Batiffol, *Primitive Catholicism;* Michiels, *L'origine de l'Episcopat,* Louvain, 1900; Harnack, *Entschung und Entwicklung der Kirchenwerfassung und des Kirchenrechts in den zwei ersten Jahrhunderten,* Leipzig, 1910.
[2] Cf. Lebreton and Zeiller, Bk. I, 96-98.
[3] *Matt* xvi, 16-19; xviii, 17-18.
[4] *Matt.* xix, 27-30; *Luke* xxii, 28-30.
[5] *John* xx, 21-22; *Matt.* xxviii, 18-20.

In point of fact, that is how the Church appears, from the first day, in the Upper Room. The Twelve formed a privileged group, in which the defection of Judas left a gap; this gap had to be filled; Peter took the initiative in the election of Matthias and directed it (*Acts* i, 15-26). On Pentecost Day it was Peter who, assisted by the eleven, explained to the people the mystery of the Spirit (ii, 14), and told the converts what they had to do (ii, 37); three thousand people were converted, and "were persevering in the doctrine of the apostles, and in the communication of the breaking of bread, and in prayers" (ii, 42). It was at the feet of the apostles that the Christians laid down the price of the possessions which they gave up (iv, 35-37; v, 2). Thus, all power was committed to their hands; their manifold cares became too absorbing, and the apostles, in order to devote themselves to the ministry of prayer and the word of God, caused seven deacons to be chosen for the ministry of tables (vi, 2 *et seq.*). These deacons also assisted the apostles in preaching, whether at Jerusalem (as Stephen) or elsewhere (as Philip).

In this group of apostles which so clearly asserted its authority from these first years, there was one leader who dominated all the rest by his supreme authority: Peter. We have seen this in the election of Matthias and in the great manifestations on Pentecost day; we shall find it again in all the events which follow: in the Temple, where he goes with John, it is he who addresses the word to the lame man, heals him, and speaks to the people (iii, 14, *et seq.*); before the Sanhedrin, it is he who speaks (iv, 7; v, 29); when Ananias and Sapphira try to conceal the price of their field, it is he who rebukes and condemns them (v, 1 *et seq.*). The Apostles, says Luke, performed great miracles; then he becomes more explicit: the sick were placed in Peter's path, so that at least his shadow might fall on them (v, 15). Peter and John are sent to Samaria; it is Peter who addresses the people (viii, 20). The decisive step in missions to the pagans, the baptism of the centurion Cornelius, is the work of Peter (x). When in the Council of Jerusalem the conditions of admission of pagans into the Church are being discussed, it is Peter who speaks first, and his opinion prevails (xv, 7).

This prominent situation of St. Peter, so manifest in the first chapters of the Acts, is less apparent in the rest of the narrative, because St. Paul is the chief centre of interest; but even there, the unparalleled authority of the head of the apostles is shown in the steps taken by St. Paul; in the care he takes to put himself in touch with Peter (*Gal.* i, 18), in the rank he assigns to Peter amongst the witnesses of the Resurrection of Jesus (*I Cor.* xv, 5), in the way, even, in which a small group of Corinthians try to abuse the respected name of Peter (*I Cor.*, i, 12).[6]

Authority and the Spirit

These powers of jurisdiction and teaching conferred upon St. Peter and the other apostles, are gifts of the Holy Spirit, charisms, ordained for the good of the Church. Of all the functions of the members of the body of Christ, the apostolate is the highest, but like the others, it derives its origin from a divine grace, and it has as its object the well-being of the body:

"Christ gave some apostles, and some prophets, and other some evangelists, and other some pastors and doctors, for the perfecting of the saints, for the work of the ministry, for the edifying of the body of Christ" (*Ephes.* iv, 11-12).

This double character, spiritual and hierarchical, is essential to the Church; this indissoluble union of authority and charism is manifest not only in the doctrine of St. Paul, but also in the facts, and that from the first day of the Church, and even before Pentecost. When the risen Jesus appears to His apostles and gives them power to bind and to loose, He says to them at the same time: "Receive the Holy Spirit" (*John* xx, 22). The highest exercise of the apostolic ministry is the gift of the Spirit; it appears at Pentecost (ii, 6-13) and later at Samaria (viii, 14), Cæsarea (x, 44), and Ephesus (xix, 6). To those who ask Paul for a letter of recommendation in proof of his apostolate, he replies: "You are our epistle, written in our hearts, which is known and read by all

---

[6] All this is not contradicted or even obscured by the incident at Antioch; cf. Bk. I, pp. 194-95. But from this incontestable primacy of St. Peter, one must not infer that his relations towards the other apostles were the same as those of the Pope towards other bishops. The Apostles received from Christ the power of universal jurisdiction, and the assurance of a personal infallibility in doctrine, privileges which they did not transmit to the bishops who succeeded them.

men: being manifested, that you are the epistle of Christ, ministered by us, and written not with ink, but with the Spirit of the living God, not in tables of stone, but in the fleshly tablets of the heart" (*II Cor.*, iii, 2-3).

Protestant writers may endeavour to oppose the Church of authority to the Church of the Spirit;[7] this opposition does violence to the history of Christian origins, and especially to the conception of the apostolate as this appears in the Gospels, Acts, and above all in the epistles of St. Paul.[8]

But if it be true that Jesus decided to found a Church which would endure as long as the world itself, and if He promised to His apostles to be with them, even "till the consummation of the world," it must surely be true that these essential characters of the Church, spiritual and hierarchical, will not disappear at the death of the apostles, and that these first leaders will have successors.

The Deacons

Besides the apostolic office, we see appearing from the first years of the Church others which, like the apostolate, have their origin in a divine call, and whose object is the building up of the body of Christ; in these also we find the union of charism and authority. Such are in the first place the deacons: we have seen that the apostles instituted these in order to hand on to them the ministry of tables which had become too

[7] This is the thesis of the postumous work of Auguste Sabatier, *Les religions d'autorité et la religion de l'esprit,* Paris, 1904.

[8] The apostolate is a charism: the apostle must have seen the Lord (*I Cor.* ix, 1-2) and have received a direct call from Christ (*Gal.* i, 1; *Acts* xiii, 2; cf. i, 26); his ministry is proved by its fruitfulness in grace and charisms(*I Cor.* ix, 2; *II Cor.* iii, 3; xii, 12). But this charism of the apostolate confers an authority which the apostle exercises; even the spiritual gifts, the most divine and most independent element seemingly in Christianity, are regulated by the apostle (*I Cor.* xii). He also regulates the celebration of the Supper, and corrects abuses in it (*ibid.,* xi, 34); by his own authority he defines the duties of married people (*ibid.,* vii, 12); he excommunicates the incestuous man (ix, 3); he sends Timothy, who will make known to the Corinthians what the apostle teaches in all the churches, and he adds: "What will you? Shall I come to you with a rod; or in charity, and in the spirit of meekness?" (iv, 17-21).

absorbing;[9] the people chose the seven, and the apostles ordained them by prayer and the laying on of hands.

In addition to the humble serving of tables, the apostles
entrusted to the deacons the ministry of preaching; and St.
Stephen, the first and best known of the seven, showed himself to be a man "full of grace and power"; the Holy Ghost
spoke and acted in him with an irresistible force; his opponents could silence him only by slaying him.

The Presbyters

A little later (*Acts* xi, 30) we find in the Church of Jerusalem some "presbyters," but we do not know when or in
what way they were instituted in the community. On the
occasion of the famine foretold by the prophet Agabus, the
Church of Antioch sent help to the church of Jerusalem; it
sent alms by Barnabas and Saul to the presbyters. In an
earlier episode (iv, 35) we saw that those who yielded up
their possessions to the community laid the price of them at
the feet of the apostles; thus we find here again the passing
on to new officials of a ministry of which the apostles at first
were in charge. And for the presbyters as for the deacons,
the administrative charge went hand in hand with a spiritual
ministry: at the Council of Jerusalem they deliberated and
decided with the apostles;[10] in 57, when St. Paul arrived at
Jerusalem with the alms of his churches, he presented himself to James, who was surrounded by all the presbyters (xxi,
18).

These various incidents show us the important part played
by the presbyters in the church of Jerusalem. To them we
must add this precept which St. James gives in his epistle
(v, 14):

[9] Cf. Bk. I, pp. 176-77; and *Acts* vi.
[10] *Acts* xv, 2: the brethren of Antioch depute "Paul and Barnabas
and certain others of the other side, to go up to the apostles and
presbyters at Jerusalem"; when they arrive at Jerusalem, they are
received "by the church, and by the apostles and presbyters" (4);
after the report of the two envoys, "the apostles and presbyters
assembled to consider this matter" (6). Peter speaks, then Barnabas and Paul, then James. "Then it pleased the apostles and presbyters, with the whole Church, to send to Antioch . . . Judas and
Silas" (22). These messengers took with them a decision which
began thus: "The apostles and presbyters, brethren, to the brethren that are at Antioch . . ." (23). This decree was promulgated
everywhere as "the decrees decreed by the apostles and presbyters who were at Jerusalem" (xvi, 4).

"Is any man sick among you? Let him bring in the presbyters of the Church, and let them pray over him, anoint-
ing him with oil in the name of the Lord. And the prayer
of faith shall save the sick man: and the Lord shall raise
him up: and if he be in sins, they shall be forgiven him."

The presbyters referred to here are not merely notable and
influential members of the community; they are ministers
charged with a liturgical function and capable of conferring
thereby spiritual graces.

Paul and Barnabas, when returning from their mission,
instituted presbyters in every church (xiv, 23).[11] The same
institution had taken place at Ephesus; the exhortation which
Paul at Miletus gave to the presbyters of Ephesus brings out
in full evidence their pastoral functions:

"Take heed to yourselves, and to the whole flock, wherein
the Holy Ghost have placed you bishops, to rule the church
of God, which he hath purchased with his own blood. I
know that, after my departure, ravening wolves will enter
in among you, not sparing the flock. And of your own
selves shall arise men speaking perverse things, to draw
away disciples after them. Therefore watch, keeping in
memory that for three years I ceased not with tears to
admonish every one of you night and day" (*Acts* xx, 28-
31).

The office of a presbyter, as set forth in this account and
discourse, is the office of a pastor and a doctor. Moreover,
here as in Pisidia, but more explicitly, the presbyters have
as their mission the continuance of the work of the Apostle,
and they are to take his place.

Lastly we must note that the same men whom St. Luke
calls presbyters in his narrative (*Acts* xx, 17) are called bishops by St. Paul in his discourse (Acts xx, 28).[12]

[11] Cf. Bk. I, p. 206.
[12] In his epistles, except the pastorals and the epistle to the Hebrews, Paul does not speak of "presbyters"; but he mentions some
who preside (*I Thess.* v, 12; *Rom.* xii, 8) pastors and teachers
(*Ephes.* iv, 11); bishops and deacons (*Phil.* i, 1). In three places
in the Epistle to the Hebrews (xiii, 7, 17, 24) there are references to superiors. Note what is said in *I Tim.* v, 17 of presbyters
who rule well. These προεστῶτες, identified with the presbyters,
seem identical also with the προϊστάμενοι of the epistles to the
Thessalonians and Romans.

In the first epistle of St. Peter, we find exhortations to presbyters very similar to those in the discourse of Paul at Miletus:

> "The presbyters therefore that are among you I beseech, who am myself also a presbyter, and a witness of the sufferings of Christ. . . . Feed the flock of God which is among you, taking care of it, not by constraint, but willingly, according to God, not for filthy lucre's sake, but voluntarily; neither as lording it over your charges, but being made a pattern of the flock from the heart. And when the Prince of Pastors shall appear, you shall receive a never fading crown of glory. In like manner, ye young men, be subject to the presbyters" (v, 1-5).

In the pastoral epistles, St. Paul sets forth the virtues which he requires in presbyter-bishops (*I Tim.* iii, 2; *Tit.* i, 6); they must be irreproachable, sober, prudent, able to instruct others, husbands of one wife, and ruling well their own households; not brutal, arrogant, quarrelsome, or covetous.[13] These presbyters are to be established everywhere; their appointment belongs to the delegates of the apostle, Titus and Timothy, who are to lay hands on them (*I Tim.* iv, 14; *II Tim.* i, 6; cf. *Acts* xiv, 23). Nowhere is there any mention of an election by the people.

What is to be noted above all in these letters is the object of this institution, which is, as St. Clement will very soon define it, the continuation of the apostolic succession, the preservation and defence of the deposit.[14]

We have just collected from the apostolic writings the indications we find there concerning the primitive hierarchy, and especially concerning presbyters and bishops; we must now discuss the interpretation of these texts.

The presbyterate in the primitive Church was not merely a title of honour attributed to old age or for services rendered.[15] A presbyter became such by apostolic institution (*Acts* xiv, 23); and when one became a presbyter, he was invested

---

[13] In his letter to Timothy, he lays it down that the candidate must not be a neophyte (iii, 6); this condition is not found in the letter to Titus; we may infer that the church of Crete was too recent a foundation to make this condition feasible.

[14] *I Tim.* vi, 10; *II Tim,* i, 14; cf. *Tit.* iii, 10.

[15] Cf. Michiels, *op. cit.,* p. 134.

with hierarchical and liturgical functions.[16] The "leaders," "presiding ones," "superiors" mentioned in the epistles of St. Paul are not distinguished from the presbyters; must they be distinguished from the bishops?

A distinction between bishops and presbyters in the apostolic Church is accepted by two groups of writers: some theologians, but only a small number,[17] and at the other extreme, a fair number of radical critics.[18] This thesis does not fit in at all well with the apostolic texts; presbyters and bishops there appear to be identical,[19] and they are understood in that sense by the best representatives of patristic exegesis, St. John Chrysostom[20] and St. Jerome.[21]

[16] *Acts* xx; *James* v, 14; and texts in pastoral epistles indicated above.

[17] Thus Franzelin, *De Ecclesia,* thesis 17.

[18] When Hatch gave his conferences in 1880, the identity of the two terms was universally accepted, as he pointed out (*The Organisation of the Early Church,* 1881, p. 39 and n. 1); his book was destined to reopen the question: by reason of the theory therein defended, he tended to separate the bishops (financial administrators) from the presbyters (members of the council or senate). Sohm (*Kirchenrecht,* p. 92) gives credit to Hatch for the differentiation introduced between these two terms, and he is right. Cf. Michiels, *op. cit.,* p. 134. J. Reville (*Origines de l'épiscopat,* p. 179) similarly writes: "All that we hope to have established is that the episcopate and presbyterate have distinct origins." This distinction will be found also in Harnack, *Entstehung und Entwicklung der Kirchenverfassung,* p. 44.

[19] *Acts* xx, 17-28; cf. *I Pet.* v, 5 (doubtful text); *Tit.* 1, 5-7; *I Tim.* iii, 2; cf. v, 17.

[20] *Hom. I,* in *Phil.* Commenting on *Phil.* i, he says: "What does this mean? Were there several bishops in one city? Not at all, but Paul gives this name to the priests, for until then the denomination was common." Cf. Michiels, *op. cit.,* p. 122.

[21] *In Tit.* i, 5 (Migne, *P.L.,* XXVI, p. 562): "The same person is priest and also bishop, and before the time when, under the instigation of the devil, there arose parties in the Church, and it was said: 'I am of Paul, I am of Apollos, I am of Cephas,' the churches were governed by the council of priests. But when each one wanted those baptized by him to belong to him and not to Christ, it was decreed in the whole world that one of the priests should by election be set over the others, and that he should have the care of the whole Church and suppress the seeds of schism"; and he quotes in support of his view *Phil.* i, 1; *Acts* xx, 28; *Heb.* xiii, 17; I *Pet.* v, 1-2. In this passage of St. Jerome and in other texts in

Accepting this identification of presbyters and bishops, one last question presents itself: were the dignitaries designed by these two names bishops or simple priests? The second alternative seems the most likely; [22] so long as St. Paul was alive, he was "the sole pastor of the immense diocese which he had won to faith in Christ. Neither in Greece or Macedonia, Galatia, Crete or Ephesus was there during his lifetime any bishop other than himself and his delegates. . . . The churches in the jurisdiction of Paul were served by deacons and governed by a council of dignitaries named indifferently presbyters or bishops, under the ever watchful surveillance and the ever active guardianship of the founder or his substitutes." [23]

These "delegates" or "substitutes" of the Apostle were the recipients of the pastoral epistles, Titus and Timothy; they were associated by St. Paul in the government of the churches, and received from him the power to ordain deacons and priests; they were therefore certainly bishops; and thus we find in the Pauline Churches, as at Jerusalem, the three distinct orders of bishops, priests and deacons.[24]

---

his works we find traces of his animosity against abuses of episcopal power; we can leave aside these features, and also what he says about the schism of Corinth, in which he finds the occasion for the distinction between bishops and priests. In his letter to Evangelus, *P.L.* XXII, 1193, he sets aside the hypothesis of a college of bishops distinct from the priests and superior to them: "Ac ne quis contentione in una Ecclesia plures episcopos fuisse contendat, audi et aliud testimonium, in quo manifestissime comprobatur eumdem esse episcopum et presbyterum: *Tit.* i, 5." On the authority of St. Jerome, cf. Petavius, *Hier.*, II, c. 4 and 5. In this work, Petavius adopts the opinion of St. Jerome; in his *Dissertations sur la dignité des evêques,* he had thought that the presbyter-bishops who governed the churches were true bishops; here he prefers to regard them as simple priests, amongst whom the apostles chose a president who became the bishop.

[22] The former alternative is chosen by Boudinhon, *Canoniste Contemporain,* 1901, pp. 390-392, and by Batiffol, *Etudes d'histoire et de théologie positive,* Vol. I, pp. 268-269; the latter by Michiels, *op. cit.,* pp. 218-230, and by Prat, *Theology of St. Paul,* Vol. I, p. 345, Vol. II, p. 306.

[23] Prat, *Theology of St. Paul,* Vol. II, p. 306, cf. Vol. I, p. 345: "These two terms are used indifferently to denote the same persons, and are applied to members of the second rank of the hierarchy—in other words, to priests."

[24] Cf. Medebielle, art. *Eglise* in *Supplément* to *Dict. de la Bible,* col. 658.

We also grasp the motive and object of this institution: Paul feels that he is at the end of his course; he is very soon going to be poured out as a libation; he wants to ensure the perpetuity of his work; he entrusts it, with a full authority, to those whom he has long associated in his work.

This apostolic succession, already attested in the letters of St. Paul, is expressly confirmed by the witnesses of St. Clement at the end of the first century:

"Christ comes from God, and the apostles come from Christ. . . . Having received the instructions of Our Lord Jesus Christ, and being fully convinced by His resurrection, the apostles . . . set out to announce the good news of the coming of the Kingdom of God. Preaching in country and cities, they tested in the Spirit their first fruits, and instituted them as bishops and deacons of the future believers" (xlii, 2-3).

"They appointed those of whom we have spoken, and then they laid down this rule, that when the latter should die, other approved men should succeed to their ministry. We do not think it right to reject from the ministry those who have been thus instituted by the apostles, or later by other eminent men[25] with the approbation of the whole Church" (xliv, 3).

This letter was written at the end of the reign of Domitian or at the beginning of that of Nerva (95-96). At that date St. John was returning from exile and taking up once more this apostolic ministry at Ephesus: "After the death of the tyrant," says Eusebius (*Ecclesiastical History*, III, 23, 6), "the apostle John left the island of Patmos and came to Ephesus: from thence he went whither he was called to the Gentiles in the neighbourhood, either in order thoroughly to establish churches there, or else to choose as clerics those who were designated by the Spirit."

We could wish to make these indications more precise by referring to the *Apocalypse*, and interpreting what is said there of the angels of the seven churches (i, 20 *et seq.*), but the symbolism of these chapters makes them difficult to in-

---

[25] These "eminent men" are the disciples, such as Titus or Timothy, upon whom the apostles conferred, together with the episcopate, the power to institute and ordain bishops.

terpret.[26] In the epistles of St. John (II and III) there seem to be traces of a conflict between the local authorities and the apostle, but from these fugitive allusions it would be dangerous to try to draw exact conclusions.[27]

§3. THE ORIGINS OF GNOSTICISM

The great Christian Gnostic systems appear only in the course of the second century; the writers of the Great Church who opposed these heretics regarded their theses as late deformations of Christian ideas,[1] and they were right. But Basilides and Valentinus had forerunners, the Gnostics combatted by St. Ignatius of Antioch, St. Jude, St. Peter, St. John and St. Paul. Even before the preaching of Christianity, Gnosticism was already prevalent in Syria, Palestine, and Egypt; the episode of Simon Magus narrated in the *Acts of*

[26] Père Allo (*Apocalypse*, p. lxv) sees in them the collective council rather than the prelates who preside over them; cf. p. 18. This is also the interpretation of Swete (p. 28), who sees in them the angel guardians of the churches, and hence a personification of the churches.

[27] Westcott writes in his Commentary (p. lvi): "Diotrephes . . . is able for a time to withstand an Apostle in the administration of his particular Church. On the other side, the calm confidence of St. John seems to rest on himself more than on his official power. His presence will vindicate his authority. Once more the growth of the Churches is as plainly marked as their independence." Streeter (*Primitive Church*, London, 1929, pp. 84-89) thinks that the local episcopate, represented by Diotrephes, was held in check by the quasi metropolitan authority of the writer of the letters, who was Bishop of Ephesus. To attribute to metropolitans at this date so great an influence is an anachronism.

[1] Thus Clement of Alexandria, *Stromat*. VII, 17, 106: "The teaching of Our Lord during his life began with Augustus and finished towards the middle of the reign of Tiberius; the preaching of the Apostles, as far as the end of the ministry of Paul, finished under Nero; the heresiarchs, on the contrary, began very much later, in the time of the king Hadrian, and lasted until the epoch of Antoninus the Elder. For instance, Basilides. . . ." Similarly Hegesippus, quoted by Eusebius, *Hist. Eccles.*, III, 32, 7; "In the time of the apostles, the Church remained, as it were, a pure virgin without spot; but after the death of the apostles, wicked error found the beginning of its organisation through the deceits of those who taught another doctrine."

the Apostles shows the remarkable diffusion of the Gnostic fancies.

Pagan Gnosticism

Gnosticism, in point of fact, was a great religious movement before Christianity, to which it was opposed in its most profound tendencies. In the first centuries of our era, it invaded the whole Græco-Roman world, coming into collision with the Hellenic and Jewish religions before attacking Christianity.[1a] Its origin must be sought in the religious syncretism which, from the time of the conquests of Alexander, and still more since the Roman conquest, had mingled and fused together the Oriental cults. The name "gnosis" indicates the object aimed at: the knowledge, or rather the vision of God; it is a divine revelation which almost always claims to be based upon some ancient message transmitted secretly by a chain of initiates; through this mysterious tradition, one is linked up with primitive peoples such as the ancient Egyptians, and through them, to the gods. Thus the hermetic books present themselves as revelations made to Hermes or received by him; others appeal to Asclepios. Similarly the Christian Gnostics place their revelations under the patronage of some apostle, or, often, of Mary Magdalene, who is supposed to have received them from the risen Christ before the Ascension.

Gnosticism claimed to be a doctrine of salvation as well as a revelation; it taught the soul how to free itself from the material world in which it is imprisoned, and to ascend once more towards the spiritual and luminous world from which it has fallen. This liberation is brought about by the communication of a heavenly revelation, accompanied often by magical formulas and rites. Participation in this gnosis is not accorded or even offered to all men; like the Mysteries, Gnosis is reserved for initiates, and this was one of its most powerful attractions.

The religious doctrine thus transmitted was characterized by a very marked dualism; matter is to be despised and hated. The supreme Deity is removed as far as possible from all contact with matter; the creation of the material world is

[1a] I here summarize the chapter dealing with the origin of Gnosticism in *Historie du Dogme de la Trinité*, Vol. II, pp. 81-93, completing this at the same time by means of the works which have since 1928 thrown light on this obscure subject.

ascribed either to an inferior deity or demiurge, or else to angels or *archontes*. Between the visible world and this god there are more or less numerous intermediaries; it is by these that the divine action is extended and abased as far as the material world, and it is also through them that the soul is able to elevate itself step by step up to the supreme deity.

These ideas admit of being adapted to many different religions or mythologies: thus in the hermetic books, the same office of the revealing and saving deity is attributed to the Logos (Book I), to the Eon (Book XI), to Agathodæmon (Book XII), and to the Sun (Book XVI). The ascent of the soul, which passes successively through the seven planetary spheres, giving the password to the *archontes* and becoming transformed into the image of the angels it meets, is a common theme which is found, with more or less marked variants, in pagan, Jewish and Christian Gnostics. The Naassene Gnostics spoken of by Hippolytus[2] laid claim to a secret revelation which James, the Lord's brother, is supposed to have entrusted to Mariamne; but at the same time they were initiated into the mysteries of the Great Mother (v, 9-10), and they repeated two hymns to Attis which they had learnt there.

Simon Magus

This elasticity which is capable of adaptation to all religions appears already in the Gnosticism of Simon Magus, which preceded Christianity and became its rival, and later on endeavoured more and more to assimilate its theology.[3]

When Philip the Deacon arrived at Samaria, he found the town led away by Simon:

"There was a certain man named Simon, who before had been a magician in that city, seducing the people of Samaria, giving out that he was some great one; to whom they all gave ear, from the least to the greatest, saying: 'This man is the power of God which is called Great.' And they were attentive to him, because for a long time he had bewitched them with his magical practices" (*Acts* viii, 9-11).

[2] *Philos.*, V, 6-11.

[3] On Simon Magus, cf. the studies of Hans Waite, *Simon Magus in der altchristlichen Literatur*, in *Zeitschrift für N.T.W.*, Vol. V, 1904, pp. 121-148, and Lucien Cerfaux, in *Recherches de Science religieuse* Vol. XV, 1925, pp. 489-511; Vol. XVI, 1926, pp. 5-20, pp. 265-285, and pp. 481-503.

Simon nevertheless had himself baptized by Philip. When Peter and John arrived, he tried to buy with silver the power of conferring the Holy Spirit. Peter rebuked him severely; Simon seemed to be penitent and humble. The New Testament says no more about him, but later works enable us to follow the development of the sect. St. Justin, who came from Nablus and knew well his compatriots, relates that "almost all the Samaritans, and a few men in the other nations, acknowledged Simon and adored him as the supreme God." [4]

This Gnosticism thus progressively exalted its hero: first of all it saw in him only an intermediate divinity, the great Power of God; then it adored him as the supreme deity. At the end of the second century, Irenæus showed this Gnosticism endeavouring to adapt itself to the Trinitarian dogma: "Simon claims to have descended amongst the Jews as the Son, in Samaria as the Father, and in the other nations as the Holy Spirit." [5]

Besides this supreme deity, a goddess named Helena was also honoured. This cult seems to have arisen at Tyre, where the Moon (Selena or Helena) was associated with the worship of the Sun; the Simonian Gnostics identified this goddess with Wisdom, while the Alexandrian Gnostics regarded her as Isis.

The Clementines and the *Acts of Peter* describe a struggle between St. Peter and Simon Magus, first in Syria and then at Rome.[6] In these creations of the imagination we can discern the memory of the bitter opposition of Gnosticism to Christianity, from Syria to Rome.

Gnosticism in the Apostolic Churches

Between the Simonian Gnosticism and Christianity there could only be an ineluctable opposition. The danger of con-

[4] *Apol.*, I, XXVI, 3; cf. LVI, 1-2. Justin was mistaken concerning the supposed statue to Simon in Rome, but we can accept his witness concerning the religion of the Samaritans and the cult which they gave to Simon.

[5] *Haer.*, I, 23.

[6] On this combat in the *Acts of Peter*, cf. Vouaux, *Les Actes de Pierre*, 1902, pp. 100-109, and on the Clementine romance, C. Schmidt, *Studien zur den Pseudo-Clementinen*, 1929, pp. 47-66, and Chapman in *Catholic Encyclopædia*, Vol. IV. An English translation of the *Acts of Peter* will be found in M. R. James, *Apocryphal New Testament*, Oxford, 1924, pp. 300-36.

tamination could be greater when the Gnosticism which attacked Christianity was less openly pagan, and when it took the appearance of a Christian or Judaising sect. Such was more generally the Gnosticism against which the apostolic writings reacted.

At the beginning, St. Paul had to defend himself above all against attacks from without; the opponents he had in view were usually Jews or Judaisers, as for instance, in the Epistle to the Galatians. But very soon there arose heretics from the very bosom of the Church; the earliest epistles hardly mention them, but from the time of the captivity, the controversy occupies a much larger place in the theology of the apostle. "The letters to the Colossians and Ephesians—the latter, more especially, exhibit an advanced stage in the development of the Church. The heresies, which the Apostle here combats, are no longer the crude, materialistic errors of the early childhood of Christianity, but the more subtle speculations of its maturer age. The doctrine which he preaches is not now the 'milk for babes' but the 'strong meat' for grown men. . . . These epistles bridge the gulf which separates the Pastoral letters from the Apostle's earlier writings. The heresies of the Pastoral letters are the heresies of the Colossians and Ephesians grown rank and corrupt." [7]

If we endeavour to trace from the apostolic writings an outline of the kind of Gnosticism which then threatened Christianity, we can perceive the following features:

(a) *Dualism,* which showed itself by contempt for the flesh; this led to a denial of the resurrection (*I Cor.* xv, 12), or to its being understood in a figurative sense, probably of baptism (*II Tim.* v, 18). From this principle divergent moral inferences were drawn: sometimes in a libertine sense: everything is allowed, because all that is fleshly is to be despised (*I Cor.* vi and x; *Apoc.* ii, 14; *II Pet.* ii, 10; *Jude* 8); sometimes, on the contrary, in the sense of a rigid asceticism, forbidding contacts deemed impure, also certain foods, and marriage (*Col.* ii, 16-21; *I Tim.* iv, 3).

(b) *Ambitious speculations,* including supposed visions or imaginations concerning the angels; [8] delighting in genealogies

---

[7] Lightfoot, *Philippians,* p. 45.
[8] These errors are above all combatted in *Col.* ii. Cf. A. L. Williams, *The Cult of the Angels at Colossæ,* in *Journal of Theol. Studies,* Vol. XI, 1909, pp. 413-438.

(*Tit.* iii, 9), and in "cunningly devised fables" (*II Pet.* i, 16).

(*c*) These resulted in *putting Christ below the angels* (*Col.* xxx), or even denying him altogether (*I John* ii, 29; *II Pet.* ii, 1; *Jude* 4). Many who did not go so far as this radical denial rejected the reality of the Incarnation: Jesus Christ had not come in the flesh. This Docetism was combatted above all by St. John, and soon afterwards by St. Ignatius.

(*d*) These heretics were *mainly Jews,* who claim to be doctors of the law (*Tit.* i, 10; *I Tim.* i, 7; *Apoc.* ii, 9). In the second letter of St. Peter, we find them appealing also to the authority of St. Paul (*II Pet.* i, 20; iii, 16). Some [9] have at times tried to reduce all this Gnosticism to a radical Paulinism; this is an insufficient explanation: Gnosticism arose above all from the speculations which were at that time widespread in Judaism and Hellenism; these attacked Christianity as they attacked every living religion; they were eliminated by it after a long struggle. This struggle was, however, not fruitless; it gave to church authority more vigour, and to dogma greater precision. The study of the apostolic Fathers, and particularly of St. Ignatius, will soon show this.

[9] E.G., MacGiffert, *History of Christianity in the Apostolic Age,* 1897, pp. 502 *et seq.*

Chapter 2

The Propagation of Christianity[1]

WHILE CHRISTIANITY WAS developing its interior life, it was continuing its territorial expansion. The persecution which broke out suddenly and cost SS. Peter and Paul their lives, did not arrest and indeed scarcely hindered the diffusion of the Christian Faith.

§1. THE EVANGELISATION OF THE ROMAN WORLD

The First Propagation of Christianity in Italy

When persecution broke out under Nero, only to die down, and then to be revived for a first time some thirty years later under Domitian, Christianity had already secured a strong footing in the capital of the Empire. St. Paul when landing in Italy had, before arriving in Rome, found Christians at Puteoli.[2] Possibly there were also some Christians at Pompeii before 77, the year of the destruction of the city.[3]

[1] Bibliography. Cf. the various Histories of the Church mentioned in the General Bibliography at the end of the book. But the essential work to consult here is Harnack's *Die Mission und Ausbreitung des Christentums in den ersten drei Jahrhunderten*, 2 vols., 4th edn., Leipzig, 1924. The sources and special works concerning the various regions in which Christian propaganda progressed in early times are indicated in the notes to this chapter.
[2] *Acts* xxviii, 14.
[3] *Graffiti* published in *C.I.L.*, IV, pl. xvi, nos. 3 and 813. The words "audi christianos" at first seems conclusive, but those which follow are still puzzling. Cf. *Bolletino di archeologia cristiana*, 1864, p. 71, where de Rossi sets forth an explanation which is not a necessary one. On the other hand, there have been discovered at Pompeii examples of a kind of word square, called a magic square, the Christian character of which seems fairly certain, though it has not yet won complete acceptance, and their discovery *in situ* is still a matter of discussion. Cf. Jalabert, *A propos des nouveaux exemplaires trouvés à Pompei du carré magique "sator"* (*C. R. Acad. Inscr.*, 1937, pp. 84 *et seq.*). Cf. also D. Mallarde, *La questione dei cristiani a Pompei* (extract from *Rivista di Studi pompeiani*, 1934-1935, Vol. I), which concludes that there are not sufficient proofs of the existence of Christianity in Pompeii.

Illyria, Spain and Gaul

Earlier still (for he speaks of it in his Epistle to the Romans written in 57 or 58) Paul had, apparently in the course of his travels the preceding year in Macedonia, gone as far as the confines of the Illyrian region,[4] and his disciple Titus visited Dalmatia while the Apostle himself was in Rome.[5] The preaching of Paul doubtless also made itself heard in Spain.[6]

In the course of the stops which his boat must have made,[7] in accordance with the sailing custom of that time, along the Mediterranean coasts of Gaul, Paul's voice very likely sounded in some synagogue or public place of Marseilles or Narbonne. One of his disciples, Crescentius, seems, according to the second epistle to Timothy, to have preached in Gaul,[8] but the towns he may have evangelised are unknown: the church of Vienne claimed him only later, and cannot make good its claim.[9]

As to the apostolic claims of so many other churches of the Gauls, their number and assurance do not suffice to justify them; they are too late in time, and are too manifestly inspired by the sentiments of an ill-informed piety and an intemperate local patriotism to call for a place in a history of the Church.

Some have fancied that Lazarus, the friend of Jesus, came into Provence, that he was the first bishop of Marseilles, and

---

[4] *Rom.* xv *et seq.*

[5] *II Tim.* iv, 11.

[6] Cf. Lebreton and Zeiller, Bk. I, p. 283.

[7] St. Jerome says that Paul made the voyage by sea.

[8] Some good manuscripts have Κρήσκης εἰς Γαλλίαν while others give εἰς Γαλατίαν. The two words can equally signify Gaul or Galatia in Asia Minor. But the latter seems more likely, from the fact that the same passage mentions together with the mission of Crescentius that of Titus to Dalmatia, i.e., to a country which was evidently still to be evangelized, whereas Galatia had already heard the Gospel. [R. St. J. Parry in his *Pastoral Epistles,* Cambridge, 1920, *in loc.,* says, "There is nothing to decide which district is meant, even if we could be certain that the point of departure was Rome."—Tr.]

[9] That the apostolic travels of Crescentius should have led him to go up the Rhone Valley is itself very plausible. But if the church of Vienne had really had such an early origin, it would not have failed to oppose this to the claims of Arles when there was rivalry for the primacy of jurisdiction in the fifth century.

that he was accompanied by his sisters Martha and Mary, whom tradition associates with the town of Tarascon and the caves of Sainte-Baume. Again, the most prominent episcopal sees in France have been generously given as founders direct disciples of St. Peter, such as Trophimus, first bishop at Arles, or disciples of St. Paul, such as Dionysius, the illustrious convert of the Areopagus at Athens, awarded the bishopric of Paris; or again of Jesus Himself, as Martial of Limoges, who is supposed to have been none other than the boy with the loaves and fishes on the occasion of the Gospel miracle of the multiplication of the loaves! These are naive legends, which edify or amuse, but have their basis only in the imagination and local pride of particular districts.

These stories are for the most part very late: the belief in the coming of SS. Mary and Martha to Provence cannot count a thousand years of existence, and the best proof of its inexactitude is the fact that it was preceded by another, the Burgundian tradition, which placed the bodies of these saints at Vezelay, whither they were supposed to have been brought from the East. There certainly was a bishop of Aix in Provence named Lazarus, but he was a contemporary of St. Augustine. The legend of the apostolic if not Athenian origin of St. Dionysius is somewhat earlier than the provençal legends: we can trace it back to the sixth century,[10] when he begins to be set forth as having been sent by Pope Clement I, the third successor of St. Peter. But what credit can we give to an account so far removed from the actual events?

The oldest apostolic claim in Gaul is that of the church of Arles, which already in the beginning of the fifth century regarded Trophimus its founder as a disciple of St. Peter. But this is unfortunately closely linked with the ambition of Arles at that time to be recognised as the first of the episcopal sees in Gaul, merely because, having become the administrative capital, Pope Zosimus momentarily invested its bishop with the title of Papal Vicar.[11]

[10] Cf. L. Levillain, *Etude sur l'Abbaye de Saint-Denis à l'époque mérovingienne*, 1. *Les sources narratives*, in *Bibliothèque de l'Ecole de Chartres*, Vol. LXXXII, 1921, p. 528, and *Le crise des années 507-508 et les rivalités d'influence en Gaule* (*Mélanges Jorga*, Paris, 1933, pp. 537-567).

[11] On the apostolic legends in general concerning the churches in Gaul, see J. Zeiller, *Les origines chrétiennes en Gaule*, in *Revue d'Histoire de l'Eglise de France*, 1926, pp. 16-33, which contains

The Spanish "traditions" of the evangelisation of the country by St. James the Great have as little foundation and are almost more unlikely than the apostolic legends of Gaul, seeing that St. James was martyred at Jerusalem before the dispersion of the apostles.[12]

Putting legends aside, it remains that some privileged regions of the West, Rome and southern Italy, the Illyrian littoral and also, apparently, the coasts of Provence and Spain, received the first announcement of the Gospel in the apostolic period. We may conjecture that the same was the case with Africa, since there were inhabitants of Cyrene amongst those who heard the sermon at Pentecost, and a great metropolis like Carthage was in constant relation with the East.[13] The relatively numerous Oriental elements in several Western cities, especially in seaports such as Puteoli, Marseilles, and Carthage, must have provided at the beginning very active agents of Christian propaganda.

Christianity in Asia

But in this second half of the first century, the East from which they came was much more thoroughly penetrated by the Christian Faith than was the West. Palestine was its original focus, and Syria, through its metropolis Antioch, was the second centre from which it spread. Asia Minor, in which so many cities had received the word from St. Paul, and perhaps from St. John, was by the end of the first century one of the parts of the Empire in which the religion of Christ had been most widely preached. The Church of Ephesus owed its foundation to St. Paul, and the Apostle

a bibliography on the subject. The only monograph of the present day on Christian origins in Gaul is that of T. Scott Holmes, *The Origin and Development of the Christian Church in Gaul during the First Six Centuries of the Christian Era,* London, 1911.

[12] On Christian origins in Spain, cf. Z. García Villada, *Historia ecclesiastica de Espana,* Vol. I, *El cristianismo durante la dominacion romana,* Madrid, 1929, 2 vols.

[13] A vague memory was conserved in the church of Carthage that its first preachers of Christianity originally came from the East. The idea that it had received Christianty from Rome seems to have originated only later on. Cf. P. Monceaux, *Histoire littéraire de l'Afrique chrétienne,* Vol. I, Paris, 1901, ch. 1, pp. 3-11, and A. Audollent, *Carthage romaine,* Paris, 1901, L. V, part I, ch. I, pp. 435-441.

John, according to the generally received tradition, governed it subsequently for many years.[14] The churches of Alexandria, Troas, Laodicea and Hierapolis, the dwelling place of Philip the deacon (later confused with the apostle of the same name) and his daughters known as prophetesses, are mentioned in the Pauline epistles. The Churches of Smyrna, Pergamus, Sardis, Philadelphia and Thyatira were, together with those of Ephesus and Laodicea, the recipients of the *Apocalypse* of John. The Christian communities of Tralles in Lydia and Magnesia in Caria appear about the year 100 in the letters of St. Ignatius of Antioch, the successor of Evodius, left in that city by St. Peter when his own apostolate called him elsewhere.

Further away from the coastal region of Asia Minor, Christianity penetrated into Pisidia with St. Paul. Iconium, Antioch in Pisidia, Lystra and Derbe possessed very early their Christian communities, and the rest of the country became Christianized rapidly. The Christian churches in Galatia were also among the fruits of the apostolate of St. Paul, who addressed to them one of his best known letters. He wrote also to the Christians of Colossæ in Phrygia, though he seems not to have evangelised them.

Bithynia on the Black Sea was evidently reached before the end of the first century, since already in the dawn of the second, Christianity was, according to the letters of Pliny the Younger, invading "not only the cities but also the towns and the countryside, emptying the precincts of the temples." [15]

Shortly afterwards, the town of Sinope had a bishop, who was the father of the heretic Marcion.[16]

Christianity also spread into the islands of the Archipelago. Paul and Barnabas had preached in 44 or 45 at Cyprus, and Paul there brought about the striking conversion of the proconsul, Sergius Paulus.

Christianity in the Hellenic Peninsula

The various countries in the Hellenic peninsula, Macedonia, Greece, and at least some of the neighbouring islands, had been evangelised at the very beginning of Christian preaching by St. Paul himself or his disciples such as Titus, who was

[14] Cf. Bk. I, pp. 240, 316.
[15] Cf. *infra*, p. 80.
[16] Eusebius, *Hist. Eccles.*, V, 13, 3.

the apostle of Crete. At any rate, the epistle which Paul addressed to Titus tells us that the apostle had placed him at the head of the Christian community constituted in the island, in which he had perhaps himself preached after his imprisonment in Rome and his voyage to Spain.

Philippi in Macedonia, Thessalonica, Berea, Nicopolis in Epirus, Athens, Corinth and Cenchrae near Corinth, had their churches towards the latter part of the first century. Those of Develtum and Anchialo in Thrace, Larissa in Thessaly, Lacedæmon and Cephalonia are mentioned in the second century. The church of Byzantium, which was to have so striking a future, cannot bring forward any proof of its existence at this time other than that of having produced the heretic Theodotus, who went to Rome about 190.[17]

True, later on its claimants to pre-eminence in the East were able to appeal to the "tradition" of a Thracian apostolate of St. Andrew, whose Acts make him die a martyr in Achaia. But these Acts are not earlier than the end of the third century, and are clearly legendary in some respects.[18] They may indeed convey to us an echo of memories which are earlier and less unworthy of belief, and the fact that Eusebius, relying perhaps on Origen, mentions the tradition[19] of a mission of Andrew in Scythia (that is, apparently, on the Roman shores of the Black Sea south of the Danube, inhabited by ancient Greek colonies) would support the hypothesis that Andrew was in touch with the Hellenic world, whose patron saint he became. But this remains wholly conjectural.

Christianity in Egypt

To the south-east of Palestine there is Egypt, destined to play a prominent part in the history of early Christendom. Did this country receive the Christian seed in apostolic times?

[17] Hippolytus, *Philosophumena*, VII, 35.
[18] Cf. J. Flamion, *Les Actes apocryphes de l'apôtre André*, Louvain-Paris, 1911. The *Acts of Andrew* have been published by Lipsius and Bonnet in *Acta Apostolorum apocrypha*, Vol. II, Leipzig, 1898, Vol. I. English translation in James, *Apocryphal New Testament*, pp. 337-363.
[19] Eusebius, *Hist. Eccles.*, III, i, 1. The text is given in the works of Origen, Migne, *P.G.*, Vol. XII, 92, but it does not follow clearly from the text of Eusebius that the statement about Andrew was already in Origen.

That is, in itself, quite likely. A passage in the *Acts* (xviii, 24-25) perhaps confirms it when it speaks of the Alexandrian Jew, Apollos, "who had been instructed (in his own country) in the way of the Lord"; unfortunately the parenthesis is not found in all the manuscripts. In any case it must be admitted that nothing is known of this primitive evangelisation. A tradition which came to be accepted, and is found in Eusebius,[20] attributes the foundation of the great ecclesiastical see of Egypt, that of Alexandria, to St. Mark the evangelist, the disciple of St. Peter. and we have a list of bishops which begins with him. We are not in a position to estimate the value of the first names on this list, but equally we must not dismiss them entirely.[21] If the letter of Claudius to the Alexandrians, which has aroused such interest and controversy, could be accepted as a witness to the reality of Christian activity at Alexandria in the year 41, this would decidedly strengthen the information given in Eusebius for this very same year. But the testimony seems ever less satisfactory,[22] and we must resign ourselves to an ignorance as to the origin of the Egyptian church which does not lessen the probability of its very great antiquity. Already in the second century the bishops of Alexandria appear in history,[23] and this great city had then a large Christian population, which implies a much earlier evangelisation.

Progress of the Evangelisation of the West in the Second Century: Gaul

In the course of this century, Christianity made good progress in the West, which hitherto had not been much affected. The churches of Gaul and Africa, in fact, figure gloriously in history well before the year 200.

The well known story of the martyrdom of Christians at Lyons in 177 shows us a church which was already of some importance in the Gallic metropolis in the reign of the Em-

[20] *Hist. Eccles,* II, 16, 1.
[21] Cf. Eusebius, *Hist. Eccles.,* II, 24; III, 14; IV, 19.
[22] Bk. I, § 3, n. 10.
[23] At least beginning with Demetrius (180). The earlier names, again, are not summarily to be rejected, but the constant ascription of exactly twelve years of episcopate by the list in Eusebius to each one of the predecesors of Demetrius after Annanius, the successor of Mark, barely conceals a chronological ignorance which must be taken into consideration.

peror Marcus Aurelius.[24] At its head was Bishop Pothinus, who came originally from Asia, where he had been a disciple of St. Polycarp of Smyrna; in Lyons he was assisted by clerics of various ranks.

We find also amongst the martyrs of Lyons a deacon of Vienne, which accordingly reveals the existence of a Christian community in that city. All this implies an evangelisation which had taken place some time before, and probably we shall not go far wrong if we think that the beginnings of Christianity at Lyons were not later than the reign of Hadrian, in the first half of the second century. An inscription, preserved at Marseilles,[25] and coming doubtless from that neighbourhood, which seems to refer to two martyrs Volusianus and Fortunatus, burnt to death, may well be at least as ancient.

Africa

The martyrological documents of Africa are concerned with events very close in time to those of Lyons, and lead to a similar conclusion. African Christianity, which gave to the church several martyrs towards the end of the second century, certainly began many years earlier. An archæological testimony confirms this in a very remarkable way: at Susa, the ancient Hadrumetum, Christian catacombs have been found in one of which there is an inscription of the Severian epoch, belonging to a tomb which is chronologically one of the last of a series numbering more than five thousand. The catacomb therefore must have come into use at least half a century previously, which would put the first evangelisation in the first half of the second century.[26] It is likely that Christian preaching reached Carthage before secondary towns like Hadrumetum.

Spain

May we think that Christianity developed in a similar way in Spain in the second century? Here there are no traces perpetuated in stone such as can be appealed to by the

[24] Cf. *infra,* p. 93.
[25] *Corpus inscriptionum Latinorum,* Vol. XII, 489.
[26] Mgr. Leynaud, *Les catacombes africaines. Sousse-Hadrumète,* 2nd edn., Algiers, 1922, pp. 9-16. The inscription in question is dated in the consulate of Lupus, who may be L. Virius Lupus, consul in 232.

churches of Gaul and Africa.[27] The darkness which envelopes the Christian origins in Spain after the preaching of St. Paul, the immediate consequences of which escape us entirely, is at most interrupted by one glimmer of light.

An entry in the Martyrology of Adon[28] states that a mission consisting of seven bishops was sent into Spain by St. Peter: the absence of this information in the Hieronymian Martyrology is not calculated to add to its credibility; the number seven and the sending by St. Peter increase our mistrust. Yet there is one point which inclines us to a more favourable judgment: the head of the mission is said to have founded the church of the *Civitas Accitana* (Guadix). Now when about the year 300 there was held at Illiberi (Elvira) a council famous in the religious annals of Spain, the Bishop of Acci presided over it: it is allowable to infer from this that the church of Acci was regarded then as the mother church of Spain, or at least of the province of Tarragona. But the inference is not a peremptory one.

In any case, the date of the mission which gave birth to the church of Acci and to those of the surrounding region is impossible to determine even approximately.

§ 2. EVANGELISATION BEYOND THE EMPIRE

Christianity in Persia

There are good grounds for believing in a very early preaching of Christianity outside the Empire, in the great kingdom which extended beyond the eastern frontiers of the Roman world, the Parthian kingdom, which at the beginnings of the third century became once more the Persian realm. The "traditions" of a threefold apostolate of Bartholomew, Thaddæus and Thomas in Persia are without solid foundation.[1] But the text in the Acts of the Apostles (ii, 9) which mentions among those present on Pentecost Day "Parthians and Medes, and Elamites, and inhabitants of Meso-

[27] A Tarragonian inscription (*C.I.L.*, II, p. 25,* no. 231*) alluding to the penetration of Christianity in this province under Nero is obviously a forgery.
[28] Under date May 15th.
[1] Cf. Lebreton and Zeiller, Bk. I, p. 331, and J. Labourt, *Le christianisme dans l'Empire perse sous la dynastie sassanide*, Paris, 1904, pp. 11-15.

potamia" supports the view that "towards the year 80, the
churches of the Greco-Roman world knew of the existence of
Christian communities in the far away lands of the east." [2]

It is likely that the missionary activity of these first propa-
gators of Christianity in Persia was confined to the Jewish
colonies of Babylonia. But it would seem that it met with
little success, seeing that it left no trace, and on the contrary
a passage in the Talmud speaks of the Babylonian region as
at that time entirely outside Christian influence.[3]

Was Christian preaching rejected by the synagogues, and
addressed instead, as elsewhere, to the pagans? This is possible, if it be true that, as the documents which give us some
knowledge, though imperfect, of Mandæism (a transformation of the old Iranian religion combined with semitic
elements) state, relations were established between the Mandæans and the Christians of early times. But in reality, what
we know of Mandæism—in spite of recent attempts which
have gone so far as to endeavour to find in it one of the
religious currents from whence Christianity itself arose[4]—
remains too uncertain to enable us to specify, or even to
establish a relation between Christianity and the oriental
movement of religious syncretism of which the Babylonian
Gnosticism shown in Mandæism constituted a phase.

In short, what had been and was again to become the
Persian kingdom was touched by Christian propaganda already in apostolic times; but the results, such as they were,
are so little apparent to us that we may well wonder whether
the seed sown by these first evangelists was not almost completely choked. In any case we cannot number Persia amongst

[2] Labourt, *op. cit.*, p. 16.

[3] *Ibid.*, p. 17.

[4] Cf. R. Reitzenstein, *Das mandäische Buch des Herrn des Grosse
und die Evangelienüberlieferung,* Heidelberg, 1919. Critique by
M. J. Lagrange, *La gnose mandéenne et la tradition évangelique,*
in *Revue biblique,* 1927, pp. 321-349 and 481-515, and 1928,
pp. 5-32. A. Loisy, *Le mandéisme et les origines chrétiennes*
(Paris, 1934) also declines to accept the thesis of Reitzenstein.
H. Lietzmann, *Ein Beitrag zur Mandäerfrage* (*Sitzungsberichte
Akad. Berlin, phil.-hist. Klasse,* 1930, pp. 596-608) has set forth
the reasons for thinking that the Mandæans were an oriental
Gnostic sect, of a relatively late date, and that it had nothing
to do with Christian origins. [A useful summary of recent Man-
dæan studies is given in F. C. Burkitt's *Church and Gnosis,*
Cambridge, 1932.]

the countries in which we find at the end of the first, or even in the first half of the second century, a properly constituted Church.

Christianity in Osroene

Between the Roman Empire and the Parthian kingdom, which became Persia once more later, there existed until the third century a little independent state, that of Edessa or Osroene, in which Christianity was planted quite early. The tradition recorded by Eusebius which puts King Abgar in correspondence with Jesus Himself, and says that his country was evangelized by the apostle Thomas and the disciple Thaddeus (Addai), has all the appearances of a legend; the fourth century veneration of the tomb of St. Thomas at Edessa and the reading there of supposed letters from Jesus to Abgar certainly do not suffice to make it authentic.[5] It is not even certain that the legend of Thaddeus may not be merely an embellishment of the acts and needs of an historic personage named Addai. Doubtless we may think that Eusebius, who was fairly well informed as to the local traditions of the countries near Syria, would not trouble to include a recently formed legend concerning the planting of Christianity in Osroene. But how are we to explain the fact that the apostle of Edessa, who is supposed to have died a martyr, is not even mentioned in the Syrian martyrology of the year 412? It is best to admit that the circumstances of the evangelisation of Osroene escape us. But the great number of the Christians in the region of Edessa at the end of the second century compels us to allow that its evangelisation had begun long before.

From Edessa, the Gospel must have been very soon carried beyond the Tigris, into Adiabene, if we may believe the Chronicle of the Church of Arbela [6] which attributes this apostolate across the Tigris to the supposed founder of the church of Edessa. But the re-appearance at the commencement of the church of Adiabene of this doubtful founder of that of Edessa, together with more than one anachronism and contradiction in various martyrological testi-

[5] Cf. J. Tixeront, *Les origines de l'Eglise d'Edesse,* Paris, 1888. The text of Abgar's letter and our Lord's reply is given in translation in M. R. James, *Apocryphal New Testament,* pp. 476-77.
[6] Edited by P. Zorell, *Orientalia christiana,* VIII, 4, no. 31 (1927).

monies, are not calculated to win [7] for the Chronicle of Arbela a credit which critics such as Harnack [8] have nevertheless not refused to give it.

As to an apostolic preaching of the Gospel on the African or Arabian shores of the Red Sea and as far as the Indies, we have already remarked that its historic reality remains uncertain, and that in any case its immediate results, if there were any, are entirely hidden from us.

[7] Cf. Paul Peeters, *La Passionaire d'Adiabène* in *Analecta Bollandiana,* Vol. XLIII, 1925, pp. 261-325.
[8] In his last edition (4th) of *Mission und Ausbreitung des Christentums,* Leipzig, 1924.

Chapter 3

The First Persecutions, and Imperial Legislation Concerning the Christians [1]

§1. THE NERONIAN PERSECUTION

WHILE THE EXPANSION of Christianity was taking place in the Roman world and beyond, the Empire, well before the end of the second century, had declared war upon the Church, beginning by putting its first head to death.

The Martyrdom of St. Peter

The martyrdom of St. Peter is, with that of St. Paul, the most important event in the first bloody persecution ordered by the imperial authority, which struck at Christians in the Empire and began in the reign of Nero.

The Burning of Rome and the Accusing of the Christians

This persecution, which might have burst forth some day or other on other excuses, since an occasion would probably have been sought sooner or later to proscribe Christianity, had an accidental immediate cause. In July, 64, a terrible fire devastated several parts of Rome; an almost unanimous and possibly well-informed opinion regarded Nero as having caused the fire, or at any rate of having helped its spread, in the desire to clear a place for the extension of his palace. To turn aside the current of hostile opinion, the emperor conceived the idea of putting the blame on the Christians, now

[1] Bibliography. The general bibliography for this chapter is the same as that of the preceding one.

Particular works to be referred to for the study of the character of the persecutions are, together with the ancient sources which give information on this subject, indicated in the notes to the chapter.

To the above may be added: A. Bouché-Leclerq, *L'intolérance religieuse et la politique*, Paris, 1911; A. Manaresi, *L'impera romano e il cristianesimo*, Turin, 1914; L. Homo, *Les empereurs romains et le christianisme*, Paris, 1931.

named as such for the first time by Tacitus[2] and described
as men "hated for their infamies" and "convicted of hatred
of the human race." [3] Whether because of the hatred which
they inspired, or more probably because of that of which
they were thought to be guilty because they had not the spirit
of the world, the hostility of public opinion towards them is
beyond doubt. Was this spontaneous? Probably it was, in
great measure: the mass of the people, perhaps because they
still confused Christians with the Jews, who were always and
everywhere disliked for their sectarianism, was certainly not
favourable. They came to impute to them the crimes of
atheism, magic, cannibalism, and other abominations. Nevertheless there may have been other factors in 64.

In the Emperor's entourage, the influence of the Judaism
which was loyal to the Empire and which would play a
prominent part a little later under the Flavian dynasty, was
already fairly strong: the Judaising sympathies of the favourite Poppea are known.[4] And the hatred of the followers of
the Old Law for those of the New did not diminish. Did
protégés of Poppea admitted into the circle immediately surrounding the emperor, think that they would serve Nero as
well as themselves "by pointing out as the authors of the
crime the Christians" [5] who took pleasure, it was said—and
the sentiments of which the *Apocalypse* of St. John is a vehement though late echo, might seem to give an appearance of
justification to such sayings—"in the ideas of heavenly ven-
geance, a universal conflagration, and the destruction of the
world"? [6] The conjecture is a plausible one; positive arguments to support it are lacking. Nevertheless, a passage in

[2] *Annales*, XV, 44.
[3] The manuscript of Tacitus long regarded as the best, the *Medi-
ceus,* has instead of the word *convicti,* that of *conjuncti,* which
would mean that the Christians were involved in one and the
same persecution for having caused the fire, and because of their
odium generis humani. Cf. E. Coq, *De la nature des crimes
imputés aux chrétiens d'après Tacite, in Mélanges d'archéologie
et d'histoire* published by the *Ecole française* in Rome, Vol. VI,
1886, pp. 115-139. The general nature of events is more or less
the same in either interpretation.
[4] Josephus, *Life,* 3; *Antiquities of the Jews,* XVIII-XX. Cf.
Tacitus, *Hist.,* i, 22.
[5] Cf. E. Renan, *L'Antichrist,* pp. 159-161.
[6] Duruy, *Histoire des Romains,* Vol. IV, p. 507 (edn. 1882, Paris).

the celebrated letter addressed to the Corinthians by St. Clement, one of the first successors of St. Peter, saying that SS. Peter and Paul perished as victims of jealousy,[7] may be a reference to this intervention of the Jewish element. In any case, from that day the Christians began to be distinguished by the Roman authorities from the Jews, who remained in possession of their privileges, while Christians were arrested, judged and condemned.

Possibly internal discords played some part in the denunciations which sent some of the Christian community of Rome to their deaths, together with their leaders: the letter of St. Clement is equally capable of being interpreted in this sense. One may infer that the disagreements, due very likely to the action of Judeo-christians, led to imprudences which helped to cause the intervention of the Roman police, if they did not go as far as positive acts of denunciation—a hypothesis which may be supported by a phrase in Tacitus concerning indications given to the authorities by some Christians— *indicio eorum.*[8]

The Martyrs

First were arrested, according to Tacitus,[9] those who admitted (*fatebantur*) perhaps the crime of arson[10]—the untrue confession may have been extorted by torture—or more probably their Christianity, which from this moment became a crime. Then, *indicio eorum* (this may just as well mean formal denunciations obtained from these first prisoners, or else simple indications drawn from their talk, their very silences, their relations, and from all that was known of their life), the arrests increased rapidly, and a great number of Christians—*multitudo ingens,* writes Tacitus, who would not wish to exaggerate greatly the number of those he regarded

[7] *First Epistle to Corinthians,* V.
[8] Cf. O. Cullmann, *Les causes de la mort de Pierre et de Paul d'après le témoignage de Clément Romain, in Revue d'histoire et de philosophie religeuse,* 1930, pp. 294-300.
[9] *Loc. cit.*
[10] The hypothesis of the guilt of the Christians has found a few defenders in our days: cf. Pascal, *L'incendio di Roma e i primi cristiani,* 2nd edn., Turin, 1901; it has no support in early writers: not one of those who have spoken of the burning of Rome after Tacitus imputes it to the Christians. Cf. A. Profumo, *Le fonti ed i tempi dell' incendio neroniano,* Rome, 1905.

as enemies of Roman society,[11] were eventually given over to the torments which Nero's cruelty had invented for them. He conceived the idea of "transforming their torture into a spectacle, and in his gardens on the Vatican he gave nightly festivals, in which the unfortunate Christians, covered in pitch and devoured by the flames, cast a sinister light on the circus performances." [12]

Peter was one of the martyrs.[13]

Eusebius, in his *Ecclesiastical History,*[14] gives the date 67 or 68, instead of 64 or 65 for this, probably merely because he attributes to Peter the famous twenty-five years as Bishop of Rome, beginning in 42. But the persecution once begun may have continued after 64, and it is not at all impossible that Paul, arrested after his return to Rome, may have suffered the capital penalty[15] just one or two years after St. Peter. But the same immemorial cult which unites them together attests the at least relative chronological proximity of their death.

§2. THE PROHIBITION OF CHRISTIANITY

Possible Extension of the Persecution to the Provinces

Did the persecution extend to the provinces? We do not possess any positive statement to this effect, but there may

[11] The Heronymian Martyrology gives 979 as the number of martyrs who perished with SS. Peter and Paul. It is difficult to estimate the value of this figure, but it is worth mentioning.

[12] L. Duchesne, *Histoire de l'Eglise,* Vol. I, p. 63.

[13] According to a tradition of which Tertullian, *De Præscriptione* 36, *Scorpiacus* 15, is our first witness, he was condemned to be crucified. This is quite in harmony with the account of Tacitus, which speaks of Christians as crucified in the Vatican gardens, and it may also be alluded to by St. John's Gospel (xxi, 18, 19): "When thou shalt be old, thou shalt stretch forth thy hands, and another shall gird thee, and lead thee whither thou wouldst not. And this he said, signifying by what death he should glorify God."

[14] Eusebius, *Eccles. Hist.*, II, XIV, 6, where he makes Peter arrive in Rome in the year 42, and attributes to him a Roman episcopate of 25 years.

[15] Clement, the successor of Peter (*Epistle to the Corinthians*), Tertullian, and the priest Caius agree in saying that St. Paul was beheaded on the Ostian Way, and buried there.

be an allusion to it in the Epistle to the Hebrews,[1] and it may also be urged that after the measures ordered by Nero the profession of Christianity was prohibited in the Empire. But the reality of this prohibition by Nero, or of an *institutum neronianum* expressly forbidding the Christian religion, has not met with universal acceptance. In point of fact, it is known only indirectly,[2] but its existence can scarcely be questioned.

The Neronian Legislation against Christianity

The questions put about half a century later by Pliny the Younger, Governor of Bithynia, to the Emperor Trajan as to the attitude to be adopted towards the Christians of his province, and the imperial rescript [3] which sent him the instructions asked for, prove the existence of an earlier legislation, the application of which had only to be clarified. Tertullian asserts, moreover,[4] in the most formal manner that Nero was the first to promulgate a law against Christians, and it cannot be doubted that the proscription of Christianity as such dates back to him: the Christians, first of all persecuted as incendiaries through the dishonest expedient of the frightened Nero, were evidently subsequently outlawed after police enquiries which ascertained their religious profession.[5]

Until then they had continued to be confused with the Jews in the eyes of the Roman authority; they were regarded doubtless as a particular sect, and thus enjoyed the privileges which enabled the Jews to retain their national religion in the Empire without performing acts of obedience in respect of the official cults. But henceforth a discrimination was made;

[1] In x, 32-38 there is reference to tribulations endured by believers for their faith. But it is not certain that this can be understood of the persecution under Domitian, inasmuch as the Epistle to the Hebrews written in the name of St. Paul was somewhat later in appearance.

[2] Cf. the full bibliography of the question in Cabrol-Leclercq, *Dictionnaire d'archéologie chrétienne*, article *Loi persecutrice*.

[3] Cf. *infra*, pp. 71-72.

[4] *Ad nationes*, 7; *Apologeticus*, 5.

[5] The Neronian origin of the prohibition of Christianity is indirectly confirmed by the text of *I Peter* v, 16, which opposes the glory of suffering *ut christianus* to the opprobrium involved in a condemnation for a crime against common law. The Epistle reflects the events in the primitive community.

possibly the Jews themselves were partly responsible for this, and this may be the most exact element in the thesis which regards the Jewish element as in some measure the cause of the outbreak of the first persecution. Henceforth Christianity was no longer regarded as a dissident form of Judaism, and had no longer any right to the favours enjoyed by the latter.[6] Consequently, the Christians were now bound, as citizens of the Empire, to comply with the minimum of religious conformity called for by the idea of the ancient State[7] or else disappear. Their faith, which allowed no concession, internal or external, to polytheism, excluded such conformity, and so there remained only outlawry, and this is undoubtedly the basis of the legislation made in their regard by Nero, and which may be summed up in one short phrase: *non licet esse christianos*, it is not lawful for Christians to exist.

§3. JURIDICAL CHARACTER OF THE PERSECUTIONS

The persecutions were not the effect merely of the application of laws previously existing.

The existence of a special legislative act explicitly prohibiting Christianity has nevertheless been much discussed. It has been said that it was sufficient to apply to Christians existing laws specifying penalties for the crime of sacrilege or of *lèse majesté*, as this would involve them in punish-

[6] Cf. above, Lebreton and Zeiller, Bk. I, pp. 29-30, 65, *et seq.;* also G. Costa, *Religione e politica nell, impero romano,* Turin, 1923, pp. 97-108. According to him, Jews and Christians were still confused together for a much longer time. He suggests that the text in Tacitus concerning the first persecution was modified, and that the *ingens multitudo* referred to included also a great number of Jews. But he brings forward no proof. Still, it is feasible that Christianity was not from this very moment regarded as a religion absolutely distinct from Judaism, but rather as a dissident form of it. The Emperor Domitian who, as we shall see, had a certain number of Christians put to death, was equally hostile to the Jews, as may be seen from the development of the *fiscus judaicus* in his reign. Cf. S. Gsell, *Essai sur le règne de l'empereur Domitien,* Paris, 1893, pp. 287-316. The enquiry which he caused to be made (cf. *infra,* p. 387) as to the descendants of the family of Jesus seems to show that he busied himself politically about Christianity regarded at least up to a certain point as a branch of Judaism.

[7] Cf. Fustel de Coulanges, *La cité antique.*

ments.[1] But sacrilege properly so called supposes a positive criminal act, which could not be found in the case of Christians; as for the crime of *lèse majesté,* closely connected, in point of fact, with that of sacrilege, committed in refusing to take part in the cult of the Emperor's divinity, we do not see Christians explicitly accused of this in the first two centuries: it is only in the third that the magistrates tried regularly to force Christians to sacrifice to the divinity of the emperor in consequence of new edicts of persecution, and condemned them if they refused to do so.

Doubtless one may say that the crime existed implicitly from the beginning, inasmuch as Christians did not recognise the Emperor as a god, and hence adopted an attitude which was bound to lead to their being regarded as defective citizens or subjects. But before the third century no text proves that the proper motive of the persecution of the Christians was a refusal which made them guilty of *lèse majesté.* They were accused rather, at first, of failing to reverence the gods of the Empire in general, and even this did not make them officially atheists, as they were judged to be by popular ignorance.

The same is true of the accusation of other especially serious crimes against common law, such as magic, incest, or infanticide: it was never more than popular rumour which imputed these to the Christians, and official justice did not take up these accusations.[2] Hence we shall not find in previous penal law the precise juridical basis of the persecutions.

Nor were they due merely to the coercive power of the magistrates.

Others have sought for this basis in the power of *coercitio,*[3] i.e., police powers which belonged to all the Roman magistrates. In order to maintain public order, these had a very

[1] Thesis of K. J. Neumann, *Der römische Staat und die allgemeine Kirche bis auf Diocletian,* Leipzig, 1890, pp. 12 *et. seq.*
[2] Contrary to what is maintained by E. Le Blant, *Sur les bases des poursuites dirigées contre les chrétiens,* in *Comptes-rendus de l'Académie des Inscriptions et de Belles-Lettres,* 1866, pp. 358 *et seq.,* according to whom Christians were condemned as guilty of homicide or of magic, as well as of sacrilege or *lèse majesté.*
[3] Theory of T. Mommsen, *Der Religionsfrevel nach römischen Recht,* in *Historische Zeitschrift, Neue Folge,* XXVIII, 1890, pp. 389-429.

extensive authority which went as far as putting to death anyone who disturbed the peace. Hence it is suggested that it was as public disturbers that the Christians, disobeying the injunction to abandon a profession of faith which was in itself a public disorder, were condemned by the decision of the magistrates, without any need of applying to them a more express law.

But if the magistrates merely had to exercise towards the Christians their power of *coercitio,* why did they more than once think it necessary to consult the prince as to the way to treat them, as we see Pliny the Younger writing to Trajan, and other governors under Antoninus or Marcus Aurelius? Moreover, Pliny speaks formally of the steps taken against the Christians as resulting from the exercise of criminal jurisdiction, *cognitio,* and accordingly, not as a result of *coercitio.* Lastly, the *coercitio* extending to the capital penalty could not be exercised in the case of a Roman citizen.

Special Legislation against the Christians

Thus we are compelled to accept[4] the reality of special legislative measures against the Christians, of which the Emperor Nero was the author, as in fact affirmed by Tertullian.[5] From his reign to that of Septimius Severus, who introduced a new regime, the juridical situation of Christians in the Roman Empire remained the same: they were proscribed, not as guilty of crimes against the common law such as incest, cannibalism or magic, as imputed to them so often by popular hostility, itself caused by difference of beliefs and customs, nor of the crimes of sacrilege or *lèse majesté,* but as guilty of professing a religion which had been forbidden:

[4] As C. Callewaert well brought out over thirty years ago, in a series of works: *Les premiers chrétiens fûrent-ils persécutés par édits généraux ou par mesures de police?* in *Revue d'histoire ecclésiastique,* 1910, pp. 771-797; 1902, pp. 5-15, 324-348, 607-615; *Le délit de christianisme dans les deux premiers siècles,* in *Revue des questions historiques,* 1903, Vol. LXXIV, pp. 28-55; *Les premiers chrétiens et l'accusation de lèse-majesté,* in *ibid.,* 1904, Vol. LXXVI, pp. 5-28; *Les persécutions contre les chrétiens dans la politique religieuse de l'Empire romain,* in *ibid.,* 1907, Vol. LXXXII, pp. 5-19; *La méthode dans la recherche de la base juridique des premières persécutions,* in *Revue d'histoire ecclés.,* 1911, pp. 5-16, 633-651.

[5] "Institutum Neronianum" is how he describes the law of persecution in *Apolog.,* 5.

christianos esse non licet. Thus it is the very name of Christian, the *nomen christianum*, that was forbidden and condemned, as Christian apologists more than once contended.

The Clarifications in Trajan's Rescript

The rescript of Trajan added to the principle of Nero about half a century later some necessary clarifications, the need of which had been shown in practice.[6] This imperial reply to the questions from a governor consisted of three points. The first two were modifications of a rule which the progress of a propaganda that could in no wise be stopped made it difficult to apply in all strictness, as is shown well by Pliny's hesitation before the prospect of too numerous condemnations.

The Emperor accordingly declared in substance: 1. Governmental authority is not to take the initiative in the processes: it is not to seek out Christians, *christiani conquirendi non sunt.* 2. Those who are accused and who declare that they are not Christians, or are such no longer, that is to say, those who have committed the legal crime of being Christians but have effaced it by apostasy, manifested by an external act of adhesion to paganism, are to be dismissed. 3. Those who confess to being Christians are to be condemned.

The letter of Pliny, and the sequence of events, show that this condemnation could only be the capital penalty, i.e., death, or one of the penalties which, like exile or forced labour in the mines involved civil death. But on the other hand, and in virtue of the second point in the rescript, we shall no more see governors before whom Christians are taken doing their utmost to obtain from them a word, or sometimes just a simple act, such as offering a few grains of

---

[6] Pliny the Younger, *Epistolæ,* X, 97 and 98. Doubts have sometimes been raised as to the authenticity of this correspondence, especially in view of the improbability of the picture which Pliny gives of his province, as already so strongly affected by Christian progapanda that the temples were deserted, and the sacrifices abandoned. We may reply with E. Babut, *Remarques sur les deux lettres de Pline et de Trajan relatives aux chrétiens de Bithynie,* in *Revue d'histoire et de Littérature religieuses,* new series Vol. I, 1910, pp. 289-305, that Pliny, who manifestly desired not to pronounce too many condemnations, may have been led to magnify the number of Christians in order to discourage repression by the very perspective of its extent.

incense to the statue of the Emperor, which could be interpreted as a disavowal, even if only a temporary one, of the
Christian faith.

Tortures were in many instances less a punishment than a
means attempted in order to extract this denial from the
accused. As for the Emperors themselves, the best of them,
as we shall see in detail in the case of Hadrian and Antoninus, if not Marcus Aurelius, who regarded Christians
with contempt rather than pity, added new precautions which
mitigated the application of a legal system the principle of
which they were nevertheless careful to maintain in all its
strictness.

Main Idea of the Legislation against the Christians

What, then, was the underlying idea which alone explains
the transformation of an expedient of the frightened Nero
into a rule of the State? It was that Christianity, a strictly
monotheistic religion, whose God would not divide his
honour with other divinities or with the world, could not be
reconciled with fundamental conceptions upon which the
Roman State rested. For this was closely associated with a
number of religious traditions, if not also of habits of life,
which were incompatible with the new faith; the mere fact
that the Christians did not worship the gods of Rome made
them rebels, or at least suspect, even before the time when
the worship or refusal of worship of the Emperor's statue
became the touchstone of their Roman conformity.

The religious position of the Jews was similar; but they
had before the year 70 formed a national body which had
received privileges and retained them after their final dispersion. Even when the obligation to sacrifice to the Emperor
could be imposed upon every citizen, they obtained legal
dispensations which safeguarded them from persecution.[7]
Doubtless the Roman authority only gradually learnt to make
a distinction between Christians and Jews. But the day came
when all confusion ceased. Christians did not, like the Jews,
form a compact national body, but a religious society
scattered abroad from its origin, the members of which were

---

[7] Instead of offering a sacrifice to the divine emperor, they offered
one to God for the emperor (cf. Josephus, *Contra Apionem*, II,
6, 77). See an account of the various privileges of the Jews in
the matter of the imperial cult, in J. Juster, *Les Juifs dans
l'Empire romain*, Paris, 1914, Vol. I, pp. 339-354.

all equally subjects who could not claim any special favour. This explains the imperial legislation against Christianity.

Juridical Origin and Form of this Legislation

The juridical origin was probably an ancient law of the republican epoch which forbade *superstitio illicita*,[8] and its form an imperial edict. Like the edicts of the prætors of the Republic, this particular edict was theoretically in force only during the reign of the Emperor who had published it. Thus it had to be renewed, and adopted, so to speak, by his successor.

This gives us, perhaps, a first reason for the intermittent character the persecutions at first displayed. Trajan decided at the beginning of the second century that there were to be no measures against Christians without previous accusation. But in the first place, these measures had to be in conformity with the imperial will. This was expressed for the first time by Nero. But then there was no severity towards Christians under the two first Flavians. The anti-Christian laws were renewed, in circumstances which we shall explain later, under Domitian; and this commencement of persecuting legislation by the two first century rulers who had left the worst reputations enabled the Christian apologists of the second century to set forth the idea that hostility towards Christianity emanated from bad emperors, and those whom every Roman had cause to hate.

But Trajan, the *optimus princeps* as he was called in his own lifetime, and whose reputation for goodness survived the Middle Ages, when faced with the question put to him by Pliny, who was worried by the prospect of the great number of capital sentences which would have to be pronounced against people who did not seem to be great criminals— Trajan could not avoid the issue, and it is by his reply that we know the principle of the laws directed against the Christians. True, the precise instructions emanating from him constitute already a modification, since he forbids the authorities to take the initiative—an interdiction so radical that the emperors themselves, when Christians boldly declared themselves by addressing to them their apologies for their faith, never answered what might seem to us to be challenges—if they ever know of these—by juridical measures. Nothing

---

[8] Cf. Tertullian, *Apologeticus*, 6.

shows better the singular and exceptional character of this legislation against the Christians than this disposition, by which the State seemed to take no cognisance of a legal crime so long as the guilty were not specifically pointed out, though it nevertheless punished with death those denounced in the appointed way. It is like a tacit confession of regret at having to punish in virtue of old ordinances, which nevertheless the State did not wish to revoke.

Chapter 4

The Persecution Under the Flavians and The Antonines[1]

THE CHURCH had come into collision with the traditions which the Empire represented, and the authorities which embodied them, in a first tragic encounter in the reign of Nero, and from that moment persecution, or more precisely, the constant danger of persecution, the effective realisation of which depended on circumstances, became its lot.

[1] Bibliography. The general bibliography is the same as that for chapter 2. In addition, there are good monographs dealing with the various Roman emperors of the end of the first and the second century: S. Gsell, *Essai sur le règne de Domitien*, Paris, 1893; R. Paribeni, *Optimus princeps. Saggio sulla storia e sui tempi dell' Imperatore Traiano*, Messina, 1926-1927, 2 vols.; G. Lacour-Gayet, *Antonin le Pieux et son temps*, Paris, 1888.

For the authentic texts of Acts of the Martyrs, see the *Acta Sanctorum* of the Bollandists, the publication of which began in Antwerp in 1643 and is being continued in Brussels; it is a collection undertaken from the first in a scientific spirit which won for it much hostility: a more searching criticism has been made in our own days. A selection of Acts of the Martyrs will be found in Ruinart, *Acta Sincera*, Paris, 1689; Dom H. Leclercq, *Les martyrs*, Paris, 1902-1911, 11 vols.; Knopf, *Ausgewählte Märtyreracten*, in *Sammlung ausgewählter kirchen-und-dogmengeschichtlicher Quellenschriften*, 2 Reihe, 2 Heft, Tübingen and Leipzig, 1901; P. Monceaux, *La véritable légende dorée*, Paris, 1928. We must also mention, for the Roman martyrological accounts, A. Dufourcq, *Etude sur les Gesta martyrum romains*, Paris, 1900-1910, 4 vols. The conclusions as to the very low historical value of most of the Roman *Gesta martyrum* has been generally accepted, but the same is not the case with those which attempt to explain their progressive elaboration.

On the Christian martyrs of Lyons in 177, it will be profitable to read C. Jullian, *Histoire de la Gaule*, Vol. IV: *Le gouvernement de Rome*, Paris, 1914, pp. 484-498.

§1. THE CHURCH UNDER THE FLAVIANS

The Roman Church under the Flavian Emperors

But just at first, being little known in spite of all, even after the bloody outburst of the year 64, and benefiting perhaps by the fact that the Emperors who followed Nero did not set out to imitate their predecessor who had left so deplorable a memory, the Church enjoyed a brief period of unquestionable tranquillity. There is absolutely no indication that in the ephemeral reigns of Galba, Otho and Vitellius, or under the two first Flavian emperors, Vespasian and Titus, Christians were attacked as such. In point of fact, it was then that at Rome, in the very heart of the Empire, Christianity, which there as elsewhere attracted mostly the humble, made also some of its most notable conquests in the highest circles of imperial society.

These conquests had moreover begun even before the first persecution. Already under Nero a great lady, Pomponia Græcina, married to a certain Plautius, a consul whose cousin espoused the emperor Claudius, had become suspect because she led a life which was too austere in the eyes of those of her circle, and had been accused of foreign superstition;[2] it is all the more probable that she had been converted to the Christian faith because subsequently we find the name of the Pomponii fairly well represented in the inscriptions in the Roman catacombs.[3] A. Plautius, her husband, claimed as head of the family the right to judge her according to ancient domestic custom, and declared her innocent. She lived until the reign of Domitian.

Converts to Christianity from the Aristocracy

The Flavians doubtless had not preconceived hostility against a religion which had issued from Judaism. Though they had brought about the ruin of Jerusalem, the siege of which had been begun by Vespasian before he came to the throne, and which had finally collapsed under the blows of

---

[2] *Tacitus*, Annals, XIII, 32.

[3] There are Christian inscriptions of a Pomponius Græcinus of the end of the second or beginning of the third century, and of of several Pomponii Bassi. Cf. De Rossi, *Roma sotterranea*, Vol. II, pp. 281, 362 *et seq.*

Titus in 70, they had admitted into their entourage the representatives of a revived Judaism, including the princess Berenice, of the house of Herod, and the historian Flavius Josephus.

Jewish ideas, which under Nero had possessed a temporary protector in Poppea, enjoyed then a return of favour in Rome, and the tendency towards religious monotheism profited thereby. The situation in Flavian Rome must have helped the progress of Christian propaganda even amongst the families of the senatorial aristocracy: after the Pomponii, it made converts amongst the Acilii: M. Acilius Glabrio, consul in the year 91, was very probably a Christian, and the oldest Christian cemetery, consecrated to the exclusive and collective use of those belonging to Roman Christianity, was a property of the Acilii on the Via Salaria.[4]

The Imperial house itself provided some converts. Flavius Sabinus, elder brother of Vespasian, was perhaps already a Christian[5] and his son, Flavius Clemens, a cousin german of Titus and Domitian, consul in 95, adopted the Christian faith. His wife Flavia Domitilla followed him, and made to the Roman Church a bequest similar to that of the Acilii, which became the cemetery on the Via Ardeatina still known to-day by their name; their two sons, pupils of Quintilian, who should have succeeded Titus and Domitian, themselves without male issue, also professed Christianity. If the tragic and premature end of Domitian, a natural epilogue to a tyrannical reign, had not annihilated the imperial hopes of these two young men, the Empire would have had at its head Christian princes two hundred years before Constantine.[6]

Another princess of the imperial house, a second Flavia Domitilla, niece of the first, would also have to be counted amongst the illustrious recruits to Christianity in Rome before the end of the first century, if her existence were more certain.[7]

---

[4] Cf. *infra*, p. 227.
[5] According to the description of his character given by Tacitus, *Hist.*, III, 65 and 75.
[6] The Christianity of Flavius Clemens and his wife Flavia Domitilla is attested by the accusation of atheism made against them by Domitian (Dio Cassius, LXVII, 14; cf. Suetonius, *Domitianus*, 15), and by the fact that the Christian cemetery named after Domitilla, was developed in land belonging to the latter.
[7] Cf. *infra*, p. 79.

The Persecution in Rome under Domitian

It was upon this flourishing Roman Christianity that, in spite of the bonds which linked some of its members to the throne itself, persecution broke out a second time in the year 95, under Domitian.

This ruler has left the memory of being a fickle tyrant; the philosophers, and all others who had the air of retaining some independence, were or became suspect to him. Moreover, he wanted to react against the spread of Jewish customs which had taken place under the rule of his father and brother. His antipathy towards the Jews was in harmony with his financial necessities, for his Treasury was exhausted after the excessive expenses he had incurred in the embellishment of Rome. Accordingly he caused to be levied with great strictness the tax of the didrachma, which the Jews, when independent, had paid to the Temple at Jerusalem, and the right to which had afterwards been claimed by Rome.[8] There were many recalcitrants amongst the proselytes who had adopted the faith of Israel but did not regard themselves as Jews.

Were the Christians who, though distinct from the Jews, were none the less still regarded as a Jewish sect, also called upon to pay the didrachma, and did their very natural resistance call for severe measures? There is, in point of fact, nothing which indicates this: it seems rather that only circumcised people were dealt with as refractory to the tax, and that if punishment was applied, it consisted only of pecuniary penalties. But on the other hand, the measures taken to compel the payment of the didrachma by all the circumcised may quite well have led indirectly to the persecution, by enabling the imperial power to take note of the number of citizens who led what was regarded as a Jewish life, whether they were proselytes of the faith of Moses or followers of that of Jesus.

Thus, so far as Christians were concerned, there was nothing to prevent the penal effect from being applied immediately; all that was required was to set once more in motion the Neronian interdict which had remained in abeyance for thirty years, but of which the murderous capabilities could be activated again at any moment. And this time also, in contrast to what the relative moderation of Trajan will pre-

[8] Suetonius, *Domitianus*, 12.

scribe a little later in requiring a previous accusation, authority took the initiative in the repressive measures. This doubtless explains why Tertullian (*Apologeticus*) says that only the emperors Nero and Domitian were the enemies of the Christians.[9] At this time there were put to death, as guilty of atheism,[10] Flavius Clemens, cousin of the emperor, and the consul, M. Acilius Glabrio, and also on this head, says Dio Cassius,[11] there were condemned "many other citizens who had adopted Jewish customs."

The double accusation of atheism and of Jewish customs seems to us not very coherent, but it is a fact that Christians were often treated as atheists, either because they did not worship the gods of the Empire, or else because, precisely as Jews, they did not render worship, at least at first, to material representations of the Deity. The sentences passed were death or the confiscation of goods. The wife of Flavius Clemens, niece herself of Domitian, Flavia Domitilla, was, according to Dio Cassius, exiled to the island of Pandataria. To another island of the Tyrrhenian sea, Pontia, the second Flavia Domitilla, niece to Flavius Clemens, was apparently likewise exiled because of her Christian faith. But this second Flavia is known only by the somewhat late testimonies of Eusebius,[12] who, it is true, cites an unknown pagan of uncertain period, Bruttius, and of St. Jerome.[13] The Acts of Saints Nereus and Achilleus, also brought forward in favour of the historic reality of the second Flavia Domitilla, do not deserve any credence.[14] It is thus possible that there may have been a legendary doubling in the tradition, and that there was only one Flavia Domitilla who was a victim of the persecution under Domitian, the wife of Clemens, exiled in one of the two islands in the Mediterranean assigned as residence for the imperial personages condemned to deportation.[15]

[9] Similarly Melito of Sardis (about 172), in a passage of his *Apology* quoted by Eusebius, *Hist. Eccles.*, IV, 26, 7, says that only Nero and Domitian made the Christian faith a matter of accusation.
[10] Dio Cassius, LXVII, 13.
[11] *Ibid.*
[12] *Hist. Eccles.*, III, 18, 4.
[13] *Epist.*, 108, *ad Eustochium.*
[14] Cf. A. Dufourcq, *Etude sur les Gesta martyrum romains*, Vol. I, Paris, 1900, pp. 251-255.
[15] Dio Cassius, LXVII, 13.

The Persecution in the Provinces: Bithynia

The persecution extended at least to some provinces: in Asia, Bithynia and the province of Asia proper were affected. The passage in Pliny the Younger which gives us information of the persecution under Trajan in Bithynia speaks of apostasies which had followed from threats some twenty years earlier: Christians were thus affected about the year 95.

Asia Minor

In Asia Minor the persecution made, according to tradition, if not a martyr, at least the most glorious of confessors in the person of St. John. A story which we find for the first time in Tertullian[16] says that John was taken from Ephesus to Rome, that he was there plunged into a vessel of boiling oil, and that he was then deported to the island of Patmos. The legendary character of the first part of this late narrative prevents us from discerning the exact memories which it may retain, if it be not a complete invention.[17] The exile to Patmos, on the other hand, has in the *Apocalypse* (i, 9) a testimony the value of which is rendered less unfavourable than many critics allow by the previous discussion on the authenticity of the Johannine writings. The *Apocalypse* is also filled on every page with the memory of those who have recently shed their blood for Jesus, and it names two of the great cities of Asia, Pergamum and Smyrna, whose churches have suffered.[18]

Palestine

Lastly, according to the historian Hegesippus, a converted Jew of the second century particularly well informed on Judeo-Christian matters, whose account is transmitted to us by Eusebius,[19] the emperor concerned himself, for reasons other than those which had motived the persecution, about

16 *De præscriptione*, 36.
17 The trial of John at Rome would be not at all unlikely in itself, seeing that the emperor insisted on himself interrogating the representatives of the family of Jesus: cf. *infra*.
18 II, 9, 10, 13. On the legitimate attribution of the martyrs of Pergamum and Smyrna to the persecution under Domitian, cf. E. B. Allo, *Saint Jean, L'Apocalypse*, Paris, 1921, pp. xcvi-ccx, 3rd edn., 1933, pp. ccxxv-ccxxviii.
19 *Hist. Ecles.*, III, 19 and 20.

Palestine, where descendants of the family of Jesus were still living.

But these attracted attention rather as descendants of David. Hegesippus asserts what may be an exaggeration of a less cruel fact, that Domitian had given orders for the destruction of all the survivors of a royal race which worried him. Some descendants of Jude, one of the "brethren of the Lord," were denounced as belonging to it. They were taken to the emperor, who after finding by interrogation that they were of modest condition, and free from any pretention to an earthly kingdom, dismissed them as inoffensive folk. The account adds that they were "respected as martyrs, they governed churches when peace was re-established, and lived until the time of Trajan." [20]

The reference here is to Judeo-Christian churches in the Palestinian region: the family of Jesus remained long in possession of the honours which the sentiment of these communities, wholly imbued with the Semitic spirit, thought it natural to give to the family which seemed to continue the earthly life of the Master Himself. We gather from this account in the oldest of Christian historians, which there is no serious reason to doubt, that Palestine like all Asia Minor was affected under Domitian by the persecution, since it mentions the "re-establishment of peace."

Peace did return very soon throughout the Empire. Domitian, assassinated in 96, was succeeded by Nerva, who adopted a policy opposite to that of his predecessor, and did not worry about Christians. Then it was, writes Eusebius,[21] that "Nerva having allowed those unjustly exiled to return to their own places, the apostle John was able to leave the island to which he had been sent, and established himself once more at Ephesus, as is stated by a tradition of our elders."

§2. THE PERSECUTION UNDER TRAJAN

Reign of Nerva

The reign of Nerva was short—scarcely two years—and so was the peace of the Church. The persecution was renewed under his successor Trajan. But it was sporadic and

[20] Cf. Lebreton and Zeiller, Bk. I, p. 314.
[21] Hist. Eccles., III, 20, 8.

intermittent in character, and this is explained by the legislation against the Christians; Trajan confined himself to making this more precise by limiting its effects in the way we have already explained.

Trajan and the Christians

Trajan has left the reputation of being one of the greatest and best of the Roman Emperors. The *optimus princeps*[1] was at once a legislator and a conqueror. But he had a very lively sense of the prerogatives of the State, and no leaning towards consideration for particular groups. From the second year of his reign, the year 99, he revived the old law forbidding unauthorised associations. This measure alone would have been sufficient to arouse once more judicial activity against the Christians.

The Question of the Martyrdom of St. Clement

Did one first and great victim pay his tribute about the year 100 in the person of the then head of Roman Christianity, St. Clement, the third successor of St. Peter after Linus and Anacletus?

Clement is known by a letter to the Church of Corinth which will be dealt with later on, and which shows the head of the Roman Church already busy with the care of other churches. But apart from that, we know nothing positive about him. Was he related to the household of Flavius Clemens in any way? It is possible that he may have been one of his freedmen, and again that he is the same as the Clement mentioned by St. Paul in his epistle to the Philippians (iv, 3). But all this is merely conjectural.

Some Greek *Acts*[2] which are not earlier than the fourth century say, on the other hand, that he was exiled by the government's orders to the Crimean peninsula in the Black Sea, where he continued his apostolate amongst those condemned to the mines, and that as a punishment for this activity he was thrown into the sea with an anchor round his neck. Neither St. Irenæus nor Eusebius nor St. Jerome, who mention Clement, say a single word which suggests this legend; we only know that the tradition of the martyrdom of

[1] Cf. above, pp. 73-74.
[2] Funk, *Patrum apostolorum opera,* Tübingen, 1901, Vol. II, pp. 28-45.

Clement away from Rome was accepted in the fourth century; but this does not carry much weight in favour of the reality and still less concerning the circumstances of this martyrdom.

Martyrdom of St. Simeon of Jerusalem

It is quite otherwise in the case of another illustrious personage of the primitive Church who perished about the same time, Simeon, Bishop of Jerusalem. He was a member of the little group of "brethren of the Lord," and had succeeded James as the head of the Church of Jerusalem, which as we have said seems to have done its best to retain authority in the family of Jesus.

Simeon was of a very advanced age in the year 107, which Eusebius gives for his martyrdom, the account of which he borrows from Hegesippus. But the figure of 120 years transmitted by him, apart from its little intrinsic likelihood, would make Simeon born before Christ. Hence there is probably some error here—such numerical errors are frequent in the texts—but this does not destroy the historical value of the narrative.

According to Hegesippus, some popular commotions against the Christians had taken place in various cities, and hostile Judeo-Christian heretics, Ebionites or others, had joined forces with them; Simeon was denounced by one of them both as a Christian and as a descendant of David. It would seem that the Roman authority was still uneasy concerning the representatives of the ancient royal race of Israel. In any case the old head of Christianity in Jerusalem was doubly accused before the imperial legate, T. Claudius Atticus, and after long torments, was crucified. The account of Hegesippus adds that his accusers were then convicted of belonging themselves to the family of David and condemned in their turn.[3]

Martyrdom of St. Ignatius of Antioch

But the chief figure in the persecution of Trajan, and the one who has left the most brilliant memory, was Ignatius, Bishop of Antioch. Like Clement of Rome, he was very closely connected with the apostolic generation of which Simeon was perhaps the last survivor, and his letters, like

[3] Eusebius, *Chronicle*, ann. 10 of Trajan, *Hist. Eccles.*, III, 32.

that of Clement to the Church of Corinth, were regarded by the early Church as almost canonical documents.

The Acts of his martyrdom merit little credence, but we know the first stages by his own letters, the authenticity of which has often been attacked, but never, as we shall see, by conclusive arguments.[4]

He was arrested in circumstances unknown to us, perhaps in consequence of some popular commotion, perhaps through a formal denunciation, and was condemned early in 107,[5] evidently by the governor of the province. He was sent to Rome with two companions, Rufus and Zosimus, to be thrown to the beasts, probably on the occasion of the great feasts given by the Emperor after his victories in Dacia, when a certain number of human victims had to lose their lives.

The bishop set out, full of a supernatural joy, certain, as he wrote to the Smyrnians[6] that "under the edge of the sword, as in the midst of wild beasts, he would be always near to God." On his journey from Smyrna, where he made a fairly long stay and met Polycarp the bishop, to Philippi in Macedonia, he wrote seven letters for which he is for ever famous, to the churches of Ephesus, Magnesia, Tralles, Rome, Troas, Philadelphia, and Smyrna.

The letter to the Romans is the best known of all. After heaping praise on Roman Christianity, which leads him to evoke the memory of Peter and Paul, he adjures the faithful of Rome, whom he cannot, he says, command like those apostles, to do nothing to oppose his martyrdom. Any such opposition was not very likely, for its success would have been very doubtful, as a pardon was almost out of the question, and a withdrawal from torture *in extremis* would not have been much use. But some protestations of devotion towards his person had probably reached the bishop, and had led him to fear that he might be saved from death. And so he protests vehemently against any such action. "Allow me," he writes, "to be immolated while the altar is ready. . . . Let me be the prey of wild beasts; by them I shall attain to God. I am God's grain: let me be ground by the teeth of wild beasts, so that I may become the pure bread of Christ." So

---

[4] Cf. *infra,* pp. 114 *et seq.*
[5] Date given in the *Chronicle* of Eusebius.
[6] *Ad Smyrn.,* 4.

it came to pass, and Ignatius was "ground" by the wild beasts, perhaps in the Colosseum, if this building, begun under Domitian, was then sufficiently advanced.

The Persecution in Bithynia and Pontus

Lastly there was one more province, or rather a group of provinces, in the Asiatic domain of Rome, in which, as we are informed by one of the most precious testimonies we possess, the persecution raged under Trajan's rule. This was Bithynia and Pontus, placed in 111 under the government of Pliny the Younger. He wrote a letter to the Emperor and received from him a reply, which are both famous, and of which we have already spoken.[7]

We learn from this correspondence that, less than a hundred years after the death of Christ, Christianity had made marvellous progress in the northern portion of Asia Minor, and this not only in the towns but also in the country parts. Pliny may have exaggerated a situation which had disturbed him, but would he have wholly invented the statement that the temples were being abandoned and that some of the ceremonies could not take place for lack of participants?

The former governors, annual proconsuls drawn by lot from among the senators, had remained inactive. But the two provinces had just changed their regime by coming under the direct administration of the Emperor: Pliny arrived there as imperial legate, *legatus Augusti proprætor*. This fact apparently emboldened the opponents of the innovators, and the denunciations began. The number of accusations, and consequently of those who should be victims, naturally worried Pliny, who was not a bloodthirsty man. Hence his questions to his prince. We know the latter's reply.

The reply is merely a simple application of an established legislation, but by the more precise instructions rendered necessary by the questions of an embarrassed magistrate it fixes a jurisprudence still vague in its details, and by limiting the initiative of the authorities it somewhat softens the rigour of principles which nevertheless remain inflexible. Trajan also rejects anonymous accusations—a very important restriction. But we cannot doubt that many Christians had already perished in Bithynia, for Pliny, whose moderation multiplied the interrogatories in the hope of obtaining an abjuration,

[7] Cf. above, pp. 67, 71.

expressly says that he had sent to death all those who persisted in their "disobedience and their invincible obstinacy." [8] He asserts nevertheless that the deserted temples are once more frequented, and that the sacrifices have begun again— official optimism, doubtless, to a large extent, but there may well have been a certain number of apostates as well as martyrs.

The Persecution in Macedonia

One European province of the Empire seems also to have experienced the rigorous measures of Trajan against the Christians: Macedonia. A letter from one of the best known bishops of the Eastern Church, Polycarp of Smyrna, written in the first half of the second century, mentions some martyrs in the city of Philippi, and also commemorates St. Ignatius, who passed by that city on his way to Rome. "Practise," Polycarp writes to the Philippians, "the patience of which you have seen models with your eyes not only in the blessed Ignatius, Zosimus and Rufus, but also in others from amongst yourselves." [9] These words do not make it absolutely certain that the Philippian martyrs were chronologically near to St. Ignatius, but they make it at least very probable.

§3. THE PERSECUTION UNDER HADRIAN

The Emperor Hadrian and the Christians

The reign of Hadrian brought no marked change in the condition of the Christians; but it somewhat diminished the danger which constantly threatened them. This voluptuous græculus[1] could have no sympathy for Christianity, but this great administrator, who would never dream of weakening a law calculated to promote public security, had an intense dislike for disorders, and he could only condemn energetically the tumultuous conditions in which the accusations against the Christians were so often made. Particularly in the East, where religious passions were more excitable and superstitions more active, the popular sentiment towards the Chris-

---

[8] Epist. cit., supra, ch. 3, § 3, n. 6.
[9] Polycarp, Ad Philippenses. On this letter, ch. 3, § 3, n. 6.
[1] This nickname had been given him because of his delight in all Hellenic things.

tians more than once culminated in violence which reached as far as public authority itself.

The second century was the period when Christianity had come forth from its original obscurity, but was not yet as well known as it would be in the next century, and it was a prey to all kinds of calumnies arising out of ignorance and misapprehension. What did the crowds not imagine about it! Ritual murders, bloody communions, sacred banquets culminating in shameful orgies, magic, ideas compared with which that of the supposed adoration of a god with an ass's head appears a mere inoffensive pleasantry—such were the rumours current about the Christians amongst the simple folk, always ready to believe the worst, and echoed sometimes even by the learned.[2] They were increased by the great complaint in which government and people joined, that Christians withdrew themselves from their fellow citizens by not worshipping the gods, and the rulers who were themselves divine. It is not surprising that such ideas caused trouble and disturbances. Accusations against the Christians were sometimes accompanied by veritable riots. An emperor like Hadrian was not the man to favour such things.

On the other hand, there were magistrates whom the cold rigour of the official doctrine did not free perhaps from all scruples as to what was to be done in presence of passionate denunciations, and were not always disposed to give way blindly to popular clamour. Some there were who asked the Emperor for fresh elucidations. The proconsul of Asia, Licinius Granianus, amongst others, wrote to Hadrian setting forth his doubts. The imperial reply reached Granianus's successor, Minicius Fundanus, about the year 124.[3] It maintained the

[2] Cf. infra, pp. 215-16.
[3] Text in St. Justin, Apology, I, 68; Eusebius, Hist. Eccles., IV, 9; Rufinus, Hist. Eccles., IV, 9. The authentic text is partly given in a Greek translation by Eusebius. This writer speaks of the letter of Granianus also in his Chronicle, Olymp. 226, thinking that the very principle of Trajan's legislation was involved, and that the rescript modified it. But that is unlikely. Dom Capelle, Le rescrit d'Hadrien et saint Justin, in Revue Bénédictine, 1927, p. 365, has again endeavoured to defend this interpretation of the rescript, which is that of St. Justin, by showing that the text annexed to his Apology was really written by him. The comparison between the language of the Apology and the introduction to the rescript seems conclusive on the matter of authenticity.

existing law, but clarified the formalities of procedure, in order to safeguard public order and to stop abuses, by forbidding the introduction of tumultuous processes, and requiring an individual and regular act of accusation, and a list of proved juridical crimes, and also by ordering the punishment of calumniators. By thus restricting the facility of denunciation and making accusers run the risk of being themselves accused of calumny should their victims suddenly apostatise, it somewhat lessened the danger which constantly threatened the Christians, though it did not remove it entirely.

Martyrs in Italy

Even so, there were certainly fairly numerous martyrdoms in the reign of Hadrian; but several of those explicitly attributed to him are known only by *Acts* of no value, while in the case of other persons, whose names come to us from sources better than that of *Passions* subject to caution, the chronological localisation is not more than probable. Such is the case with Pope Telesphorus, who seems to have been put to death under Hadrian, as his pontificate apparently ended in 136, though it may have lasted till 138 or even later, which would bring his end to the reign of Antoninus.[4] A certain Alexander, sometimes wrongly identified with the first pope of this name, was also probably a Roman martyr in the time of Hadrian, together with his companions Hermes, Quirinus, Eventius and Theodulus. Getulus, his wife Symphorosa, and their seven sons, perished in Sabina.

Other martyred saints are honoured in Umbria. Local traditional cults and inclusion in the martyrologies guarantee the historic reality and death for the Faith of some, but their *Acts* appear subject to such doubt that it is best merely to register their names.

But it does not at all follow that Justin correctly interpreted the rescript itself: his very benign interpretation might favour his apologetic thesis, but all the known facts contradict the thesis of a substantial modification of previous legislation. Cf. Callewaert, *Le rescrit d'Hadrien,* in *Revue d'histoire et de littérature religieuses,* Vol. VIII, 1903, pp. 152 *et seq.,* who also shows that the doubts sometimes entertained on the authenticity of the rescript, mainly because of the defective interpretation given to it, are without foundation.

[4] Martyrs known by St. Irenæus (Eusebius, *Hist. Eccles.,* V, 6).

The Jewish Rebellion of Bar Kokhba and the Christians

We also lack details concerning a local but violent persecution which in Hadrian's reign caused Christians to suffer for another reason. The bloody Jewish revolt of Bar Kokhba had fearful results for them: Justin in his first *Apology*[5] writes that Bar Kokhba "caused Christians, and Christians only, to suffer the last torments if they would not deny and blaspheme Jesus Christ."

§4. THE PERSECUTION UNDER ANTONINUS

The Emperor Antoninus and the Christians

The Emperor Antoninus, who succeeded his adoptive father Hadrian in 138, undoubtedly tended by nature to be more benevolent in regard to the Christians. He did not indeed modify the rigorous legislation under which they still remained, but like Hadrian, and perhaps with greater willingness and desire to avoid the shedding of blood, he forbade any giving way to popular commotions against them, as is shown by four rescripts addressed by him to the cities of Larissa, Thessalonica, Athens, and the provincial assembly of Achaia.[1] He has also been credited with a much more favourable rescript addressed to the provincial assembly of Asia, forbidding denunciations; but although Eusebius has preserved this document in his *Ecclesiastical History* (IV, 13), attributing it, however, to Marcus Aurelius, its apocryphal character is plain. The principles of the legislation itself were not changed. The Christians did indeed make at this time a great effort to persuade people to recognise the harmlessness, if not the beneficial character, of their religion. But these apologetic endeavours, the first of which in date was that of Marcianus Aristides, a contemporary of Hadrian, and which are dealt with in detail in a later chapter, did not have the wished-for result.

Martyrdom of St. Polycarp of Smyrna

The imperial orders themselves were not always obeyed.

---

[5] XXXI, 6.
[1] Eusebius, *Hist. Eccles.*, IV, 26, 10.

The most illustrious martyr who suffered under Antoninus,[2] Polycarp Bishop of Smyrna, was a victim of a veritable popular uprising, to which Quadratus, the proconsul of Asia, gave way. We know of this event, so glorious for the church of Smyrna, through a letter it sent to the church of Philomelium and all the communities "belonging to the holy universal Church."[3] Twelve Christians were denounced, condemned, and thrown to the beasts in 155; one of them, however, named Quintus, weakened at the last moment, sacrificed to the gods, and swore by the genius of the emperor. But the crowd was not satisfied, and called for the bishop.

The request was out of order, but the proconsul allowed it nevertheless. Polycarp was dragged to the amphitheatre, and in the governor's box was called on to shout, "Down with the atheists." Polycarp consented to do so, having no difficulty in agreeing with the populace in a declaration which he nevertheless made in an altogether different sense. But when he was ordered to curse Christ, he replied: "For eighty-six years now I have served him; he has never done me evil. How could I blaspheme my king and my saviour?" He was finally burnt alive on a fire of wood made ready by a crowd consisting of alike Jews and pagans.

There were also under Antoninus other victims of pagan

[2] The martyrdom of St. Polycarp was long put in the reign of Marcus Aurelius, on the strength of a statement in Eusebius. Waddington, *Fastes des provinces asiatiques,* Vol. I, Paris, 1872, pp. 219 *et seq.,* and also in *Mémoires de l'Academie des Inscriptions et Belles-Lettres,* Vol. XVI, 1867, p. 219, showed, by the list of governors of the province of Asia, that the martyrdom took place under Antoninus. Although the ancient chronology has still been defended by J. Reville, *La date du martyre de saint Polycarpe,* in *Revue de l'histoire des religions,* III, 1881, p. 369, it must be abandoned. The confusion between Antoninus and Marcus Aurelius, who was also known by the name of his adoptive father, Antoninus, is not at all surprising. Cf. also F. X. Funk, *Patres apostolici,* Vol. I, 3rd edn., Tübingen, 1913, pp. xciv *et seq.*

The more exact dating of Polycarp's death was the work of C. H. Turner's paper in *Studia Biblica,* Vol. II, 1887, pp. 105-55. Turner showed that the only date which accounts for all the data is February 22nd, 156. There is an annotated translation of the *Martyrdom* in Owen, *Some Authentic Acts of the Early Martyrs,* Oxford, 1927, pp. 31 *et seq.*

[3] Eusebius, *Hist. Eccles.,* V, 18, 9.

hatred: at Jerusalem, Mark the Bishop; in Rome, Popes Hyginus and Pius I, and about 160, a Christian priest or catechist called Ptolemy, and two laymen one of whom bore the name of Lucius. Their condemnation is narrated at the beginning of the second *Apology* of Justin: a husband, angry at the conversion of his wife, accused Ptolemy of having perverted her, and as the accused confessed to being a Christian, he was immediately condemned to death by Lollius Urbicus, the prefect of the city; the two other Christians, who were present in the crowd, manifested their belief and shared the same fate.

§5. THE PERSECUTION UNDER
MARCUS AURELIUS

Marcus Aurelius and the Christians

The reign of Marcus Aurelius witnessed more martyrdoms, and some of them are amongst the most famous in all the history of the persecutions. It was not that Marcus Aurelius in any way added to the legislation concerning the Christians: he maintained it, like his predecessors, but perhaps with more contemptuous inflexibility. He was humane as a philosopher, but had nothing but a haughty disdain for a sect which seemed to him to set little store by intelligence, and welcomed sufferings with a readiness which he regarded as an undignified affectation. Moreover, as a ruler he was fully conscious of his duties towards the Empire, and could not suffer rebels. Hence his severity.

But the much greater frequency in his reign of the applications of a principle always in force is not to be imputed to him alone. It has its explanation in the circumstances, the growth of popular animosity, due perhaps itself to public misfortunes, war, epidemics, or cataclysms the responsibility for which was laid by superstition on the Christians. Perhaps also the progress of Christian propaganda had something to do with it, for popular ignorance continued to regard Christians as enemies of the gods, of morality, and of the Empire. And this animosity more than once forced the hands of the magistrates.

Martyrs in Rome

This was the case, in the last years of the reign, in the trial of the martyrs of Lyons. But some fifteen years earlier, possibly in 162, there were put to death at Rome, after a regular denunciation, St. Felicitas and seven other martyrs regarded by tradition as her sons, and in any case related to her.[1]

Between 163 and 167, a legal accusation made by the Cynic philosopher Crescens similarly brought about the appearance before the prefect of Rome, Junius Rusticus, confidant of Marcus Aurelius, of the Christian philosopher and apologist Justin. He was arrested with some other believers, probably his disciples, amongst them being a woman, Charity, and a slave of Cæsar's household, Evelpistus. The essential question, "Are you a Christian?" brought the reply: "Yes, I am." Then followed the sentence: "Those who have refused to sacrifice to the gods and obey the orders of the Emperor are to be scourged and taken away to suffer the penalty of death, in conformity with the laws." The execution took place immediately.[2]

Martyrs in Greece

The Churches in Greece also suffered, for a letter from Dionysius, Bishop of Corinth, to Pope Soter about 170, thanks the latter for sending help to the Christians condemned to the mines, and another letter of the same Dionysius mentions the martyrdom of Publius, Bishop of Athens.[3]

Martyrs in Asia Minor

Sagaris, apparently bishop of Laodicea in Asia Minor, where he was buried, perished in the proconsulate of Sergius Paulus, i.e., between 164 and 166; another Asiatic, Thraseas, Bishop of Eumenia, suffered probably at the same time.[4]

[1] On the historical value of the *Passion* of St. Felicitas, see a summary of the various views in P. Allard, *Histoire des persécutions pendant les deux premiers siècles*, Paris, 1909, 3rd edn., p. 378, n. 2. It is worthy of note that the base of a small column coming from a ciborium and found in the ancient Catacomb of Priscilla bears the names of the martyrs Felix, Philip, Vitalis and Martial, mentioned in the *Passion* as sons of Felicitas. [English tr. of the *Passion* in Owen, *op. cit.*, pp. 74 *et seq.* Another by W. H. Sheering, London, 1931.—Tr.]

[2] *Acta Sancti Justini*, in Otto, *Corpus Apologetarum Christianorum sæculi secundi*, Vol. III, Jena, 1879, pp. 266-278. Engl. tr. in Owen, *op. cit.*, pp. 47 *et seq.*

[3] Eusebius, *Hist. Eccles.*, IV, 23.

[4] Eusebius, *Hist. Eccles.*, V, 24.

Other Christians in Italy and Greece were condemned to forced labour in the mines. Doubtless the denunciations multiplied, and the hostility of the populace increased. Theophilus, Bishop of Antioch under Marcus Aurelius, says that "the Christians were constantly persecuted. The most pious were continually stoned, and sometimes even put to death." [5] This doubtless refers to popular violence. But the events of 177 at Lyons shows that this could always lead to action by the magistrates.

The Martyrs at Lyons in 177

The martyrs of Lyons have, so to speak, told their own story in an ever-famous document, the letter of the church of Lyons to the churches of Asia, Phrygia and Rome,[6] one of the most beautiful documents of Christian antiquity, in which an account of the cruellest sufferings is given in a very simple manner; nevertheless it breathes all the ardour of the combat entered into for the love of Christ, and in it we find men threatened with the worst torments still anxious about all that concerned the universal church in their time. In particular they concerned themselves with the Montanist prophetic movement then troubling Asia Minor, and endeavoured to bring back to unity those who were going astray.

The church of Lyons was indeed, as far as we can judge from the information in the letter, partly of Asiatic origin and composition. Its head, Bishop Pothinus, over 90 years of age in 177, had been a disciple of St. Polycarp of Smyrna, and the names of several of its members show them to be Orientals, such as the Phrygian doctor Alexander, "long established," nevertheless, "amongst the Gauls."

The indigenous element was also represented;[7] and there were in this young Christian community some notable Gallo-Romans such as Vettius Epagathus, a Roman citizen, described in the letter as a Christian wholly filled with the Holy Spirit. There was also amongst the faithful summoned before the Roman magistrate at Lyons at least one representative of the church of Vienne, the deacon Sanctus. Were the two churches really one community, under one head, in spite of

---

[5] *Ad Autolychum,* III.

[6] In Eusebius, *Hist. Eccles.,* V, 24, English tr. in Owen, *op. cit.,* pp. 53 *et seq.*

[7] In the list in the *Hieronymian Martyrology,* about half the names are Greek, and the other half Latin.

the fact that they were in two different civil provinces, that of Lyons and Narbonne? Possibly so, and perhaps this is the most natural explanation of the one common measure taken against them. But there is nothing which formally excludes the hypothesis of two distinct churches, or that members of the one, that of Vienne, were involved in consequence of their momentary presence in Lyons in the process against their brethren.

From the point of view of public law, however, a common trial before one governor of people belonging to two different provinces might cause some surprise. But this admits of explanation: the Christians of Vienne—and it must be borne in mind that we know only one, the deacon Sanctus, who definitely came from there—may have been arrested at Lyons where they happened to be at the moment; or if the two churches had only one head, they may have been proceeded against as accomplices of their brethren at Lyons.

These latter found a more aggressive attitude taken up towards them by the pagans in the last years of the reign of Marcus Aurelius. The most ridiculous calumnies were reechoed, and vexations multiplied: exclusion from the baths, markets, and even from the "houses" (which doubtless means that people refused to let houses to Christians, or expelled them from private meeting places),[8] and ill treatment of every kind: "They were insulted, beaten, dragged about, robbed, stoned, and confined together." [9]

The agitation increased at the beginning of August, on the eve of the feasts of Rome and Augustus, the annual manifestation of imperial loyalty which the Christians were bitterly accused of not observing. Did the movement become so hostile that the local authorities decided that they must intervene by taking the initiative in arrests though this was excluded by the imperial rescripts? Or were the Christians taken before them? We know that the governor was absent, and that the municipal magistrates and the tribune of the urban cohort stationed at Lyons took them, tortured them, and kept them in prison awaiting the return of the imperial legate. About ten of those tortured gave way, but most of these repented afterwards. But one serious feature was that

[8] Thus Owen, op. cit., p. 138 n. He adds, however, that the word is thought by some to refer to public buildings.—Tr.
[9] Eusebius, loc. cit., 6.

some pagan slaves employed by the Christians, some of whom were of sufficient social rank to have servants, when put to the question, consented to confess to having witnessed scenes of incest and anthropophagy. Nothing further was necessary to persuade more than ever people already disposed to believe wholly in the reality of these crimes.

The tortures were repeated for several days, in the course of which the aged bishop Pothinus, "who could scarcely breathe because of the exhaustion of his body, but who was upheld by the ardour of the Spirit," [10] died in prison, and the apostates, ashamed of their weakness, proclaimed once more their faith in Christ. The legate when he returned pronounced the inevitable sentence of death: Sanctus the deacon of Vienne, Maternus the neophyte, the very young slave Blandina, and the Asiatic Attalus of Pergamum, one of the most prominent members of the community in Lyons, were condemned to the wild beasts.

But before Attalus died, it was discovered that he was a Roman citizen: troubled, it seems, by this discovery, and by the number of executions still awaiting, the legate wrote to the Emperor. The reply was as it was bound to be: the confessors of the faith were to die, but renegades were to be set at liberty. [11] Very few of these latter remained, for almost all, at their last appearance, returned to the side where death awaited them, to the astonishment of the pagans and the joy of the other Christians.

Those of the condemned who were Roman citizens were beheaded, except Attalus who, in spite of his status, was thrown to the beasts with the general body. Alexander, the Phrygian doctor, perished in the same manner. The last to suffer, whose apostasy was doubtless hoped for right to the end, were Ponticus, a lad of fifteen years, and Blandina, the young slave, who constantly animated her companions by the example of her courage and by her words. She suffered at the last alone: "Like a noble mother who had just exhorted

[10] *Loc. cit.*, 29.

[11] If the governor had not himself proceeded to this relaxation, called for by the legislation of Trajan, it may have been because he had submitted to pressure from the hostile populace, or else, as Babut remarks (*art. cit.* above, ch. 3, § 3, n. 6 of the article) because he regarded the Christians as guilty of crimes against common law, as attributed to them by popular hostility, and that this seemed to justify their proscription.

her children and sent them to their King, she repeated herself the whole series of their combats, and hastened to them, full of joy and exulting in her end." [12] By the heroism with which she bore the tortures, she won the admiration of the pagans themselves, for these "confessed that never amongst them had a woman endured such manifold and cruel tortures." [13]

The Christian community in Lyons, almost fifty brethren of which[14] thus died, seemed to be decimated. But it was to be reconstituted almost at once under the direction of the priest Irenæus, who, having escaped the persecution, was charged to carry to Pope Eleutherus a letter similar to that addressed to the churches of Asia and Phrygia. Shortly afterwards Irenæus became bishop of Lyons.

More Martyrs at Rome

Finally, towards the end of the reign of Marcus Aurelius, between June 177 and March 180, a time suggested by a note in the martyrology of Ado, there were new martyrs in Rome: St. Cecilia, of the illustrious Roman family of the Cæcilii, and the three companions joined with her in the earliest martyrological tradition, Valerian, Tibertius and Maximus. The *Passion* which represents Cecilia as the virgin spouse of Valerian, brother to Tiburtius, is only a late romance; but the account it gives of the death of Cecilia, condemned to be suffocated in the bath of her own house, and finally decapitated, has been at least partially confirmed by remarkable archæological discoveries. Cecilia was buried near to the papal crypt in the cemetery afterwards named after Pope Callistus, in a piece of land belonging to her family; the latter subsequently presented it to the Church, and this explains the proximity of the saint's burial place to that of the Popes of later times.[15]

The Episode of the "Thundering Legion"

In contrast with all these quite certain facts of the persecution, a legendary account, which was once regarded with

[12] Eusebius, *loc. cit.,* 55.
[13] Eusebius, *loc. cit.,* 56.
[14] The *Hieronymian Martyrology* (ed. Rossi-Duchesne, n. 73), gives forty-eight names.
[15] On the value of the *Acts* of St. Cecilia, cf. A. Dufourcq, *Etude sur les Gesta martyrum romains,* Vol. I, Paris, 1900.

some favour though it merits none, attributes to the Emperor Marcus Aurelius a change of attitude towards the Christians, which came about in a very unexpected manner. This is the story of the famous prodigy of the "Thundering Legion," narrated in Tertullian's *Apologeticus*[16] and Eusebius's *Ecclesiastical History*[17] as follows: During a campaign against the Quadri in 174, the Roman army, on the point of perishing by thirst, and attacked by the enemy, was saved by a providential storm due to the prayers of the Christian soldiers of the *Legio XII Fulminata*. Thereupon Marcus Aurelius sent a message to the Senate, informing them of this miraculous event, and in gratitude published a kind of edict of toleration which even enacted penalties "against the accusers of the Christians." This is an invention the improbability of which is evident, especially in view of the fact that a pagan tradition attributing the army's salvation to Jupiter coexists with the Christian tradition, and that the latter is again at fault in supposing that the name of *Fulminata* was given to the Twelfth Legion in consequence of the prodigy, whereas it possessed it previously.

That does not mean that everything is to be rejected in a tradition found immediately after the events: the danger in which the imperial troops were, and the rain which descended in a named place, the memory of which is recalled by the Antonine column in Rome, are not to be called in question. And why should we refuse to allow that this salutary rain may have been asked for from heaven not only by pagan soldiers but also by their Christian comrades who may have been very numerous in a detachment of the legion coming from Syria, where the Twelfth Legion was stationed at that time? But whether Marcus Aurelius knew of it or not, he did not in any way deviate from the principles put in force by his predecessors and recalled by himself in regard to Christians.

§6. PERSECUTION AND PEACE UNDER COMMODUS

The Emperor Commodus and the Christians

But better times came to the Church with the reign of the son and successor of Marcus Aurelius, Commodus. There

[16] 5.
[17] V, 5, 2-6.

might have been a tendency among early Christian apologists to represent as persecutors only those emperors who had left the worst memories, and Nero and Domitian filled this office well. The quite relative moderation of the Antonines suggested a very tempting contrast; these great Antonines, conscientious rulers deeply imbued with the Roman tradition, were none the less and even because of that, fundamentally intractable towards Christianity.

Commodus, on the contrary, though son by blood of Marcus Aurelius, was not in the same moral line: he was careless of his real duties as sovereign, in contrast to Domitian, and much prone to violence, and the Roman Senate in condemning his memory could call him more impure than Nero and more cruel than Domitian.[1] But his political indifference itself explains why he showed himself to be less inflexible than his immediate predecessors in regard to a religion these had looked on as a danger to the State. Certainly his rule marks an incontestable change in the relations between the Church and the Empire.

African Martyrs

But this did not take place all at once. In the beginning of the reign of Commodus, we find the first Christian martyrs in Africa whose memory has come down to us.

Twelve Christians in the little town of Scillium, in the part of Numidia dependent on the proconsular province, were delated in 180 to the proconsul, Vigellius Saturninus, who resided at Carthage. They boldly professed their faith and refused to sacrifice to the gods or to swear by the genius of the emperor, and accordingly they were condemned to die by the sword, and were executed on the spot.[2] It is quite likely that the martyrs of Scillium were indeed the first martyrs in the African Church, for Tertullian asserts that Vigellius Saturninus began the measures of bloody repression in this province.[3] We might infer from this that this church

[1] "Sævior Domitiano, impurior Nerone" (*Historia Augusta, Vita Commodi*, 19, 21).
[2] Passion of the Scillitan martyrs in Ruinat, *Acta Sincera*, pp. 77-81; Aube, *Etude sur un nouveau texte des Actes des Martyrs Scillitains*, Paris, 1881. Cf. De Smedt in *Analecta Bollandiana*, Vol. VIII, 1889, pp. 6-8. English tr. in Owen, *op. cit.*, pp. 71 *et seq.*
[3] *Ad Scapulam*, 3: "primus hic gladium in nos egit."

was then at least relatively young, which would not exclude the possibility that there was a previous period in which a small number of faithful may have lived obscurely without being disturbed.

Many have put before the martyrs of Scillium, who appeared before the governor of Africa on July 16th, a group of martyrs of Madaura put to death on July 4th of the same year, 180. Unfortunately these latter martyrs, who bear native names, and the leader of which, Namphamo, has been called *archimartyr*, i.e., doubtless protomartyr of Africa, were most probably not witnesses to the Christian faith who became victims of the imperial persecutions, but fanatical followers of the Donatist schism, executed probably in the fourth century for having taken part in the crimes committed by the most extreme members of the sect known as the Circumcellians.[4]

Martyrs in Asia Minor

A few years later, about 184 or 185, the province of Asia was once more the scene of persecutions. The proconsul Arrius Antoninus, who was himself to be accused of aspiring to the Empire and was put to death in 188, acted according to Tertullian [5] in an especially cruel way.

Did he favour denunciations? Did he use torture more rigorously to obtain confessions or apostasies? Did he condemn his victims to more exquisite tortures? We know that as a kind of protest, the Christians of a town in Asia, where he was holding his assizes, presented themselves one day in a body at his tribunal to be dealt with by him. Their great number made him afraid: he arrested a few and sent the others away, saying to them: "Miserable people, if you wish to die, have you not sufficient ropes and precipices?" [6]

Martyrdom of Apollonius at Rome

Rome had an illustrious martyr under Commodus in the person of the senator Apollonius, a new example of the penetration of Christianity into the highest ranks of Roman aristocracy. Denounced as a Christian by one of his slaves,

---

[4] Cf. J. Baxter, *The Martyrs of Madaura*, A.D. 180, in *Journal of Theological Studies*, Vol. XXIV, 1924, pp. 21-37.
[5] *Ad Scapulam*, 5.
[6] *Ibid.*

whose reward was merely to be executed himself, in accordance with the stipulations of an ancient law which forbade slaves to delate their masters, Apollonius read before a full meeting of the Senate an Apology for the Christian Faith, but he was none the less finally beheaded, in virtue of the existing legislation, still in force, as is shown by his *Acts*.[7]

The Peace of the Church under Commodus

Nevertheless, the political situation underwent a change. Commodus had a favourite, Marcia, who had entered his palace as a slave and finished by becoming his wife, though without the title of Augusta. Now Marcia was a Christian by faith if not by baptism; her conduct had not perhaps been always in conformity with the Gospel ideal, but she was doubtless well disposed, and in any case she did what she could to ameliorate the lot of her brethren.

And so from this moment, in spite of the evident paradox in such a situation, there were Christians in the Imperial court. One of them, the freedman Proxenes, even became Commodus's chamberlain.[8] This favour accorded to Christians by a prince indifferent to a political tradition more than a century old evidently did not pass unnoticed, and the magistrates took account of this change of atmosphere. An African proconsul, for instance, made no secret of the excuses he accepted in order to absolve the Christians deferred to his tribunal.[9] Marcia herself obtained from Commodus the pardon of confessors condemned to forced labour, juridically a capital penalty, in the mines of Sardinia. Pope Victor (189-197) gave a list of these confessors, and the priest Hyacinth,

---

[7] The martyrdom of Apollonius, known through Eusebius (*Hist. Eccles.*, V, 21) and various redactions of his *Passion*, presents some difficulties. But the torture of the *delator*, if he was indeed the slave of the accused, is understandable, as is also the reading of the Apology, if Apollonius did indeed belong to the Senate. More embarrassing is the attributing of the introduction of the process before the Senate to the prefect of the prætorium, whereas the competent authority was the prefect of the city. But the prætorian prefect may have acted by delegation from the emperor. The literature of the subject is given in Duchesne, *Histoire ancienne de l'Eglise,* Vol. I, p. 251, n. 3.

[8] J. B. de Rossi, *Inscriptiones christianæ Urbis Romæ,* 5.

[9] Tertullian, *Ad Scapulam,* 4.

foster-father and friend of Marcia, went to free the prisoners, amongst whom was a future Pope, Callistus.[10]

For the first time, a pardon was granted to Christians condemned for their religion, without any denial, even feigned, of their Faith; and the two powers, ecclesiastical and imperial, agreed in the application of the decision made. An unexpected *modus vivendi* seems to have been established between the Church and the Empire. It was due doubtless to a relaxing of the rigid principles from which none of the Antonines had previously thought himself able to deviate. But the increase in the number of the Christians, shown by the very multiplicity of the condemnations, their penetration even into the interior of the palace,[11] and the ease with which the provincial authorities adapted themselves to the new situation might well have signified that the previous system would not work. The one bad emperor in the second century became, doubtless without knowing it, more just than all his glorious predecessors by performing the first act of benevolence towards the Church that she had as yet enjoyed.

Henceforth, in order that rigours should once more be applied, at least with some fulness and some duration, new imperial initiatives would be required, although the preceding legislation had not been abrogated.

[10] St. Hippolytus, *Philosophoumena,* IX, 11.
[11] Cf. Irenæus, *Adversus hæreses,* IV, 30, 1 (1065).

Chapter 5

The Apostolic Fathers and Their Times [1]

WHEN PASSING from the history of Jesus to that of the apostles, we noted the infinite distance separating the Master from the disciples. "One is your master, Christ": these words of Jesus come home with an irresistible force to anyone who compares the discourses of the Lord reported in the Gospels with the letters of the Apostles. In turning from the apostolic writings to study the early documents of the history of the Church, we have a similar feeling—less keenly, no doubt, but still strongly. Coming out of the Holy of Holies, we were still in the Sanctuary; now we are in the Temple precincts. The apostles, guided by the Holy Spirit, spoke in its name with an infallible authority. Now they are all dead, and their successors, even the greatest and holiest, realise that they are beneath those whom they replace. St. Clement writes to the Corinthians: "Let us have before our eyes the excellent apostles," and he celebrates the glory of Peter and Paul (*Clem,*. V); St. Ignatius, similarly, writes in his letter to the Romans (*Rom.* iv, 3): "I do not give you orders, as did Peter and Paul: they were apostles, I am only a condemned man." The years which follow in the course of the second century do not lessen this distance but increase it; they magnify the incomparable authority of the apostles. Very soon apocryphal works will circulate under their venerated names: *Preaching of Peter, Apocalypse of Peter, Letters* of the Apostles, *Acts* of Paul, John, Peter, or Thomas; all these pious frauds manifest the unequalled prestige of the apostles themselves.

This will be confirmed by Catholic theology: it recognises that down to the death of the last apostle, the deposit of revelation was progressively enriched, that, as St. Paul writes, "the mystery of Christ was not in other generations known to the sons of men as it is now revealed to his holy apostles and prophets" (*Ephes.* iii, 4-5). After the death of the apostles,

[1] Bibliography. See the notes at the beginning of the treatment of each of the Apostolic Fathers.

there will be no new addition: "As soon as we believe," Tertullian will say, "we have no more need to believe anything further. For the first article of our belief is that there is nothing further which we ought to believe." [2]

At the same time, this deposit is not lifeless or inert; as St. Irenæus will shortly say, "It is as a precious deposit contained in an excellent vessel; the Spirit ever renews its youth and communicates its youthfulness to the vessel containing it." [3] Hence when studying the history of the Church, our effort will be to reach towards this deep life which the documents reveal to those who understand them. When leaving His apostles after the appearance in Galilee, the Lord promised to remain with them until the consummation of the world. The whole development of history since then manifests the realisation of this promise; if our exposition is faithful to its subject, it will bring out this divine life which rejuvenates the pagan world and reveals itself by its fruits of truth and grace.

§1. ST. CLEMENT OF ROME [4]

We are fortunate to find at the outset of this history some documents of undeniable authenticity, which give us through

[2] *De præscriptione,* VII, 13.

[3] St. Irenæus, IV, 24, 1.

[4] The letter of St. Clement has been transmitted to us in Greek in two manuscripts. The *Alexandrinus,* in fifth century uncials, is, as everyone knows, one of the chief authorities for the New Testament; cf. F. C. Kenyon, *Handbook to the Textual Criticism of the New Testament,* London, 1912, pp. 72-77; Lightfoot, *The Apostolic Fathers,* I, 1, London, 1890, pp. 116-21; but there is a great gap in this manuscript (LVII, 6—LXIII, 4). In 1875 a second manuscript was discovered, to which we owe the *Didache*: the *Hierosolymitanus,* written in 1056; its contents enable us to fill up the gaps in the *Alexandrinus.* With the Greek texts we can compare the early Latin, Syriac and Coptic versions.

There are numerous editions: Lightfoot, *The Apostolic Fathers,* Part I, *St. Clement of Rome,* 2nd edn., London, 1890, 2 vols.; O. von Gebhardt and A. Harnack. *Clementis Romani Epistulæ,* Lipsiæ, 1876, 2nd edn., 1900; Funk, *Patres Apostolici,* Tübingen, 1901. The text was published once more in 1924 by Bihlmeyer; also by H. Hemmer in *Clément de Rome,* Paris, 1909. Excellent English version, with notes by W. K. Lowther Clarke, published by the S.P.C.K. in 1937. Another by Lightfoot.

Abundant bibliography in O. Bardenhewer, *Geschichte der*

the mouths of the two illustrious bishops Clement and Ignatius the witness of the two great churches of Rome and
Antioch. We could not desire a better "introduction to the
early history of the Church." [5]

St. Clement and his Letter

The first of these documents does not name its author, but
presents itself as a letter from the church of Rome to that of
Corinth. But this anonymity is dispelled by a very firm and
very early tradition, almost contemporary with the letter
itself.[6]

Clement, the author of the letter, was Bishop of Rome, as

---

altkirchlichen Literatur, Vol. I, pp. 110-113; cf. Rauschen-
Altaner, Patrologie, pp. 56 and 58. Recent studies by Harnack,
Das Schreiben der Römischen Kirche an die Korinthische aus
der Zeit Domitians, Leipzig, 1929, and by Fr. Gercke, Die Stel-
lung des ersten Clemensbriefes innerhalb der Entwicklung der
altchristl. Gemeindeverfassung, Leipzig, 1931.
[5] The title of Harnack's last work, a translation and commentary
of the letter of Clement (see n. 4).
[6] "The original manuscripts and the Latin and Syriac versions
put at the head of the epistle the name of St. Clement: Epistle
of Clement to the Corinthians. In view of the character of the
Alexandrine manuscript and the early date of the versions, we
may infer that already in the second century and even in the
first half of that century the tradition was fixed in this respect"
(Hemmer, op. cit., p. xxiii). About 170, Dionysius of Corinth
writes (apud Eusebius, Eccles. Hist., IV, 23): "To-day we have
kept the holy day of Sunday, during which we have read your
letter; we shall continue to read it always as a warning, together
with the first which Clement wrote to us." Cf. on the bearing of
this testimony, W. J. Ferrar, in Theology, Aug., 1928, p. 282;
Hermas, Vis. ii, 4, 3: "Thou shalt write two little books and
thou shalt send one to Clement and the other to Grapte; and
Clement will send it round to the other cities, for it is to him
that this belongs"; cf. Harnack, op. cit., p. 50. Irenæus (about
180), III, 3, 3: "In the time of this Clement there were very
serious divisions amongst the brethren who were at Corinth, and
the Church which is in Rome wrote to the Corinthians a very
strong letter exhorting them to peace, renewing their faith, and
the tradition which they had recently received from the apostles."
Numerous other citations are collected in Lightfoot, op. cit.,
Vol. I, pp. 148-200, beginning with the significant comparisons
of the letter of Clement with that of Polycarp (in 110), pp.
149-152.

is stated by the majority of those who quote his letter.[7] More-over, this is clear from the letter itself: only the bishop could thus speak in the name of his Church. His place in the epis-copal succession at Rome is less easy to determine: the best attested tradition puts him third, after Linus and Anacletus.[8]

Of the man himself, his origin, and religious formation, we know only what we can gather from the reading of his letter. Eusebius and St. Jerome [9] have rightly stressed the close contact between the letter of Clement and the Epistle to the Hebrews; it is also related to the Book of Wisdom. It reveals a very deep Christian faith in its author, yet he is one who delights to base himself on Jewish tradition and to feed himself thereby; hence it is not without reason that Clement has been regarded as a Christian convert from Judaism.[10] On the other hand, as regards the surrounding

[7] The citation of Dionysius of Corinth here is especially interest-ing: writing in 170 to Soter, Bishop of Rome, he assures him of the public reading given to his letter, as of "the first written by Clement."

[8] Irenæus, *Hær.*, III, 3, 3; *Hist. Eccles*, III, 4, 9, after Hegesippus (Hemmer II). A second tradition, coming no doubt from the Clementine romances, makes him the immediate successor of Peter: Tertullian, *De præscr.*, 32 (Lightfoot, *op. cit.*, p. 174). A third puts him immediately after Linus: Liberian catalogue. This transposition doubtless arises from a confusion wth Cletus (Lightfoot, *op. cit.*, p. 170; cf. Augustine, *Epist.*, 53, 2; Lightfoot, *op. cit.*, p. 174). Attempts at harmonisation: (1) Rufinus, *Præf. in Recogn.* (Lightfoot, p. 174): Clement succeeded Peter as apostle, Linus and Cletus succeeded him as bishops. (2) *Apost. Constitut.*, VII, 46 (Lightfoot, *op. cit.*, p. 344); Linus was ap-pointed by Paul, Clement by Peter. (3) Epiphanius, *Hær.*, XXVII, 6; Clement, with a view to peace, yielded his rank to Linus, and resumed it only after the death of Cletus, cf. *Epist.*, LIV, 2: it is better to yield one's place than to give rise to a schism. This is an ingenious comparison—doubtless too ingenious.

[9] *Hist. Eccles.*, III, 37-38; *De viris illustribus*, 15.

[10] Cf. Hoennicke, *Judenchristentum*, pp. 291 *et seq.*; Lightfoot, *op. cit.*, pp. 58-60; Tillemont, *op. cit.*, Vol. II, p. 149; Hemmer, *op. cit.*, p. xi. On the opposite side: Harnack, *op. cit.*, p. 51. The author of the letter cannot be identified with the Clement of *Phil.*, iv, 3 (cf. Lightfoot, *op. cit.*, p. 4, 52-58, and *Philippians*, p. 168).

Lightfoot, *op. cit.*, p. 60, and Harnack, p. 51, conjecture that Clement was a freedman of the imperial household; this is only a conjecture, but it is ingenious; the deputies sent by Clement

paganism, he shows a sympathetic understanding of all that is noble and good; he allows and admires the heroism of the great pagans Codrus, Lycurgus, Decius and others (ch. liv). Still more does he praise the world, the work of God (ch. xx-xxii); his Christianity is not at all that of which the pagans will make a bugbear, as the religion of a *gens lucifuga;* he is a man of the widest and most truly human sympathies.[11]

This humanism, discreetly revealed in the letter, has been transformed and elevated by the Christian faith; the language, accustomed to prayer, takes a liturgical tone. The great prayer (LIX-LXI) is one of the most revealing documents for early liturgy; we hear therein the voice of a bishop who, at the close of the exhortation he has just addressed to the community at Corinth, turns towards God, as he is accustomed to do at the end of his homilies, and invites his Christian hearers to pray and praise together with him.[12]

It is indeed a homily that we have in this document. Clement knows that it will be read at Corinth in his name in the assembly of the brethren, and he addresses these absent Christians, as he would address his own in Rome, exhorting them, rebuking them, but also persuading them to pray to God with him.

This exhortation already displays the characteristics the Roman Church's documents will always have: a wise and paternal gravity, a conscious responsibility; a firm insistence but at the same time mildness in reproaches, and in the ex-

would also be of Cæsar's household; Claudius Ephebus, Valerius Bito, and Fortunatus; Claudius and Nero were of the gens Claudia, and Messalina of the gens Valeria. On the death of Clement we have no certain information; the only indication in favour of a death away from Rome is the absence of any tomb, or of any indication of the burial of the saint at Rome; cf. Tillemont, *op. cit.,* pp. 159-160; Allard, *op. cit.,* Vol. I, pp. 173-180; Lightfoot, *op. cit.,* Vol. I, pp. 86 *et seq.*

[11] Many thoughts and turns of phrase show a Stoic influence. Bardy, *Expressions stoiciennes dans la Ia Clementis,* in *Recherches de Science Religieuse,* Vol. XIII, 1922, pp. 73-85; commentary by Knopf, ch. xix, xx, xxviii, xxxiii; cf. *Histoire du Dogme de la Trinité,* Vol. II, p. 254.

[12] This great prayer does not stand alone in Clement's letter; we find therein, especially in ch. xx and xxxiii, other portions of a very marked liturgical character; and we find a very manifest echo of it in the formulas of prayer in the *Apostolic Constitutions. Cf. Hist. du Dogme de la Trinité,* Vol. II, p. 251.

position of doctrine, care to preserve in its integrity the heritage of the traditional deposit.[13]

The Roman Primacy

The date and occasion of the letter are fixed definitely by the document itself: a discord had broken out within the church of Corinth, and had resulted in the deposition of the presbyters (ch. xlvii); these facts had come to the knowledge of the Church of Rome, which had decided to intervene; it had nevertheless delayed to do so, because of the persecution to which it had been subjected (ch. 1). "The letter must have been written during a pause in the persecution, or immediately after its end, in the last days of Domitian or the beginning of the reign of Nerva, i.e. in 95 or 96." [14]

Was the intervention of the Church of Rome spontaneous, or had it been requested by the Corinthians? We cannot say; [15] what is certain is that Rome was conscious of its

[13] This faithfulness in transmitting the deposit received from the apostles is recognised already by St. Irenæus (III, 3, 3) as one of the characteristics of this "very strong letter." Lightfoot (*op. cit.*, pp. 396-397) has repeated and confirmed this praise: "It was the special privilege of the early Roman Church that it had felt the personal influence of both the leading Apostles, St. Paul and St. Peter—who approached Christianity from opposite sides—the Apostle of the Gentiles and the Apostle of the Circumcision. Comprehensiveness therefore was its heritage. . . . Comprehensiveness was especially impersonated in Clement, its earliest and chief representative." This "comprehensiveness" does not wholly efface the personal character of this letter, and Harnack is mistaken (*op. cit.*, p. 50) in regarding this view of Lightfoot as failing to recognise the personal merits of Clement.

[14] Knopf, *op. cit.*, p. 43. This conclusion is generally accepted.

[15] Batiffol, *L'Eglise naissante*, p. 154: "Had the Roman Church been asked by Corinth to intervene? The epistle does not say so; if the presbyters deposed by the sedition of the Corinthians had had recourse to Rome, it was perhaps better for Clement not to say so. In this hypothesis we should have here a noteworthy appeal to Rome, the very first in the history of the Church. But it is also possible that Rome derived its knowledge of the scandal at Corinth by public report, and that its intervention was spontaneous (XLVII, 7). In this hypothesis we should understand better that the intestine revolution at Corinth was most unusual, but also that Rome already felt itself in possession of that superior and exceptional authority which it never ceased to claim subsequently, and which was religiously obeyed at Corinth on

authority, and the responsibility which this involved; Corinth also recognised it and bowed to it. [16] Batiffol has described this intervention as "the Epiphany of the Roman Primacy," [17] and he is right. [18]

The Ecclesiastical Hierarchy

This is not the only lesson that may be learnt from this document: we find in it also a strong affirmation of the ecclesiastical constitution of the Church:

"The Master commanded us to perform the offerings and the divine service not haphazardly or without order, but at fixed times and hours. He himself determined where and by what ministers these ought to be carried out. . . . To the high priest, special functions have been entrusted; to priests their own places have been assigned; the Levites have their own duties; layfolk are bound by precepts peculiar to lay-folk" (XL).

In these Biblical recollections, it is the ecclesiastical hier-

---

the occasion of this first intervention." We may remark that the apostle John was still alive; it was not John, however, who intervened at Corinth, but the Bishop of Rome.

[16] This is clear from the letter of Dionysius of Corinth, quoted in n. 6.

[17] Batiffol, op. cit., p. 146.

[18] In an article published since the above was written, L'intervention de l'Eglise de Rome à Corinthe vers l'an 96, in Revue d'Histoire ecclésiastique, Vol. XXXI, 1935, pp. 267 et seq., Père R. Van Cauwelært has recently called again into question the value of the letter of Clement as a support for the Roman primacy. He explains the Roman intervention at Corinth by the very special relations which existed between the two cities arising from the fact that Corinth was a Roman colony. But there is no proof that these relations involved a specially close intimacy between the two churches. Civic relations were essentially relations between Latins, as Père R. Van Cauwelært himself expressly recognises. But the early Christian community in Rome was more than half Greek: Greek remained its official language until nearly 200, and the Letter of Clement is in Greek. Had it been in Latin, this point might have favoured the new thesis. Cf. J. Zeiller, A propos de l'intervention de l'église de Rome à Corinthe, in Revue d'histoire ecclésiastique, ibid., pp. 762 et seq. Père Van Cauwelært nevertheless upholds his point of view (Réponse aux remarques de M. J. Zeiller, in Revue d'histoire ecclésiastique, ibid., pp. 765 et seq.).

archy that Clement has in view.[19] The origin of this hierarchy, and in particular of the powers of government, is more
clearly set forth in chapters XLII and XLIV:

> "The apostles were sent to us as messengers of good
> news by the Lord Jesus Christ; Jesus Christ was sent by
> God. Christ, then, comes from God, and the apostles from
> Christ; these two missions come harmoniously from God's
> will. Having received the instructions of our Lord Jesus
> Christ, and being fully convinced by his Resurrection, the
> Apostles, strengthened by the word of God, went forth,
> with the assurance of the Holy Spirit, to announce the
> good news of the coming of the Kingdom of God. Preach-
> ing therefore through country and cities, and having tested
> their firstfruits by the Holy Spirit, they appointed these as
> bishops and deacons of the future believers" (XLII).

> "Our Apostles knew by Our Lord Jesus Christ that there
> would be strife concerning the episcopal office. For this
> reason, in their perfect foreknowledge, they instituted
> those of whom we have spoken, and then laid down the
> rule that after their death, other approved men should
> succeed to their ministry. Those who have been thus in-
> stituted by the apostles, or later on by other eminent men,
> with the approbation of the whole Church, and who have
> served blamelessly the flock of Christ with humility, tran-
> quillity and charity, and who have had good testimony
> borne to them for a long time—such men, we consider,
> cannot justly be deposed from their ministry" (XLIV).

Already we see here how deeply rooted is the assurance of
the succession which links the whole ecclesiastical hierarchy
through the apostles to Christ, and through Christ to God;
here we have the foundation for the traditional thesis set
forth by Irenæus and Tertullian: "Quod ecclesiæ ab aposto-
lis, apostoli a Christo, Christus a Deo accepit." [20]

---

[19] Batiffol, *op. cit.*, p. 152. "It is controverted whether the high
priest here figures the bishop, or Christ: it is clear, at any rate,
that the priests stand for the presbyters, and the levites for the
deacons. In any case, Chistian services belong to a hierarchy
distinct from the laity: there are clerics, and layfolk."

[20] *De præscr,* XXI, 4. In his History of the Papacy (*Geschichte
des Papsttums,* Tübingen, 1930, Vol. I, pp. 10 *et seq.*), Caspar
recognises an apostolical succession here, but tries to make it a

These two prominent features of the ecclesiastical constitution, the Roman primacy and the divine origin of the hierarchy, are not demonstrated here as theses which opponents deny and which have to be proved; they are truths generally admitted by Christians; Clement can bring them forward with full assurance against the seditious persons at Corinth.

The Christian Faith and the Christian Life

The aim of the letter, the summoning back of the divided and rebellious Christians to concord and obedience, had led Clement to bring out into full light the constitution of the Church. It was desirable that we should first of all stress the great importance of his teaching here, but it must not lead us to overlook all that surrounds this central thesis, for in a hortatory [21] form we have a picture of the Christian life and Christian faith which is of the greatest value to the historian. The Church is seen to be directed towards an ideal of peace, submission to God and to earthly rulers, and of fraternal concord, which even persecution does not disturb. The duty of obedience and union is recalled without weakness, but the strongest counsels or precepts are set forth in a benevolent, peaceable and truly paternal tone; the praise with which the letter begins is not a mere *captatio benevolentiae* but is above all the sincere expression of esteem and affection for the Church of Corinth. There is only one severe feature: the advice given to the authors of the sedition to leave Corinth; even this is presented not as a condemnation inflicted upon them, but as an act of charity asked from them:

"Is there among you some one who is noble, compassionate, and filled with charity? Let him say: 'If I am the

---

purely spiritual succession such as that which links up the teachers in a philosophical school to its founders. But this is to mistake the character of the Christian Church, which is not a philosophical school, but the Body of Christ, a visible society, governed by hierarchical heads.

[21] It is difficult to summarize this letter; but here are the chief developments: I-III, prologue; IX-XXXVI, moral considerations in order to prepare for the return to peace; XXXVII-XXXVIII, transition: the Body of Christ; XXXIX-LXI, teaching directly aiming at remedying the division amongst the Corinthians; LXII-LXV, conclusion.

cause of the sedition, I will leave, and go wherever you wish. I will carry out the decisions of the people, only let the flock of Christ live in peace with the appointed presbyters!' He who will act thus will gain for himself great glory in Christ, and every place will welcome him. . . ." (LIV).

Then, in order to give encouragement, Clement mentions examples of devotion given by pagans and Jews, and in these examples again we note with Hemmer the "breath of humanity which inspires Clement, and leads him to do justice to the devotion of Codrus, Lycurgus, Decius, and other pagan heroes."

Not men alone, but also inanimate creatures teach us peace, concord, and harmony (ch. XX-XXI).

Still, it is true that the usual sphere of Clement's thought is sacred history; it is there he seeks by preference for his models and also for examples of God's punishments, as we see from the beginning (ch. IV) and throughout the epistle. These recollections of the Old Testament are moreover a common possession, and doubtless Clement utilises many developments which are already traditional.

What is more personal are the properly Christian features; these are not so numerous, but they are set forth prominently. This is the case with the example of the excellent apostles Peter and Paul (ch. V) and of the Roman martyrs (ch. VI); and above all with the examples and lessons of Christ himself:

"Let us fix our gaze on the blood of Christ, and know how precious it is to God his Father, because having been poured out of our salvation, it has brought to the whole world the grace of repentance" (VII, 4).

"Above all let us remember the words which the Lord Jesus spoke to us to teach us fairness: . . . 'Be ye merciful, that ye may obtain mercy. . . .' " (XIII, 1).

"Christ belongs to those who are humble, and not to those who exalt themselves above the flock. The sceptre of the majesty of God, the Lord Jesus Christ, did not come with the pomp of pride or boastfulness, though He might have done, but in humility, as the Holy Spirit spake concerning him" (XVI, 1-2).

"The sovereign Creator and Master of the universe

willed that all these things should remain in peace and concord, for He is good towards all, but especially towards us who have recourse to his mercy through Jesus Christ our Lord, to whom be glory and majesty for ever and ever, Amen" (XX, 11-12).

"Such is the way, my beloved, in which we find our salvation, Jesus Christ, the high priest of our offerings, the protector and help of our weakness. Through him we fix our gaze on the heights of heaven; through him we see as in a mirror the spotless and sublime countenance of God; through him the eyes of our heart are opened; through him our mind, hitherto closed and darkened, opens to the light; through him the Master has willed that we should taste the immortal knowledge, who, being the effulgence of God's majesty, is so much higher than the angels as he hath received a more excellent name. . . ." (XXXVI, 1-2).

We recognise in the last sentence an echo of the Epistle to the Hebrews: Christ is our high priest, the mirror in which we contemplate the splendour of God; He is infinitely above the angels, and this transcendence is then proved by Clement by the Biblical texts already quoted in the Epistle to the Hebrews.[22]

A little further, we have a eulogy of charity which recalls the teaching of St. Paul (*I Cor.*, xiii), and which concludes in the contemplation of the charity of Jesus Christ:

"Let him who has the charity of Christ fulfil the commandments of Christ. Who can describe the bond of the divine charity? Who is able to express its sublime beauty? The height to which charity raises us is ineffable. Charity unites us closely to God; charity covers a multitude of sins, charity suffers all things, bears all things; there is nothing low in charity, nothing proud; charity does not make a schism, charity does not create sedition, charity does all things in concord; in charity the perfection of all the elect of God is consummated; without charity nothing is pleasing to God. By charity the Master has raised us up to Him; because of the charity He had for us, Jesus Christ our Lord, by the will of God, gave His blood for us, and His flesh for our flesh, and His soul for our souls" (XLIX).

[22] On all this cf. *Histoire du Dogme de la Trinité,* Vol. II, p. 270.

This is indeed a Christian sermon.[23] Doubtless the thought of Christ is not so constantly present to the mind of Clement as it was to Paul, but when He does appear He dominates everything: He is the "sceptre of the majesty of God" and the radiation of His glory; to mankind He is the Redeemer and Saviour. This exalted Christology will be more concealed in the apologists: desirous above all to demonstrate to catechumens or even to pagans the preliminaries of the faith, they will postpone the great theological theses to a later teaching; but the witness of the apostolic Fathers, and in particular of Clement and Ignatius, warns the historian not to think that silence comes from forgetfulness, or that the second Christian century, before Irenæus, lost sight of the theology of the apostles.

The dogma of the Trinity is equally attested in this letter. We note particularly this solemn declaration in which Clement confirms his moral teaching:

"Accept our counsel, and you will not regret doing so. For as truly as God lives, and the Lord Jesus Christ and the Holy Spirit, the faith and hope of the elect, he who humbly carries out . . . the commandments given by God, will be included and counted among the number of those saved by Jesus Christ. . . ." (LVIII, 2).[24]

The Jews swore by the life of Jahveh; Clement swears by the life of the three divine Persons, in whom he sees "the faith and hope of the elect"; we feel here the energy of the

[23] Bousset, *Kyrios Christos,* 1921, p. 291, is mistaken in seeing in the primitive Roman Church as it appears in Clement, the religion of the Jewish Dispersion. So also Lietzmann, *Geschichte der alten Kirche,* Vol. I, p. 209: "This community did not spring from Paulinism, but received from it only a very superficial impress. It developed directly out of the Greek synagogue, and it sets forth a conception of Christianity such as we should expect to find amongst the proselytes." Against this, cf. *Hist. du Dogme de la Trinité,* Vol. II, p. 280.

[24] This important text was already quoted by St. Basil, *De Spiritu Sancto,* XXIX, 72 (Migne, *P.G.,* XXIX, p. 201). As this chapter and the following ones are lacking in the *Alexandrinus,* the authenticity of this text was long questioned, but the discovery of the Jerusalem MS. and the Syriac version has removed all doubts. Cf. on the doctrinal importance of this text, *Hist. du Dogme de la Trinité,* Vol. II, pp. 277-279.

Christian soul which, pressed by grace, professes by faith the Trinity of divine Persons, and by hope tends towards them; it is the same energy that we shall find at the end of the second century in Athenagoras; "We are moved by the sole desire to know the true God and His Word . . ., to know the community between Father and Son, and the union and distinction of these united terms, the Spirit, the Son, and the Father." [25]

Two other texts [26] also remind the Christians of their Trinitarian faith. As Harnack puts it: "The author sets forth the profession of the Trinitarian faith; he does not comment on it, evidently because he felt no difficulty in this formula, any more than St. Paul had done." [27] And certainly there is no indication of any hesitation here in Clement or the Corinthians. They believe in God, Father, Son and Holy Spirit; they aspire to know Him; this is the faith and hope of the elect.

The Christian life which these texts reveal to us expands into the great prayer (ch. LIX-LXI); we shall study this later on, when we deal with prayer and the liturgy.

§2. ST. IGNATIUS OF ANTIOCH [1]

Of all the witnesses of the Christian Church at the beginning of the second century, there is none more qualified than

[25] *Legatio*, c. XII.
[26] "The apostles, fully convinced by the resurrection of our Lord Jesus Christ, and strengthened by the word of God, with the assurance of the Holy Spirit" (XLII, 3); "Have we not one only God, and one only Christ, and one only Spirit (of Grace) poured out upon us, and is there not one only calling in Christ?" (XLVI, 6).
[27] *Der Erste Klemensbrief*, in *Sitzungsberichte der kon. Preuss. Akad.*, 1909, III, p. 51, n. 4.
[1] Editions: Lightfoot, *Apostolic Fathers*, Part II, 3 vols., 1889; Gebhardt-Harnack, Funk-Bihlmeyer (*supra*, p. 103, n. 4); Lelong (1910); Bauer (1920). English translation by Dr. Srawley, published by S.P.C.K., 1919. Historical and theological studies: T. Zahn, *Ignatius von Antiochien*, Gotha, 1873; E. von der Goltz, *Ignatius von Antiochien als Christ und Theologe*, Leipzig, 1894; H. de Genouillac, *Le Christianisme en Asie-Mineure au début du IIe siècle*, 1907; Rackl, *Die Christologie des hl. Ignatius v. Antiochien*, Freiburg, 1914; Lebreton, *Histoire du Dogme de la Trinité*, Vol. II, pp. 282-331.

the illustrious Bishop and martyr, St. Ignatius of Antioch; and no testimony is more explicit than his. For a long time this testimony was suspect; Renan could still write: "The question of the epistles of St. Ignatius is, after that of the Johannine writings, the most difficult of those connected with primitive Christian literature," [2] and he answered the question negatively.[3] But thanks above all to the work of Lightfoot, the critical problem has been studied more closely, and definitively settled, and this has assured definite progress in the early history of the Church.[4]

The confusion which so long paralysed the efforts of critics arose in great part from the state of the manuscript tradition.[5]

[2] *Les Evangiles*, p. x.

[3] *Ibid.*, p. xvii; cf. p. 492.

[4] In one of his last works, Loofs wrote: "There was a period of new biblical, theological and historical researches in which one seemed to be retrograde if one did not set out to interpret in the light of Philo and the literature deriving from him, all the references to the Logos met with in the christological texts of early Christian literature. That has changed now that the authenticity of the letters of Ignatius has been definitively established" (*Paulus von Samosata*, Leipzig, 1924, p. 312).

[5] The manuscript tradition presents three different forms:

The *short* recension, containing three letters, Polycarp, Ephesians and Romans, in a very abridged form.

The *mean, mixed* or *long* recension, containing in a longer form the three letters mentioned above, and in addition, Magnesians, Trallians, Philadelphians, and Smyrnians.

The *long* or *longer* recension, containing in a still longer form the seven preceding letters, and in addition: Mary of Cassobola to Ignatius, Ignatius to Mary of Cassobola, Ignatius to the Tarsians, to the Antiochenes, to Hero, and to the Philippians.

This last form, obviously interpolated, was the first to be published, in 1498, by Lefèvre d'Etaples; the mean form, the only authentic one, in 1644 by Ussher; the short form in 1845 by Cureton.

To Lightfoot (in 1885 and 1889) belongs the merit of having elucidated the critical problem and bringing forward the decisive testimonies which established the authenticity of the seven letters (*op. cit.*, Vol. I, pp. 135-232). O. Pfleiderer, in the first edition of his *Urchristentum*, 1887, pp. 825-835, had declared the letters of Ignatius to be "as certainly unauthentic as the pastoral epistles"; in his second edition (1902), pp. 226-232, he recognises them as authentic. Lightfoot (*op. cit.*, Vol. I, p. 423) thus con-

But it is evident that the decisive reason for this opposition lay in the desire to defend a theological thesis threatened by these documents.[6]

St. Ignatius and his Letters

The circumstances in which these letters were written are very clearly determined: in the course of a persecution of which we know nothing otherwise, and which speedily died down,[7] Ignatius, Bishop of Antioch, was arrested; he was taken to Rome to be condemned to wild beasts. He made a first stop at Philadelphia,[8] a second at Smyrna, where he was received by Polycarp, the bishop, and met also by representatives of the churches of Ephesus, Magnesia and Tralles. When he was there he wrote to these three churches and to the church of Rome. Next he was taken on to Troas, from whence he wrote to the churches of Philadelphia and Smyrna, and also to Polycarp. He passed by Philippi on the way to Dyrrachium, and lastly reached Rome. At his request, the Christians of Philippi wrote to Antioch to congratulate the Christians there on the return of peace; they sent their letter

---

cludes his study of the question: "While external and internal evidence combine to assert the genuineness of these writings, no satisfactory account has been or apparently can be given of them as a forgery of a later date than Ignatius."

There is another grouping of the epistles, adopted by T. W. Manson in *A Companion to the Bible* (Edinburgh, 1939, p. 127): The *Long Recension* (13 epistles), the *Short* (the genuine 7), and the *Syriac* (3 only).

[6] J. Reville admitted this in his *Origines de l'Episcopat*: "The real reason, and the only really strong one, which from the beginning of modern historical criticism to our own day, has caused the disqualification of the epistles of Ignatius in their first recension is the ardent episcopalianism which inspires them from one end to the other" (p. 478). He himself accepts the authenticity but rejects the testimony: "To take literally the information furnished by the epistles on the ecclesiastical state of their time is about as reasonable as to represent the state of our modern society from the violent diatribes against the Republic of Freemasons by a militant clerical, or against the *bourgeois* by a revolutionary socialist" (p. 480). The clerical would at least know what was going on in his Church, and the Socialist in his party: that is all we ask from Ignatius.

[7] Ignatius to Polycarp, VII, 1.

[8] *Philad.*, III, 1; VII, 1; VIII, 1.

to Polycarp, who replied to them, and at the same time sent them at their request the letters of Ignatius which he possessed; in this way there was constituted the first *Corpus Ignatianum.*[9]

These letters, which are about fifteen years later than that of Clement,[10] are like that, and even more so, occasional papers; they were not written after long preparation, but in haste, by a prisoner condemned to wild beasts and closely guarded: "chained to ten leopards, that is, ten soldiers who show themselves to be the more wicked as one does them more good" (*Rom.* v, 1). We must not expect to find in them an elaborate exposition of the Christian doctrine, nor a complete description of ecclesiastical organisation, but we shall find there a most sincere and clear testimony concerning the Christian life and faith, that of a martyr who is already suffering for Christ, and desires only to die for him, who dearly loves the Church, and who warns it with the farsightedness of a man inspired by God, and with the authority of a bishop.

[9] Harnack recalls these facts in his studies on early collections of letters: *Die Briefsammlung des Apostels Paulus und die anderen vorkonstantinischen Christlichen Briefsammlungen,* Leipzig, 1926, pp. 28-35. Polycarp to the Philippians, 13: "You and Ignatius have written asking that if anyone is going to Syria he may also take your letter. . . . The letters of Ignatius, both those he has addressed to us and the others which we possess, are being sent to you at your request; they are included with this letter. . . . If you on your side have certain news of Ignatius and his companions, please communicate it to me." This text is quoted by Eusebius, *Hist. Eccles.,* III, 14-15. On this letter of Polycarp we have also the testimony of Irenæus (III, 3, 4), and of Eusebius (*Hist. Eccles.,* IV, 14, 8). Now Irenæus was a disciple of Polycarp, as he reminds Florimus (*Hist. Eccles.,* V, 20). The letter of Ignatius to the Romans is quoted by Irenæus (V, 28, 4) without mention of the author's name, and also by Origen (*De Orat.,* 20, *In Canticum, Prol.*). In *Hom. VI in Luc.,* Origen quotes *Ephes.,* XIX. These two last citations are expressly attributed to Ignatius. The seven letters are enumerated by Eusebius, *Hist. Eccles.,* III, 36, 2.

[10] The date of these letters is that of Ignatius's martyrdom; this date belongs to the reign of Trajan (98-117), but it is difficult to be more precise. Cf. Lightfoot, *op. cit.,* Vol. II, p. 472.

The Church and the Churches

We find many common features between these letters and that of Clement: there is the same desire for order and peace in the Church by submission to the hierarchy, and the same love of unity. But there is also a great difference between the two bishops: Clement does not confine himself to exhorting: he gives authoritative advice which is to be followed. Ignatius's attitude is not the same: in spite of the prestige of his situation as a confessor, he adopts always a great reserve so far as he himself is concerned. Thus he writes to the Trallians (III, 3): "In my love for you, I refrain from more severe remarks which I might address to you concerning your bishop; I will not presume to command you like an apostle, being only a condemned man." Even these counsels, which he multiplies to other churches, disappear from the letter to the Romans; here we find only prayers, supplications, and veneration for the Roman Church. We may infer from this that in the mind of Ignatius, the various churches are mutually independent, and that a bishop, even of Antioch, and a confessor of the faith, can give only counsel to other churches, while the Roman Church alone has a rank apart, an authority which is over all the others, which justified the step taken by Clement, and calls for submission and deference from Ignatius.

If we pass from the churches as a whole to the local organisation of each church, we find everywhere a definitely constituted hierarchy. Ignatius requests that it shall be respected; he does not need to promote its establishment: it already exists.

A few texts, chosen from a great number, will give the sense and force of the directions of Ignatius:

"The youthfulness of your bishop ought not to lead you to treat him with too much familiarity, in him you must reverence the very power of God the Father. In this way act, as I know, your holy presbyters; they do not presume upon his youth, but being inspired by the wisdom of God, they are subject to him, or rather it is not to him they are subject, but to the Father of Jesus Christ, to the universal bishop" (Magn., III, 1).

"All must reverence the deacons as Jesus Christ, the bishop as the image of the Father, the presbyters as the

Council of God and the college of the apostles. Without them there is no church" (*Trall.*, III, 1).[11]

We learn from Clement and the *Didache* that the episcopate is not only a ruling authority but also a priesthood;[12] it has the same character in Ignatius; hence the indispensable place of the bishop in the administration of the sacraments:

"Do nothing without the bishop in what concerns the Church. Regard as valid only that Eucharist which is celebrated under the presidency of the bishop or of his delegate. Wherever the bishop is, there let also the community be, just as wherever Christ Jesus is, there is the Catholic Church. It is not permitted to baptize or to celebrate the agape apart from the bishop; but all that he approves is pleasing to God, and all that you do is secure and valid" (*Smyrn.*, VIII, 1-2).[13]

Authority and the Charisms

Lastly, we note the no less important fact of the union between the charisms and the hierarchy. Ignatius, the bishop who everywhere preaches obedience, is at the same time the enthusiastic confessor, full of desire for martyrdom; he is also a seer, whose vision has penetrated the heavens: "Though I am a prisoner of Jesus Christ, I am able to know heavenly things, and the hierarchy of angels, and the ranks of principalities, and things visible and invisible, but I am not thereby a true disciple" (*Trall.*, V, 2).[14]

At the end of his book on the idea of the apostolate, the

[11] Cf. *Ephes.*, IV, 1; VI, 1; *Philad.*, III, 1; *Smyrn.*, VIII, 1; *Polyc.*, VI, 1.

[12] *Clement.*, XLIV, 4; *Didache, XV.*

[13] Cf. *Philad.*, IV. Amongst all the churches made known to us in these documents, there is one where the monarchical episcopate does not appear, namely, that of Philippi. Cf. Michiels, p. 367: "There is (in the letter of Polycarp) no mention of a bishop, but there is of priests and deacons. It seems to us that certain reasons compel us to infer from this silence the non-existence of a bishop at Philippi. No other satisfactory explanation has been advanced." Cf. H. de Genouillac, *op. cit.*, p. 143; Duchesne, *Histoire ancienne de l'Eglise*, Vol. I, pp. 88 *et seq.*

[14] Cf. *Philad.*, VII, 2: "They suspected that I spoke thus because I knew already of the schism which was to break out; but I take to witness him for whom I bear these bonds, that I had learnt

Protestant historian H. Monnier wrote: "There came to pass this strange thing: the Spirit, in the second century, went over to the side of the bishops, deserting the cause of those inspired by profession. Ignatius and Polycarp, the known founders of the monarchical episcopate in Asia, are full of the fire of the Spirit: they prophesy, and have visions, while the free missionaries of their time are doubtful personages, whose vocation derives from their own caprice. And in the rest of this struggle between growing Catholicism and free Inspiration it is evident to us that Catholicism represents the true interestes of the Church. . . . Free Inspiration had created the Church, but at this moment it was becoming a danger; it had either to discipline itself or disappear. That is why the best among the Spirituals put their gifts at the service of the Church, and ended by being absorbed into its hierarchy." [15] The study of the apostolic times and in particular of St. Paul, has shown what we are to think of this supposed sovereignty of Inspiration at the beginning of the Church; but it is interesting to note that at the period to which we have come, namely, the early years of the second century, the Catholic organisation of the Church is evident even to observers the least predisposed in its favour.

Ignatius found already some opponents who wished to refer only to Scripture: "I have heard some people saying: 'If I do not find (this point of belief) in the records, in the Gospel, I will not believe it!' And when I say to them: 'It is written,' they reply to me: 'That is precisely the question.' For me, the records are Jesus Christ, the inviolable records are his Cross, his death, his resurrection, and the faith is by Him; it is by these things that I desire, thanks to your prayer, to be justified" (*Philad.*, VIII).[16]

---

nought from man. It was the Spirit which said aloud: 'Do nothing without the bishop. . . .' " *Polyc.*, II, 2: "If you are both flesh and spirit, you ought to treat gently the things that come before you; as for things invisible, pray that they may be revealed to you, so that you may lack nothing, but possess the spiritual gifts in abundance." Cf. *ibid.*, I, 3: "Devote yourself to constant prayers, ask to grow in understanding, watch, and let your spirit never sleep."

[15] *La notion de l'apostolat des origines à Irénée*, 1903, p. 374. Cf. *ibid.*, p. 245.

[16] Batiffol, *l'Eglise naissante*, pp. 162 *et seq.*; on the following text, *ibid.*, p. 166.

This Church is not a friendly group of scattered communities with no bond between them: it is truly a unity created by Jesus Christ: "Where the bishop is, there ought also to be the people, just as where Jesus Christ is, there is the Catholic Church"[17] (*Smyrn.*, VIII, 2). "Jesus Christ is the Mind of the Father, just as the bishops established in the confines (of the world) are the Mind of Jesus Christ" (*Ephes.*, III, 2).

The Roman Primacy

Moreover, this unity rests upon the special dignity of the Roman Church; in this matter the witness of Ignatius is of great weight.[18] It is evident in the first place in the initial address of the letter, which is of a solemnity and high tone which distinguishes it from all the others:

"Ignatius, also called Theophorus, to the Church which has obtained mercy in the bounteous power of the Father most High and Jesus Christ his only son, to the Church which is beloved and illuminated by the will of Him who willed everything that exists, according to the love of Jesus Christ our God, to that Church which presides in the region of the Romans, worthy of God, worthy of honour, worthy of blessing, worthy of praise, worthy to be heard, worthy in purity, presiding in love, which has received the law of Christ, which bears the name of the Father, and which

[17] This is the first occurrence of this expression; it signifies the "universal Church" in contrast to particular churches; so in *Mart. Pol.*, *inscr.* VIII, 1; XIX, 2. Very soon it will signify the Great Church in contrast to the heretics; thus *Muratorian Canon*, 66, 69 (ed. Lietzmann); Clement of Alexandria, *Strom.*, VII, 106, 107; cf. *Mart. Pol.*, XVI, 2 (doubtful text). Cf. note by Bauer on *Smyrn.*, VIII, 2.

[18] It has often been studied: Funk, *Der Primat der römischen Kirche nach Ignatius und Irenæus*, in *Kirchengeschichtliche Abhandlungen*, Paderborn, 1897, Vol. 1, pp. 2-12; Chapman, *Saint Ignace d'Antioche et l'Eglise romaine*, in *Revue bénédictine*, Vol. XIII, 1896, pp. 385-400; Batiffol, *Eglise naissante*, pp. 167-170; H. Scott, *The Eastern Churches and the Papacy*, London, 1928, pp. 25-34. Interpreted differently by Harnack, *Das Zeugnis des Ignatius über das Ansehen der römischen Gemeinde*, in *Sitzungsber. der Akademie*, Berlin, 1896, pp. 111-131; H. Koch, *Cathedra Petri*, Giessen, 1930, p. 175; E. Caspar, *Geschichte des Papstums*, Vol. 1, Tübingen, 1930, pp. 16-17.

I salute in the name of Jesus Christ, the Son of the Father, to those who are attached in body and soul to all His commandments, filled for ever with the grace of God, and purified from every foreign dye, I wish a full and holy joy in Jesus Christ our God."

The impression we get from the reading of this address is confirmed by the letter as a whole: all the other epistles are full of recommendations and counsels; we find none such here, but only respectful requests; this complete change of attitude can only be explained by the singular veneration which the bishop of Antioch has for the Roman Church. Lastly, we must quote: "You have never envied anyone; you have given instructions to others. What I desire is that what you counsel and ordain may be always practised" (*Rom.*, III, 1); and still more this final recommendation: "Remember in your prayers the church of Syria which, having me no longer, has only God as its pastor. It will have no other bishop besides Jesus Christ and your charity" (*Rom.*, IX, 1). We will not exaggerate the importance of these words, but we must remark that Ignatius addresses them only to the Romans: from the other churches he asks only prayers.[19]

After re-reading these texts, we can without imprudence subscribe to this conclusion of an Anglican writer, S. H. Scott: "The Roman Church had a primacy, and that primacy was owing to its connection with St. Peter." [20]

Circumstances had led St. Ignatius to multiply his recommendations of unity between Christians, and of submission to the hierarchy, and thus no testimony is more explicit than his, or more valuable to us concerning the life and organisation of the Church at the beginning of the second century. But as we have already seen, this great bishop was at the same time a spiritual man and a prophet. As he himself recommends to St. Polycarp (*Polyc.*, II, 2), if he is flesh as well as spirit, this is in order to govern with gentleness those amongst whom he lives, while also contemplating invisible things. This contemplation is for him both a much desired grace and an imperious need. His whole theology is illuminated by it.

[19] On all these texts we can accept the commentaries of Duchesne, *Eglises séparées*, pp. 127-129, recalled by Batiffol, *op. cit.*, p. 170.
[20] *The Eastern Churches and the Papacy*, p. 34.

The Flesh of Christ

This theology naturally has traces of the controversies which then loomed large. In Asia as a whole, and above all in the churches of Tralles and Smyrna, Ignatius felt the menace of Gnosticism, and reacted against it with all his might. Deceived by their dreams, these people had gone so far as to deny the real life and real flesh of Jesus Christ; the Bishop of Antioch, like his master St. John,[21] sees in these denials the complete opposite of Christianity: [22]

"Refuse to listen to the speech of those who do not speak to you of Jesus Christ the descendant of David and the Son of Mary, who was really born, who really ate and drank, who really suffered persecution under Pontius Pilate, who was really crucified and died before the eyes of heaven, earth, and the lower regions; who really rose from the dead. . . . If He suffered only in appearance, as is said by certain atheists, that is, certain unbelievers, who themselves are only an appearance, why am I in bonds? Why am I impatient to fight against the wild beasts? Then I die in vain, and what I say of the Lord is a lie!" (*Trall.,* IX).

"He really suffered, just as He really rose again, although some unbelievers, who are themselves only an appearance, say that He suffered only in appearance. . . . As for me, I know and believe that, even after his resurrection, He had a body. . . . After His resurrection, He ate and drank with His disciples like a corporeal being, although by the spirit He was united to His Father. . . . If it was only in appearance that Our Lord did all that, it is only in appearance that I am in bonds. Then why am I surrendered and given over to death by fire, sword and wild beasts?" (*Smyrn.,* II).

The Eucharist

These Christological errors had their immediate effect on the doctrine of the Eucharist, and Ignatius follows the controversy into this domain:

[21] Cf. *Histoire du Dogme de la Trinité,* Vol. I, pp. 482-485.
[22] *Ibid.,* Vol. II, pp. 80-81.

"They abstain from the Eucharist and from prayer, because they do not admit that the Eucharist is the flesh of our Lord Jesus Christ, which flesh suffered for our sins, and which the Father in His goodness raised up again. So those who deny the gift of God find death in their disputations. It were better for them rather to love, in order to rise again" (*Smyrn.*, VI).

In St. Ignatius as in St. John, these uncompromising affirmations of the reality of the flesh of Christ, in His life here below as also in the Eucharist, are penetrated with a belief in the vivifying activity of this flesh:

". . . You all break one bread, which is the medicine of immortality, an antidote which preserves us from death, and assures us of life for ever in Jesus Christ" (*Ephes.*, XX, 2).

Life in Christ

This belief unceasingly affirmed by Ignatius[23] is the deep source of his own life: if he repels Docetism with such energy, it is because the real flesh of Christ, denied by this heresy, is the indispensable principle of life: "Without him we do not possess true life" (*Trall.*, IX, 2): "The only thing necessary is to be found in Christ Jesus, for eternal life" (*Ephes.*, XI, 1).

Once more we find in the theology of Ignatius, as in that of Paul and John, and indeed in all Christianity, the indissoluble union of flesh and spirit: this defender of the hierarchy is, as we have said, a spiritual man; similarly, this defender of orthodoxy is also the great mystic who writes to the Romans (III, 3): "Nothing that is visible is beautiful. Even our God Jesus Christ is manifested better now that He has returned to the bosom of the Father." And there is in him a desire, deep as life itself, to disappear and to hide in the

[23] *Ephes.*, III, 2: "Jesus Christ, our inseparable life"; VII, 2: "in death, true life"; *Magn.*, I, 2: "I desire for the churches union with the flesh and spirit of Jesus Christ, our eternal life"; *Trall.*, IX, 2: "We who believe in him will be raised up by the Father in Christ Jesus, without whom we do not possess true life"; *Smyrn.*, IV, 1: "Jesus Christ, our true life." Cf. *Ephes.*, XI, 1; XIX, 3; *Magn.*, V, 2; IX, 2; *Trall.*, II, 1, etc.

divine silence where God alone is heard; then he will be a "word of God," but as long as he lives in the flesh he is but a "voice" (*Rom.*, II, 1); or as he says further on: "It is when I shall have disappeared from this world that I shall be able to be called truly faithful" (III, 2). The dreadful death in store for him attracted him irresistibly: "Let me become the food of the beasts; by them I shall attain to God. I am the bread of God, I must be ground by the death of the beasts in order to become the stainless bread of Christ. . . . Then shall I be truly a disciple of Jesus Christ, when the world sees no longer my body. Entreat Christ for me, that by the beasts I may become a victim offered to God" (*Rom.*, IV, 1-2).

Christ and Martyrdom

In this impatient thirst for death, silence, and complete disappearance, we must not suspect the influence of the perverse mysticism spread everywhere by Gnosticism: God is not for Ignatius an abyss in which he is to lose himself, He is the Father who is calling him in Christ and who is waiting for him; his faith is radiant with light: this Christ, whose real human nature he defends with such vigour, is He who takes hold of him by his life and by his resurrection; it is He who, present in his faithful one, leads him on towards God:

"Let naught of things visible or invisible seek to deprive me of the possession of Jesus Christ! Come fire, and cross, and bodily combat with wild beasts, lacerations, tearings, dislocation of bones, mutilation of members, crushing of the whole body, come the worst torments of the devil upon me, provided only I possess Jesus Christ! . . . Him I seek, Him who died for us; Him I want, who rose again for our sakes! The hour draws near for my birth. Forgive me, brethren; hinder me not from living, do not desire my death; bestow not upon the world or the seductions of matter him who desires to be God's. Let me grasp the pure light; when I shall attain to it I shall be truly a man. Let me imitate the suffering of my God. If anyone has Him in his heart, let him understand my desires, let him be compassionate in my pain, since he himself knows it. . . . My love has been crucified, and there is not within me any fire for matter, but a living water, which murmurs within me and says to me: 'Come to the Father.' I have no more pleasure in corruptible food, nor in the joys of this life. I desire the bread of God, which is the flesh of Jesus Christ, the son of David, and for drink I desire his blood, which is love incorruptible" (*ibid.*, V-VII).

These flaming words of the great martyr were read over and over again in the early Christian church in the times of the martyrs;[24] there is none more vehement or more poignant, but what gives them superhuman beauty is the faith which inspires them; the man who speaks thus has directed all the activities of his life towards union with Christ; if he hears the murmur of living water which comes from Christ's bosom[25] and calls him to the Father, it is because all other love has been crucified in him. And Christ was not only passionately loved as a Master, but also as God: "Let me imitate the passion of my God!" And the faith which shines out so clearly in the face of death sheds a warm light on all the other letters. It is this that we must now briefly study.[26]

What we find here is what we have already found in Clement, "the faith and hope of the elect"; but these Christian mysteries appear in Ignatius in a more vivid light. The difference arises doubtless from the character of these letters: they are not, like the epistle of Clement, official documents or liturgical in style; they are short notes, written in haste by one condemned to death, with all the unconstrained zest of a martyr exhorting his brethren in the faith. Moreover, and this is very important, the fifteen years which separate Ignatius from Clement were marked by a noteworthy progress in the history of the Christian revelation, for during them there appeared the Gospel of St. John, which had a great influence on St. Ignatius. Lastly, in these churches of Syria and Asia where the holy martyr lived and wrote, theological problems were more keenly discussed than they were at Rome, and in a more technical form. Ignatius, full of impatience to be united to Christ by an imminent death, does not stay to dis-

[24] Irenæus, V, 28, 4; Acts of Perpetua and Felicitas, XIV; Origen, *De Orat.*, XX; *In Cant. Prolog.*
[25] Compare with this text that in the letter of the Martyrs of Lyons, speaking of the deacon Sanctus: "The heavenly spring of living water which comes from the bosom of Christ refreshed and fortified him" (*Hist. Eccles.*, V, 1, 22).
[26] A more detailed study will be found in *Histoire du Dogme de la Trinité*, Vol. II, pp. 282-331.

cuss these problems, but he is aware of the danger, and is anxious to preserve the faith of Christians.

God the Father and Jesus Christ

What strikes the reader of these letters in a vivid way from the first is the ever-present mention of "God the Father and the Lord Jesus Christ." [27] Towards one and the other the faith and love of the holy martyr go out with the same force; life here below is life "in Christ" or "in God"; the end he aims at is to "attain to God," or to "attain to Christ." [28] Christians are the temples of God, and the temples of Christ; God dwells in them, and so does Christ.[29]

Thus in the Christian life we already find the inseparable union of Father and Son; both are our life here below, both are the goal at which we aim, the object of our hope in heaven. And yet they are not confused together: Jesus Christ, the Son of God, is the one Mediator who unites us to his Father: "Be subject to the bishop, and to one another, as Jesus Christ was to his Father according to the flesh." [30] By reason of his Incarnation, the Son of God appears to us indeed in a state of subjection and suffering which is due to his human nature: "He who is above all seasons, outside time, and invisible, became for us visible; being impalpable and

[27] These two terms are frequently united in this form (*Philad., inscr.* I, 1; *Polyc., inscr.*) or in equivalent forms: "God the Father and Jesus Christ" (*Ephes.,* XXI, 2; *Magn. inscr.; Trall.,* I, 1; XII, 2; *Philad.,* III, 2; *Smyrn., inscr.*); "God the Father and Jesus Christ our God" (*Ephes., inscr.*) or "our Saviour" (*Magn. inscr.*).

[28] Life "in Christ": *Ephes., inscr.,* I, 1; III, 1; VIII, 2; X, 3; XI, 1; XI, 2; XII, 2; XX, 2; XXI, 2; "in God," *Ephes.,* VI, 2; *Magn.,* III, 3; XIV; *Trall.,* IV, 1; VIII, 2; *Pot.,* I, 1; VI, 1. "Attain to God," *Ephes.,* XII, 2; *Magn.,* XIV, 21; *Trall.,* XII, 2; XIII, 3; *Rom.,* I, 1; II, 1; IV, 1; IX, 2; *Smyrn.,* XII, 1; *Pol.,* II, 3; VII, 1. "Attain to Christ," *Rom.,* V, 3; VI, 1.

[29] "Temples of God," *Philad.,* VII, 2. "God present in us," *Ephes.,* XV, 3. Christians are "Godbearers and Christbearers," *Ephes.,* IX, 2. "You have in you Jesus Christ," *Magn.,* XII. Cf. what we have said above concerning Jesus Christ as our life, p. 124.

[30] *Magn.,* XIII, 2. These last words, "according to the flesh," are lacking in the Armenian version and are suppressed by Lightfoot; but they are found in the Greek text, and the ancient Latin version, and are retained by the other editors: Bauer, Krueger, Funk-Bihlmeyer.

impassible, He became for us passible, and endured for us all kinds of sufferings." [31]

This distinction between the Father and the Son is not a consequence of the Incarnation: in His eternal pre-existence[32] the Son is distinct from the Father and is generated by Him: [33] "Before the ages, He was with the Father, and has appeared at the end" (*Magn.*, VI, 1); "there is only one God, who has manifested himself by Jesus Christ His Son, who is His Word, coming forth from silence, who in all things pleased Him who sent him." [34]

As we see from this last text, the Son of God is also His Word; God is the infinite and peaceful silence; [35] the Word has come forth by the Incarnation and has come to us to speak to us; He is "the true mouth through which the Father has truly spoken" (*Rom.*, VIII, 2). Now He has returned to the bosom of the Father; He has disappeared from this world, but more than ever He is active and is calling us (*Rom.*, III,

[31] *Pol.*, III, 2. We find the same idea in *Ephes.*, VII, 2: inasmuch as He is flesh, Jesus Christ had a beginning, He is in the flesh, born of Mary, passible; inasmuch as He is spirit in death, He is without beginning, God, true life, born of God, impassible. Cf. *Hist. du Dogme de la Trinité*, Vol. II, p. 294, n. 2.

[32] *Pol.*, III, 2. Cf. *Histoire du Dogme de la Trinité*, Vol. II, pp. 302-304.

[33] Attempts have sometimes been made to interpret the theology of St. Ignatius in a Modalist sense, thus G. Krueger, Kroymann, Bethune-Baker, and above all Loofs, *Paulus von Samosata*, pp. 293-322. This interpretation does not do justice to Ignatius's thought: cf. *Histoire du Dogme de la Trinité*, Vol. II, p. 305-312. It is still more often said that in Ignatius filiation affects Christ only as man; this again is inexact; it is manifest that, considered in his "spirit," that is, in his divine nature, Christ is ἀγέννητος (*Ephes.*, VII, 2); but this term had not in the time of Ignatius the precise sense of "ungenerated" which it took on after the Arian controversy; it signifies "unproduced," and applies to all three divine Persons. Cf. *ibid.*, pp. 312-319 and 635-647.

[34] *Magn.*, VIII, 2. Cf. *ibid.*, VII, 2 (in an exhortation to unity): ". . . the one Jesus Christ who has come forth from the One Father, though remaining united to Him, and who has returned to Him."

[35] Cf. *Ephes.*, XIX, 1, speaking of the great mysteries of the life of Christ, the virginity of Mary, her child-bearing, and the death of the Lord: "These are resounding mysteries, which have been wrought in the peaceful silence of God." Cf. *Histoire du Dogme de la Trinité*, Vol. II, p. 321.

3); He enlightens us by His Spirit[36] and leads us towards the Father.

In this theology of Ignatius we can recognise the influence of St. Paul and above all of St. John; and this Christian tradition is vivified by the intimate action of the Holy Spirit; the imminence of martyrdom brings out the depth of this life, the ardour of desire, and the assurance of faith. This fruitful tradition will be transmitted to heirs worthy of it, St. Polycarp and St. Irenæus.

§3. ST. POLYCARP [1]

The Witness of Tradition

St. Polycarp is of exceptional interest to us: he appears early in the second century, in touch with St. Ignatius: we follow him to Smyrna and Rome through the recollections of St. Irenæus, and lastly the letter of the Church of Smyrna tells us of his martyrdom in 155. Thus he is for us, in this second century of which we know so little, the embodiment of tradition, as he was for his contemporaries.

When Ignatius stopped at Smyrna, Polycarp received him with such veneration that the martyr afterwards sent him from Troas a special letter; in the praises he gives him, and the advice he tenders him, we see already the bishop of Smyrna as he henceforth appears:

> "I honour thy piety, solidly established as on an unshakable rock. . . . Take care of unity, the greatest of goods; assist all others, as the Lord assists thyself. . . . Pray without ceasing . . . watch, and let thy spirit never sleep. . . . Bear the infirmities of all, like a perfect athlete. . . . " (I, 1).
>
> "As for invisible things, pray that they may be revealed to thee. . . ." (II, 2).

[36] On the Holy Spirit, the most explicit text is *Philad.*, VII, 1-2: "Some have wished to deceive me according to the flesh, but the Spirit is not deceived, it comes from God, it knows whence it comes and whither it goes, and it penetrates hidden secrets. . . ." Cf. above n. 14, and *Histoire du Dogme de la Trinité*, Vol. II, pp. 326-331.

[1] The editions of St. Polycarp are the same as those of St. Ignatius; we may add to them the historical studies on the saint's martyrdom: H. Delehaye, *Les Passions des martyrs et les genres littéraires*, Brussels, 1921, pp. 11-59.

"Do not be dismayed by those who, in spite of a trust-
worthy appearance, teach error. Stand firm as an anvil
under the hammer. A great athlete triumphs in spite of the
blows which fall upon him. We ought all the more to endure all things for God, so that He may support us. . . ."
(III, 1).

That is how Polycarp appeared throughout his life, and
when he faced death forty years later. He was the perfect
athlete, firm as an anvil, firm as a rock, upon whom rested
the churches of Asia; he was the irreconcilable enemy of
error;[2] he was also a man of prayer, "whose spirit never
slept," one whom the Church of Smyrna celebrated after his
death as "an apostolic and prophetic doctor" (*Mart.*, XVI, 2).

Letter to the Philippians

The letter of Polycarp to the Philippians is especially valuable to us because of the guarantee it gives to the letters of
St. Ignatius. But it is also interesting in itself, inasmuch as
it shows us Christian morals and preaching at the beginning
of the second century. The bishop of Smyrna is full of veneration for "the blessed Ignatius, Zosimus and Rufus" (IX,
1), still more for "the blessed and glorious apostle Paul" (III,
2); if he writes to the Philippians, it is to grant their desire
(III, 1). He exhorts them to rectitude in the faith (VII, 1),
to the memory of the death and resurrection of the Lord (I,
2; II, 2); he particularly urges them to follow the example of
Christ:

"Let us have our eyes constantly fixed on our hope, and
the pledge of our justice, Jesus Christ: He it is who bore
our sins in His own body on the wood, who committed no
sin, and in whose mouth was found no guile (*I Pet.* ii, 24,
22), but He suffered all things for our sakes, that we may
have life in Him. Let us therefore imitate His patience, and
if we suffer for His name, let us give glory to Him. For

[2] Thus he writes in his letter, VII, 1: "Whosoever interprets in the
sense of his personal desires the words of the Lord, and denies
the resurrection and the judgment, is the first born of Satan."
Many years afterwards, he will reply to Marcion in the same
terms: "Dost thou recognise me?—I recognise the first born of
Satan" (Irenæus, III, 3, 4; Migne, *P.G.*, VII, p. 853).

that is the example He has set forth to us in His own person, and we have believed therein." [3]

When he sets forth to the Philippians the imitation of Jesus Christ, Polycarp also reminds them of His teaching, especially according to the Sermon on the Mount: "Judge not, that you be not judged; forgive, and it will be forgiven you; be merciful, in order to obtain mercy; you will be served according to the measure you mete out to others. Blessed are the poor, and those who suffer persecution for justice, for the kingdom of heaven is theirs" (II, 3).

The Church of Philippi had been saddened by the scandal of the presbyter Valens and his wife; Polycarp seizes the occasion in order to condemn avarice, and to recommend chastity and sincerity. And once more he urges his correspondents, in face of the threatened persecution and of heresy, to persevere in faith and patience.

Witness of Irenæus

This letter is the only writing we possess of Polycarp's; but his disciple Irenæus gives us a glimpse of his glorious career during the forty or forty-five years separating the martyrdom of Ignatius from that of Polycarp. In order to bring back to the faith one of the friends of his childhood, Florinus, who had fallen into the Gnostic heresy, Irenæus wrote to him thus:

"These doctrines, Florinus, to say nothing more, are not sound in thought; these doctrines do not agree with the Church; they involve those who believe in them in the greatest impiety; the heretics, even those outside the Church, have never dared to bring these doctrines into the light of day; these doctrines have never been transmitted to you by the presbyters who were before us and who lived with the apostles. For when I was still a child, I saw you with Polycarp; you shone at the imperial court, and endeavoured to gain his approbation. Indeed I remember better those times than recent events. For the things one learns when one is young become one with the soul and unite themselves with it, so that I can say in what place the blessed Polycarp used to sit in order to speak, how he came in and went out, what was the character of his life,

[3] Cf. V, 2: "Let them walk in the way of truth marked out by the Lord, who became the servant of all. . . ."

his physical appearance, the talks he had with people, how he told of his relations with John and with the others who had seen the Lord, how he reported their words and all that he had learnt from them concerning the Lord, His miracles and His teaching; all this Polycarp had gathered from those who had seen the Word of Life, and he related it all, in conformity with the Scriptures. I carefully listened to all these things then, by the grace of God given me; I have kept them in memory, not on paper but in my heart. Continually, by God's grace, I recall them faithfully, and I can testify before God that if this blessed and apostolic presbyter had heard things such as these, he would have cried out and stopped his ears, saying as he often did: 'O good God, unto what times hast thou reserved me, that I should endure all this!' And whether he was sitting or standing, he would have fled from the place where he had heard such words. This can be shown moreover by the letters which he sent to the neighbouring churches to strengthen them, and to certain brethren, to warn and exhort them" (*Hist. Eccles.*, V, 20, 4-8).

This letter, written in the time of Pope Victor about 186, is one of the most interesting documents in the early history of the church of Asia; it shows the veneration which at the end of the first and the beginning of the second century surrounded the presbyters who had seen the Lord with their eyes and could repeat his words; and after them, the witnesses of that past generation, and amongst them all, Polycarp, "the blessed and apostolic presbyter." It shows us how this influence spread round him into the neighbouring churches, and above all it confirms what we know already of this faithful disciple, "firm as a rock." But this firmness did not make him unfeeling; he suffered, as did St. Ignatius and St. John, when anything divided and troubled the Church: "O good God, to what times hast thou reserved me!" All this is confirmed again by the testimony full of veneration that Irenæus gave to his master.[4]

[4] *Haer.*, III, 3, 4 (Migne, *P.G.*, VII, 851-855), reproduced by Eusebius, *Hist. Eccles.*, IV, 14: "Not only was Polycarp a disciple of the apostles, who had lived with several of those who had seen the Lord, but also he was appointed by the apostles as bishop in the church of Smyrna, for Asia, and we ourselves saw him in our childhood. . . ."

St. Polycarp in Rome

In this passage, Irenæus recalls the journey made to Rome by St. Polycarp under the pontificate of St. Anicetus; he speaks of it more fully in a letter he wrote later to Pope Victor:

"The blessed Polycarp paid a visit to Rome under Anicetus; there were between them some differences of little importance, and they quickly came to agreement; on this question (of the Pasch) they did not desire to quarrel. Anicetus was unable to persuade Polycarp not to observe what he had always observed with John the disciple of Our Lord and the other apostles whom he had known; Polycarp, on his side, could not persuade Anicetus, who said to him that he was obliged to retain the custom of the presbyters who had preceded him. This being so, they remained in communion with each other, and with the Church. Anicetus gave the Eucharist to Polycarp, evidently out of respect, and they parted in peace, and in the Church all were at peace, whether they retained the observance or not" (*Hist. Eccles.*, V. 24, 16-17).[5]

We shall return later to this Easter question, and the peace-making intervention by St. Irenæus; what we note here is the part played by St. Polycarp in this matter, his attachment to tradition, his care for the unity of the Church, and lastly, the veneration with which he was regarded.

This veneration, which surrounded the old bishop at Rome, was still more marked at Smyrna. In the account of his martyrdom, we read how the bishop removed his clothes and bent down to take off his shoes: "He did not usually do this himself, for on every occasion the faithful contended for the honour of touching him, so great was the veneration accorded to him, even before his martyrdom, because of the holiness of his life" (*Mart.*, XIII, 2). ·

[5] On this incident, cf. G. Bardy, *L'Eglise romaine sous le pontificat de saint Anicet*, in *Recherches de Science religieuse*, Vol. XVII, 1927, pp. 481-511, especially pp. 496-501.

Martyrdom of St. Polycarp

The year which followed his visit to Rome[6] saw the martyrdom of St. Polycarp. All Asia was roused; the church of
Philomelium asked for an account of his death. The Church
of Smyrna entrusted Marcianus, one of its members, with the
writing of the account, and sent it round to all the churches.
This is "the earliest hagiographical document we possess, and
all agree that there does not exist a more beautiful one. It is
enough to read it and to weigh each phrase to be convinced
that this account is what it claims to be, the work of a contemporary who knew the martyr, saw him in the midst of the
flames, and touched the remains of the saint's body with his
own hands." [7]
Other martyrs had already been tormented; one only had
yielded, a Phrygian named Quintus, who had denounced himself, a practice disapproved by the Church; the others had
been wonderfully constant. Amongst the spectators, some
were moved with pity (*Mart.*, II, 2), but others, exasperated
by the courage displayed, cried out: "Away with the atheists!
Go and find Polycarp!" (*ibid.*, III, 2).
The bishop had, at the urgent request of the faithful, withdrawn to the country. He was betrayed by a young lad, saw
the soldiers coming, and would not flee; he made them eat,
and asked to be allowed to pray to God; "he was so full of
the grace of God that for two hours we could not cease, and

[6] On the date of the martyrdom of St. Polycarp, cf. Lightfoot, *op.
cit.*, Vol. I, pp. 644-722; Harnack, *Chronologie*, Vol. I, pp. 334-
356: "There is scarcely a date in the early history of the Church
which is so universally accepted as that of the martyrdom of
Polycarp, the 23rd February, 155" (p. 334): Corssen, *Das Todes-
jahr Polycarps*, in *Zeitschrift für N. T. Wissensch.*, 1902, pp.
61-82, confirms this conclusion. We read in the *Acts*, XXI: "The
martyrdom of the blessed Polycarp took place . . . on the seventh
of the kalends of March, on a great sabbath day . . . under the
proconsulate of Statius Quadratus." The proconsulate of Quadratus is dated, according to the speech of Aelius Aristides and an
inscription at Ephesus, in the years 154-155; the 7th of the
Kalends of March fell on a sabbath day in the year 155.
[7] Delehaye, *Les Passions des Martyrs*, pp. 12-13. This beautiful
account has often been translated: by Racine, when staying in
1662 with his uncle, the chanoine Sconin at Uzès; by Lelong in
Textes et Documents, 1910; by Dom Leclercq, *Les Martyrs*, Vol.
I, p. 65.

those who heard him were struck with admiration" (*ibid.*, VII, 3). He was taken away; Herod the *irenarch* or "High Sheriff," took him into his carriage and endeavoured to persuade him. Eventually Polycarp said: "I will do nothing of what you advise me to do"; and he was brutally thrown out of the carriage. He arrived at the stadium; a heavenly voice was heard by the Christians: "Courage, Polycarp, play the man!"

The proconsul, Statius Quadratus, tried again to shake him, and finally called upon him to curse Christ. Polycarp replied: "For eighty-six years now I have served Him, and He has never done me any ill. How could I blaspheme my King and my Saviour?" He was thereupon declared to be a Christian, and at the request of the populace, he was condemned to be burnt alive. In this way was to be verified the prophetic vision he had had three days earlier: he had seen his pillow on fire, and turning towards the faithful he had said to them: "I am to be burnt alive."

The crowd, mainly of Jews, hastened to prepare the fire; Polycarp was bound on it, "like a holocaust acceptable to God." He raised his eyes to heaven, and prayed:

"O Lord, God Almighty, Father of Jesus Christ, Thy well beloved and blessed Son, who has taught us to know Thee, God of angels, powers, and of all creation and all the race of the just who live in Thy presence! I bless Thee because Thou hast thought me worthy of this day and of this hour, worthy to take part amongst the martyrs in the chalice of Thy Christ, to rise again to eternal life of body and soul in the incorruptibility of the Holy Spirit. May I be this day admitted amongst them in Thy presence, as a fatted and acceptable victim, the destiny which Thou hast prepared me and made me to see in advance, and which Thou bringest about now, O God who liest not, true God! For this grace and for all things I praise Thee, I bless Thee, I glorify Thee through the eternal and heavenly High Priest, Jesus Christ Thy well beloved Son. Through Him may glory be to Thee, with Him and the Holy Spirit, now and for ever, Amen." [8]

[8] On this prayer, cf. *Histoire du Dogme de la Trinité*, Vol. II, pp. 197-200.

The fire was lit, and the flames surrounded the martyr's body; it seemed as though it was "not flesh that was burning, but bread that was being baked, or an ingot of gold or silver that was being purified in a furnace; and we smelt a delightful odour, like that of incense or some other precious perfume." The *confector* killed Polycarp with a dagger; from the wound blood flowed so abundantly that it extinguished the fire. When the faithful went to remove the body from the fire, it was taken away from them, at the instigation of the Jews; who said: " 'Christians would be capable of leaving the Crucified to give worship to Polycarp!' They did not realise that we could never give up Jesus Christ, who suffered for the salvation of those who are saved in the whole world, the innocent for the guilty, and that we could not give worship to another. For Him we adore as being the Son of God; as for the martyrs, we love them as disciples and imitators of the Lord, and they are worthy of it because of their supreme attachment to their King and their Master." [9]

But the Christians could at least gather the bones of the martyr, and put them in a suitable place. "There we meet together, as far as the Lord permits, in joy and gladness, to celebrate the anniversary day of the martyrdom." [10]

The Lessons of the Martyrdom

This account is not only one of the most moving in early Christian literature, but also one of the most instructive. It shows us the attitude, at once prudent and firm, recommended by the Church to the faithful in face of persecution. The opinion of pagans was still on the whole violently hostile: the courage of the martyrs called forth pity from some spectators, but in the case of the majority, hatred was increased and exasperated: it was the crowd that clamoured for the arrest of the bishop, and then for his condemnation to death by fire. Amongst these opponents, the Jews were the most bitter: the death of the martyr did not satisfy them, they demanded that his body should be destroyed.[11]

[9] Cf. *Histoire du Dogme de la Trinité,* Vol. II, pp. 204 *et seq.*
[10] The Church of Smyrna continued faithful to the celebration of this anniversary, even in the worst days of the persecutions: it was on the day of this feast that the priest Pionius was arrested with several other Christians in 250, during the persecution of Decius: *Acts,* II, 1, ed. Knopf, p. 59.
[11] This request was addressed to the governor by "Nicetas, father

The martyr sought his strength only in prayer; Polycarp, prepared so long for this desired hour, did not tire of prayer, but continued in it when the officers arrested him, when he was bound to the fire, and when he was waiting for death: at this supreme moment his prayer was already an act of thanksgiving, and spontaneously the liturgical formulas which he had so often pronounced came back to his lips. The Christian populace which was so deeply attached to him venerated him still more when sanctified by martyrdom; and yet there is an impassable gulf between him and Christ; no text reveals better than his profession of faith, so full of adoration, what Christ is to His believers: "Him we adore as the Son of God; as for the martyrs, we love them as disciples and imitators of the Lord."

§4. THE CONTROVERSY WITH THE JEWS AND THE LETTER OF BARNABAS

The writings which we have studied in the preceding sections have brought before us great bishops, Clement, Ignatius and Polycarp. They have deserved our study: in the person of these leaders, the Christian Church itself appears before us. The other documents which we find, under the names of apostles, have not the same origin, and do not bring us the same knowledge: the letter of Barnabas is a spurious work; Hermas is an unknown person; the *Didache* is an anonymous work. The Church no longer appears in the person of its great men, but it is still present; these writers are unknown or without interest, but the books themselves are witnesses which enable us to see the Christian people, their struggles, their aims, and their prayers.

The letter of Barnabas will not detain us long.[1] This little

---

of Herod and brother of Alce" (XVII, 2). This Alce seems to be the one mentioned by Ignatius, *Smyrn.*, XIII; *Polyc.*, VIII. Cf. Lightfoot, *op. cit.*, Vol. I, p. 366. Christianity had therefore penetrated into the family of the irenarch; the reaction of hatred was only the more violent.

[1] This letter is contained in two MSS., both discovered in the nineteenth century: the *Sinaiticus*, discovered by Tischendorf in 1859 and the Jerusalem MS. discovered by Bryennios in 1875. Edited by Gebhardt-Harnack; Funk-Bihlmeyer; Oger, Paris, 1907; Windisch, Tübingen, 1920. In this last work is an abundant annotation; also in the translation by Veil, *Apocryphes du N. T.* by

book is set forth modestly and humbly without the author's name: "As for me, it is not as a doctor, but as one of yourselves that I will give you some instructions." [2] This anonymous and modest doctor was, especially at Alexandria, identified with St. Barnabas;[3] this apostolic attribution gained for some time great credit for this little work; the confusion has been long dispelled, and for ever, but the epistle is nevertheless not without its interest.

It was composed, it seems, at Alexandria, probably shortly before the revolt of Bar Kokhba (130-131).[4] It comprises two parts of unequal length and importance: the four last chapters (XVIII-XXI) contain a moral exhortation in which we find the distinction between the two ways of good and evil, presented in the form in which we find it in the *Didache*. The first part, much longer (ch. I-XVIII) is also much more original, and gives the letter its chief interest: it is a controversial work against Judaism; not a scholastic dissertation, but a moving exhortation in face of a great and pressing danger:[5] "The days are evil; the enemy is active and powerful" (ch. II, 1). "The great scandal spoken of in Scripture has come nigh" (ch. IV, 3). "I therefore beg you, I who am one of you, and who love you more than my own life: take care of yourselves, and be not like some people who heap sins upon sins, and who say that the Testament belongs to those (Jews) as to ourselves. It is ours, but those have lost it for ever" (ch. IV, 6-7). We hear in this work not the peaceful speculations of a catechist, but "the cry of alarm by the shepherd." This alarm gives the letter its great interest, and

---

Hennecke, Tübingen 1904, and 1923. The theological teaching has been studied in *Histoire du Dogme de la Trinité*, Vol. II, pp. 332-345. Literary study in Puech, *op. cit.*, Vol. II, pp. 22-31.

Quotations in text follow the French edition. An English translation by Lightfoot of the whole letter will be found in *Excluded Books of the New Testament*, London, 1927.

[2] I, 8; cf. IV, 6 and 9; VI, 5.

[3] This identification appears already in Clément of Alexandria; cf. Harnack, *Gesch. d. altchristl. Literatur*, Vol. I, p. 60, and *Histoire du Dogme de la Trinité*, Vol. II, p. 344, n. 4; it was adopted by Origen, and also explains why it finds a place in the *Sinaiticus* after the New Testament.

[4] Cf. *Histoire du Dogme de la Trinité*, Vol. II, p. 332, n. 3.

[5] Cf. the just comments by Veil (*Handbuch*, p. 208, and *Neutestamentl. Apokryphen*, 1924, p. 503).

also accounts for the exaggerations in which the controversialist indulges.

Symbolical Interpretation of the Law

In order to preserve his correspondents, whose peril moves him so deeply, the writer defends the radical thesis which the Church never approved, and the danger of which will soon be revealed by Marcion, that the old alliance never existed as a positive law willed by God subjecting the Jewish people to certain practices or ceremonies; it had only a symbolical value, which the Jews failed to realise, in attaching themselves to the letter: the circumcision demanded by God was not a carnal circumcision (ch. IX, 4); the alimentary prescriptions were only allegories (ch. X); the true sabbath is the rest of God after six thousand years, inaugurating a new world (ch. XV). The only Temple acceptable to God is not an edifice in stone such as the Temple of Jerusalem, which God interdicted through His prophets, but the spiritual temple of our souls (ch. XVI).

All this is not only weak, but dangerous, as will soon appear; but it must not be overlooked that Barnabas was only following the example of numerous Jewish exegetes, who likewise allegorised the Law;[6] in utilising this weapon of allegorical exegesis he thought he could defend the Church and save it from Judaism; in reality he was destroying the historical facts on which the Church was based; the Church has rejected this allegory, this gnosis to which Barnabas invites the faithful.[7] The apologetic argument of Barnabas contains another feature, however, of permanent value: the divinity of the Son of God, and the infinite value of His Passion.

[6] Philo, *De migr. Abrah.*, 89 (I, 450). Philo rejects this allegory, which sees only the symbol and denies the reality, and certainly Barnabas goes beyond Philo, but only by travelling further, along the same road. Cf. Heinisch, *Der Einfluss Philos auf die älteste christliche Exegese,* Münster, 1908, especially pp. 60, 106, 262.

[7] I, 5: "I am writing to you briefly in order that, together with the faith, you may have a perfect gnosis." IX, 8-9. "What says the gnosis? Learn it. It says: 'Hope in him who must manifest himself to you in the flesh, Jesus. For man is a land which suffers. . . .' " The gnosis is here presented by Barnabas as a gift deposited by God in the soul of the master, and communicated by the latter to those who are worthy; it is in the light of this gnosis that the author develops his allegorical exegesis. Cf. *Histoire du Dogme de la Trinité,* Vol. II. pp. 344-345.

Theology

To the disciples of Barnabas, as to those of St. Paul, the Passion of Jesus appeared first of all as a scandal; the apologist effaces nothing, but on the contrary brings it out into full light, and shows the divine power of it:

> "If the Lord endured that His flesh should be given up to destruction, this was in order to purify us by the forgiveness of sins, which takes place through the sprinkling of His blood" (V, 1).
>
> "If the Lord endured to suffer for our souls, though He is the Lord of the whole world, and the one to whom God said at the foundation of the world: 'Let us make man to our own image and likeness,' how could He endure to suffer at the hand of man? Learn this. The prophets, receiving grace from Him, prophesied about it, and it is in order to abolish death, and to manifest the resurrection from the dead, that He endured to suffer, for He had to appear in the flesh in order to fulfil the promise given to our fathers, and to prepare for Himself a new people, and to show while still upon earth that it is He who will bring about the resurrection, and will judge" (V, 5).[8]

He recognises also in the Incarnation a manifestation of God: our minds, incapable of sustaining the immediate vision of the godhead, are able to contemplate it veiled in flesh (ch. V, 10). By these great theological ideas, Barnabas is linked up with the most authentic Christian tradition; he echoes St. Paul, and prepares the way for St. Irenæus.[9] By his anti-Jewish polemic, he testifies, not indeed to the deep thought of the Church, but at least to the danger which Judaism constituted for it, and the Church's reaction to the danger.

[8] This passage calls up numerous reminiscences in the literature of the second century and those which followed: Irenæus, *Demonstr.*, VI and XXXVIII; G. Hippolytus, *Anaphora of the Apostolic Tradition,* etc. Cf. *Histoire du Dogme de la Trinité,* Vol. II, p. 339, n. 2.

[9] E.g., in his doctrine of the "recapitulation"; we find in Barnabas (V, 11) the verb ἀνακεφαλαίω, familiar to St. Paul (*Rom.* xiii, 9; *Ephes.* i, 10) and to St. Irenæus, but not found elsewhere in the apostolic Fathers or apologists.

This fact must be borne in mind by the historian: the violence and success of the Marcionite propaganda will be understood better if Barnabas has been read: the condemnations imprudently formulated in this epistle against the Jewish legalism, will be pronounced by Marcion against the very author of the Law; not only the Jews will be affected, but also their God. The excessive character of these exaggerations will show the Church the danger in this unwise apologetic, and will keep her clear of it once and for all.[10]

§5. THE MORAL REFORM AND PENANCE IN THE ROMAN CHURCH. THE SHEPHERD OF HERMAS [1]

The Book and the Author

Of all the writings of the Apostolic Fathers, there is none more instructive than the *Shepherd* of Hermas, but there is none more difficult to interpret. In this first half of the second century which is so obscure to us, this book presents in simple and sincere pictures, not indeed high theological doctrines, but Christian life in its simplest, commonest, and

[10] We must remark in conclusion that this Jewish danger, and the strong reaction against it, can be explained by what we know of the great influence of the Jews at Alexandria: previous to the Christian preaching this great influence is shown by the life and work of Philo; in the first centuries of the Christian era it continued and threatened the Church: it was at Alexandria above all that the apocryphal Gospels, with their Judaising tendencies, were read.

[1] Editions: Hilgenfeld, Leipzig, 1866; Gebhardt-Harnack, 1877; Funk, Tübingen, 1881; Lelong, 1912; German translations and notes by Weinel, *Neutestamentl. Apokryphen,* pp. 217-229; Dibelius, Tübingen, 1923. On the old Latin translation, see Turner in *Journal of Theol. Studies,* XXI, 1920, pp. 193-209. A quarter of the Greek text has been found in a fourth-century papyrus, cf. C. Bonner, *A papyrus Codex of the Shepherd of Hermas,* University of Michigan, 1934.

Chief studies: T. Zahn, *Der Hirt des Hermas,* Gotha, 1868; A Stahl, *Patristische Untersuchungen,* Leipzig, 1901, pp. 223-359; d'Alès, *L'édit de Calliste,* 1914, pp. 52-113; Puech, *op. cit.,* Vol. II, pp. 71-95; Lebreton, *Histoire du Dogme de la Trinité,* Vol. II, pp. 346-387. [Good discussion also in Cayré, *Manual of Patrology,* Paris, 1936, pp. 83-96. English translation by Lightfoot in *Excluded Books of the New Testament,* London, 1927.—Tr.]

at the same time its deepest form. While arousing our curiosity in this way, it also presents as many arduous problems as it offers aspects: its date, its composition, its character, its doctrine—all are matter for discussion. It is not that the style is difficult—it is simple and abrupt, like that of a man of the people; but the thought is often incomplete, often also obscured by additions: the writer was evidently not quite satisfied with what he had said, but instead of effacing it, he added to it new developments which often agree ill with the first text.

This explains the fortune of this work: it was accepted almost everywhere with great favour in the second century; in the third, the West rejected it, and in the East it kept its place only in Egypt; from the fourth century it disappeared very quickly.[2] What the early Fathers loved in it was not its theology, but its moral teaching, its conception of the Christian life; that constitutes its value, and that is why it calls for our attention here.

The Book of Hermas as we have it consists of a series of five Visions, ten Commandments, and ten Parables or Similitudes; the writer himself suggests another division which corresponds better to his plan: in a first part, the Church appears under various symbols, in four successive Visions; the second part, the longer and more important, contains the revelation of the Shepherd: after a Vision which constitutes an introduction, the Shepherd teaches Christians their duties and exhorts them to penance; this is the theme of the Commandments and the Parables.

This short outline already enables us to realise the character of the book: it is an apocalypse, full of visions and revelations; but at the same time it is an autobiography. The writer calls himself Hermas; he was a slave freed by Rhoda, became rich, married a shrewish woman, and had several children who turned out badly; they apostatised, denounced their parents, and ruined them. Hermas had, it seems, been brought up in Christianity, but he had been only a poor kind of Christian; when he was ruined, he was converted.[3] It was

---

[2] On all this tradition cf. *Histoire du Dogme de la Trinité*, Vol. II, pp. 346-348, and above all Harnack, *Gesch. der Literatur*, Vol. I, pp. 51-58.

[3] *Vis.*, III. 6, 7: "When thou wert rich, thou wert good for nothing; now thou canst serve, thou art fit for life."

his anxiety for his children that led him to preach; he had the joy of seeing them converted (*Sim.*, VII, 4), and the angel revealed to him the re-establishment of his fortune. To these details in the book itself, the *Muratorian Canon* adds another: Hermas was a brother of Pope Pius (about 140-154). This last indication would put the composition of the book in about the end of the first half of the second century.[4] The work indeed was not all composed at once; the different parts which go to make it up are separated by fairly large intervals, and reveal great changes in the state of the Church and the preoccupations of the author. At the beginning of the work, a violent persecution is in progress; in the second, we have the after-effects of this trial, the reconciliations which the apostates implore and the Church grants or refuses. At the beginning the author has in view the final catastrophe; later on it is penance that preoccupies him, the conditions it requires, the renewal to which it should lead: in the family of Hermas himself, the situation is different, and the apostate children have repented.

This succession of episodes rather loosely linked together is the cause of a certain lack of consistence in the book, and a lack of coherence in the doctrine, which it is difficult to unify; but it has for a historian the interest of a film which is slowly projected before his eyes, and brings out through the witness of a freedman of Rome the moral preoccupations of Christianity.

Moral Reform

That is indeed what we must look for in the first place: Hermas has no theological training, and speculative questions do not interest him; we are not surprised to find that from the doctrinal standpoint he is extremely inconsistent; but he is

[4] This is also the date suggested by the book itself: the description of the persecution, which applies better to the system inaugurated by Trajan than to the procedure of Domitian (Lelong, *op. cit.*, pp. xxix-xxxii), and the new Gnosticism, not yet a great danger (*ibid.*, p. xxxvii). Against this date there is the mention of Clement (*Vis.*, II, 4, 3). This is certainly difficult to explain, but this difficulty cannot prevail against the arguments on the other side; it can be solved if we suppose that the first visions belong in Greek text to the time of Clement and were put forth under Pius. Cf. Lightfoot, *Clement*, Vol. I, pp. 359-360; Turner, in *Journal of Theol. Studies*, Vol. XXI, pp. 193-194.

a sincere and fervent Christian, very much occupied with the moral problems arising out of life around him; he sets them forth as he sees them; we could not desire a more sincere witness.

Like all moralists, Hermas is a righter of wrongs, and the first impression he gives us is a severe one: the Church first of all appears to him in the guise of an infirm old lady seated in a chair; but from the second vision onwards she regains her powers, and in the third vision she is "young, beautiful and gay": the message of the Lord has been heard, hearts have revived, and have taken new life.[5] From so rapid a transformation it will be inferred that the evil was less deeply rooted than it seemed. This impression is strengthened in the course of the book; we find there under various forms and symbols the examination of conscience of the Roman Church; this examination shows us that the majority of Christians are good people who have never lost their baptismal innocence, and have no need of penance.[6]

Thus in the eighth parable, we have a great willow tree which represents the Law or the Son of God; the archangel Michael has detached some branches from this tree and given them to mankind: this is the law taught to the faithful; the branches which they have received and carry represent symbolically the state of their consciences. Several bring back branches which are split, dried up, or at least have lost their leaves; these are those Christians who are sinners or negligent. "Others carry their branches green and as they had received them from the angel; this is the case with most people." [7] The just are therefore a majority in the Church.

Strength and Weakness

This statement has all the more weight because of the delicate nature of Hermas's conscience: the scene with which

[5] *Vis.* III, 11-13.

[6] Cf. Lelong, *op. cit.*, p. lviii; Duchesne, *Hist. ancienne de l'Eglise,* Vol. I, p. 229.

[7] *Simil.*, VIII, 1, 16. Hermas himself interprets this symbol thus (*ibid.*, 3, 8): "Those who have given back the branches as they received them, are the saints and the just, who have lived in perfect purity of heart and in the faithful observance of the commandments of the Lord." Above these again Hermas distinguishes those who have brought back branches covered with new shoots, or even with fruits: these are the confessors and martyrs.

the book opens (*Vis.*, I, 1), the remorse arising from a look or a desire, shows that the Christian ideal was strong within him, with all its exigencies.

Yet this Church has also its weaknesses; we find the details in the third vision, and in the eighth and ninth parables. The general impression is well set forth in *Vision, III, 11*:

> "Why did the woman appear to thee in the first vision as old, and seated in a chair? It was because thy mind was aged, already exhausted and without power, because of thy softness and thy doubts . . . (she was seated in a chair) because every infirm person by reason of his weakness sits in a chair in order to support his weakened body." [8]

Thus, the most widespread and serious fault is hesitation, or discouragement, such as that of old men who have no more hope, who ask "if all this is real or not" (*Vis.*, III, 4, 3). Hence the great aim of the first chapters is to strengthen hope, and this not so much by the preaching of penance as by the announcement of the end: "The Tower will be quickly built" (*ibid.*, III, 8, 9). In the rest of the work, the perspective widens and the effort is directed more and more towards penance.

Riches

The softening and lukewarmness arises above all from contact with the world: the Church has numerous members, it gathers them from all ranks of society; the rich are particularly liable to deteriorate:

> "Those who brought back their branches with one half green and the other dried up are men occupied with business, and who have become almost foreign to the society of the saints" (*Sim.*, VIII, 8, 1).

> "Those who have brought branches with two-thirds dried up and the other green are men who, after embracing the faith, have amassed riches and won the esteem of the pagans. This has been a source of great pride, and they have become haughty; they have abandoned the truth, and

[8] In *Vis.*, II, 4, 1, Hermas explained this aged character of the Church by saying that she is the oldest of creatures; there he was considering rather the transcendent Church; here the Church Visible.

left the society of the just in order to share in the life of the pagans, finding this way easier. Nevertheless they have not denied God, but have persevered in the faith, although they do not the works of the faith . . ." (ibid., IX, 1).

"From the third mountain, which is covered with thorns and thistles, there come these believers: some are rich, the others are men full of the bustle of affairs. The thistles represent the rich; the thorns, those who are entangled in the multiplicity of affairs. These last, those who are hampered by a mass of business of all kinds, do not frequent the servants of God, but walk at a distance, at random, stifled as they are by their occupations. As for the rich, these have little to do with the servants of God, lest these should ask something from them. Such men will enter only with difficulty into the kingdom of God" [9] (ibid., IX, 20, 1).

In the persecution, "their business and their riches lead them to deny their Master"; they will enter into the Tower when they will have been deprived of their riches; "thy own example will bring this truth home to thee: when thou wert rich, thou wert good for nothing; now thou canst serve, thou art fit for life" (Vis., III, 6, 5-7). This last trait confirms the impression we get from the others: the rich whom Hermas criticises are those of his own circle: prosperous merchants, absorbed by business, and puffed up by their quickly won fortunes, but upset by persecution, unless this saves them by despoiling them. Even apart from these times of crisis, these rich people run the risk of feeling out of their element in the midst of the lowly folk who surround them in the Christian community; they are always obsessed by the fear that they are going to be called upon to give something; they are inclined to regret their fine pagan surroundings, and to cast an envious glance over the wall of the Church towards the world outside.[10]

[9] Cf. Vis., III, 11, and Sim. 1.
[10] We may recall here what St. James had already written concerning the attentions sometimes multiplied to the rich, to the despite of the poor: "If there shall come into your assembly a man having a golden ring, in fine apparel, and there shall come in also a poor man in mean attire, and you have respect to him that is clothed with the fine apparel, and shall say to him: 'Sit thou here well'; but say to the poor man: 'Stand thou there, or sit under my footstool': Do you not judge within yourselves, and are

Ambition

Another evil which Hermas strongly denounces is ambition, with the dissensions to which it gives rise. In the maternal exhortation the Church addresses to all her children, she especially warns the leaders, and those who occupy the first places: "Take care, my children, that your divisions do not lead you to loss of life!" (*Vis.*, III, 9, 7). In the parable of the willow tree, the Shepherd emphatically points out the same danger:

> "Those who have brought back their branches green, but slit, are men who have always remained faithful and good, but quarrel bitterly amongst themselves for the first places and for honours. They are foolish thus to dispute for priority. But at heart these men are good; thus, as soon as they have become aware of my commandments, they have purified their hearts and have hastened to do penance. Accordingly they have been allowed to dwell in the Tower; but if ever one of them should fall again into discord, he will be expelled from the Tower and lose his life" (*Simil.*, VIII, 4-5).

These last words show that the evil is much less serious at Rome than it was at Corinth;[11] Clement could then give to the ringleaders no other counsel than to leave the country; at Rome, exhortations have sufficed, and there is peace.

Many other vices are rebuked by Hermas, especially in the Parables VIII (6, 4 *et seq.*,) and IX (15, 3 and 19 *et seq.*); but they are less characteristic of the state of the Roman Church at this time. What is most interesting to observe is the persecution, the dangers it creates, the terrible trial it represents, and the results it brings.

---

become judges of unjust thoughts? Hearken, my dearest brethren: hath not God chosen the poor in this world, rich in faith, and heirs of the kingdom? . . . But you have dishonoured the poor man" (*James* ii, 2-6). The rich St. James has in mind are also merchants who go from town to town, promising themselves great profits, and boasting of their riches (IV, 13-17). On the penetration of the rich into the Church, cf. Harnack, *Mission und Ausbreitung*, pp. 559 *et seq.*

[11] Lelong accordingly exaggerates when he writes (*op. cit.*, p. xxxvi): "There took place at Rome in the time of Hermas what had taken place at Corinth at the time of Clement."

Persecution

In the Visions, the Church appears as threatened by an imminent persecution; a great tribulation is expected, to be followed, it is hoped, by a definitive triumph.[12] The second part of the book carries us a few years further on; the persecution has struck the Church; not the fiscal inquisition inaugurated by Domitian, but the persecution of the Christian name, as determined by the procedure laid down by Trajan; this name is the pride of the Christian and the reason for his martyrdom. The martyrs appear in the ninth parable; they are the believers who come from the eleventh mountain:

> "These are the men who have suffered for the name of the Son of God, and who have displayed all the eagerness and generosity of their hearts in suffering and sacrificing their lives. . . . All those who have suffered for the Name are glorious before the Lord, and have seen all their sins blotted out. . . . All those who, when haled before the magistrates and subjected to the questioning, have not denied but have suffered willingly, rejoice before the Lord with a much greater glory. . . . But there are others who showed themselves timid and hesitant; only after debating in their hearts whether they ought to deny or confess did they decide to suffer; these last have as their symbol the less beautiful fruits, because of this thought which arose in their hearts" (*Sim.*, IX, 28, 2).

Fear has not been entirely removed; the persecution still threatens the Church; the parable ends with an ardent exhortation:

> "You who suffer for the Name, ought to give thanks to God that He has judged you worthy to bear this name, and to receive the healing of all your sins. Consider yourselves therefore happy; indeed, think that you have done a great work when you suffer for God. The Lord gives you life, and you do not think of this. For your sins have weighed you down, and if you had not suffered for the name of the Lord, they would have made you dead to God. It is to you I speak, you who know not whether you ought to deny or confess; confess that you have a Master, if you do not

[12] *Vis.*, II, 2, 7: III, 4; and above all *Vis.*, IV, the sea-monster.

wish to be cast into prison as renegades. If the pagans punish a slave who has denied his master, what, think you, will the Lord, who is the Master of all things, do to you? Cast these thoughts out of your heart, in order that you may live always for God" (*Sim.*, 28, 5).

Turning over the pages of this book, we seem to mingle with the crowd of Christians in Rome; we feel ourselves constrained by the bitterness of the persecutions, but we also realise the pride and power of the faith in the hearts of these neophytes.

The Hierarchy

If we try to find in the Shepherd some indications of the constitution of the Church, we note first of all that the monarchical episcopate is not directly mentioned; but we shall not overlook the fact that the writer was brother to the Bishop of Rome.[13] He speaks on several occasions of the heads of the Church, presbyters and pastors;[14] he does not spare them from rebuke; he warns them above all against love of first places, vanity, ambition;[15] he stigmatises the untruthful deacons who have dissipated the goods of widows;[16] but he praises the charitable bishops who open wide their houses to the brethren, who maintain widows, and who lead a holy life.[17] We find traces still of the rivalry which at the end of the first century occasionally broke out between the

[13] Turner (*art. cit.*, p. 194) rightly says: "As the *Shepherd* was published by Hermas during his brother's tenure of the see, and as it seems probable that in Mandate IX he is intending to glance at conditions actually prevailing within the Roman community, then the conclusion is natural that Hermas comes before the public at this particular time both because his relationship to the bishop will attract attention to his revelations, and because in his capacity as a seer he can do something to assist his brother in the difficulties of his position."

[14] Presbyters: *Vis.* II, 2, 6; III, 9, 7; II, 4, 2-3; pastors, IX, 31, 5-6. He uses the titles "presbyter" and "bishop" in the same sense: *Vis.*, III, 5, 1; cf. the notes by Funk, and Lelong, p. lxxxii.

[15] *Vis.*, III, 9, 7; *Simil.*, VIII, 7,4.

[16] *Simil.*, X, 26, 2.

[17] *Ibid.*, 27, 2. Other features in this indication of the hierarchy will be found in *Vis.*, II, 2, 6; III, 5, 1; IV, 3; IX, 7. Cf. Dobschuetz, *Urchristl. Gemeinden*, p. 233; Weinel, *Neutest. Apokryphen*, p. 330.

prophets and the presbyters (*Vis.*, III, 1, 8), and already we notice a struggle between the martyrs and the hierarchy (*ibid.*, 9); this will be more pronounced in the third century, in the time of Cornelius and Cyprian.

The Church the Mother of the Christian

Beyond all these human inequalities, faults, and virtues in the leaders of the Church, Hermas contemplates the Church herself, the Mother of the Christian.[18] Like a mother, the Church exhorts her Christian children:

> "Hear me, my children; I have brought you up in great simplicity, innocence and holiness, thanks to the mercy of the Lord, who has poured out justice upon you. . . . Make peace to reign amongst you, so that I also may be able to go joyfully before the Father to give an account of all of you to your Lord" (*Vis.*, III, 9, 1).

We see from these last words that the office of the Church towards the Christian is the same as the office of Christ, that of a mediator with the Father;[19] this is because the Church is one with Christ. Hermas expresses this by the symbol of the Tower which is the Church, and the rock which is Christ: "The Tower was formed as of one single stone; no join could be seen in it; one would have said that the stone had been drawn from the Rock itself; the whole gave me the impression of a monolith" (*Simil.*, IX, 9, 7). "Thou seest," he says again, "that the Tower forms one mass with the Rock." [20]

---

[18] On this belief, so dear to the Christians of the second century, cf. Lebreton, *Mater Ecclesia,* in *Recherches de Science religieuse,* 1911, pp. 572-573.

[19] See also *Simil.,* X, 2, 2: "Et hic (Pastor) apud me de his bene interpretetur et ego apud dominum."

[20] Cf. Durell, *The Historic Church,* Cambridge, 1906, pp. 99 *et seq.* This affirmation of the identity between the Church, the body of Christ, and its head, could appeal to the teaching of St. Paul, and will remain dear to all Christians. Hermas also affirms that the Church was the first of all creatures to be created, and that the world was formed for her (*Vis.,* I, 4, 1); this conception reappears in a more definite form in the *IIa Clementis.* Cf. *Histoire du Dogme de la Trinité,* Vol. II, p. 388, 392.

Penance

Of all the moral problems dealt with by Hermas, there is one which dominates all the others, that of penance and reconciliation. This is the chief object of the message transmitted to the Roman Church.[21]

This message is set forth with great energy; but it formulates at the same time two theses which at first sight are impossible to harmonise: there is no other penance than baptism, and yet another penance is offered. Hermas is himself aware of his contradiction, at least apparently, and sets it forth clearly:

"I have heard, O Lord, some masters teach that there is no other penance than that which we made when we descended into the water and there received the pardon of our previous faults." "Thou hast well understood, it is so. For he who has received the forgiveness of his sins ought to sin no more but remain in innocence. But since thou wishest to know the last word of all, I will discover also this to thee: . . . For those who were called before these days, the Lord established this penance, and set me over it. But I say to thee that if any one should, after this great and solemn call, yield to a temptation of the devil and sin, there is a penance; but if he falls again indefinitely, to do penance again, let him hope not for fruit; his salvation is indeed compromised." "I revive," I cried, "after the very precise explanations you have just given me, for I know that, if I do not commit new sins, I shall be saved." "Thou wilt be saved," he said to me, "as also will those who act thus" (*Command.*, IV, 3).

The last words of this passage reveal its significance: what causes Hermas anxiety is the danger in which are those believers who have sinned after their baptism, and amongst these he includes himself. Are these lost beyond recall? They

[21] Cf. A. d'Alès, *L'édit de Calliste*, 1914, pp. 53-113. In the *Shepherd*, three portions especially concern the question of penance: the third Vision: the construction of the Tower (d'Alès, *op. cit.*, p. 54); the fourth Commandment: chastity; there is no other penance besides baptism (*ibid.*, p. 67); the eighth and ninth Parables: the branches, the twelve mountains, and the Tower (*ibid.*, p. 87).

would be, if one had to adhere rigorously to the principle laid down at first: there is only one penance, baptism; but the Lord, knowing "the weakness of man and the malice of the devil," has instituted another penance, and has set the Shepherd over it. This merciful institution, which remedies past faults, must not encourage future sins: to those, then, who have not yet received baptism, or who have just received it, the principle is repeated: there is no other penance besides baptism. Does this mean that the penance preached by Hermas is, so to speak, a Jubilee, which will never be repeated? Certainly not;[22] and the proof is that later on the same promise of reconciliation will be made, accompanied by the same warning: this is the last pardon.[23] In all these texts we see the pressing exhortations of a preacher, and we must not look for the precision of a canonist.

What we note above all is the strength of the Christian ideal: a grave fault after baptism is an unworthy falling back; an indefinite perspective of such faults cannot be considered, but since unfortunately these falls have taken place in the past, the guilty ones are restored, with the warning that such a fault must never be repeated.[24]

This reparation of sin is regarded and can only be regarded as a return into the Church;[25] this is already the teaching of the third Vision: one can be saved only by entering into the Tower; and "the Tower which you see being built is Myself, the Church." [26]

---

[22] This comparison of the Jubilee, first advanced by Batiffol, *Etudes de théologie positive,* Vol. I, p. 57, has been adopted by Lelong, *op. cit.,* p. lxiv, but is rightly rejected by d'Alès, *op. cit.,* p. 79.

[23] *Simil.,* IX, 26, 5.

[24] There is no reference in the *Shepherd* to the three unpardonable sins (apostasy, adultery, homicide) which will appear as such in Tertullian.

[25] This essential point is misunderstood by Lelong, *op. cit.,* pp. lxxiii-lxxv, but is well established by d'Alès, *op. cit.,* pp. 104 *et seq.*

[26] In the eighth Parable, VIII, 6, 6, we see penitent believers who are admitted into "the external precincts" of the Tower: in this symbol we probably have the situation of those who cannot be readmitted into the Church but who remain on the threshold in penance and prayer; cf. d'Alès, *op. cit.,* pp. 111 *et seq.*

Theology

The problems we have so far studied are the constant subject of the preoccupations of Hermas; but we have noticed
therein more than one obscure point, especially in the question of penance and the reconciliation of sinners. If we pass
from moral problems to theological conceptions, we must be
prepared for more serious confusion: these high speculations
are entered upon by Hermas only occasionally, in order to
illuminate the moral questions which occupy him: thus in the
fifth parable he preaches the meritorious character of fasting
and works of supererogation; in order to explain this he sets
forth to Christians the example of Christ, and doubtless
nothing is more excellent, but, too anxious about the moral
lesson, he forgets theology: Jesus appears to him as a faithful
servant who, having been charged by God to care for his
vineyard, did more than his duty, more than the Master of
the vineyard had asked of him: ordered to surround it with
a fence, he dug it, weeded it, and cleaned it of noxious plants;
the Master of the vineyard, touched by this zeal, made his
servant a co-heir with his son.

This may lead to very useful moral resolutions, but it is
difficult to harmonise with the Christian Faith. Hermas himself sees this and perhaps hears those around him saying:
"Why, O Lord, is the Son of God represented as a servant in
the parable?" He feels the objection strongly, and to parry it,
he has recourse to his usual procedure; he does not strike
out, but he adds; he tries to enunciate more correctly the
mystery of the Incarnation, and above all he hastens to draw
from the new interpretation he presents a new moral lesson:
just as the flesh, that is, the humanity of Christ, served in all
faithfulness and purity the divinity it bore within itself, so
also the Christian must keep without stain the spirit which
dwells in him: the moralist is pleased with this useful instruction; the theologian is less satisfied with the theological conception it suggests.[27]

[27] If the parity proposed by this interpretation were pressed, the
divinity of Christ would be reduced to a sanctification similar to
that accorded to all Chrstians; this would do violence to the
thought of Hermas just as much as to Christian doctrine; hence
we must be careful not to interpret too strictly the imprudent expressions of the writer. Cf. *Histoire du Dogme de la Trinité,* Vol.
II, p. 372.

Anyone who is familiar with the *Shepherd*, and the embarrassment of thought, and still more of expression, in which the writer is involved, will not be too surprised at these obscurities and incoherences, and above all he will take care not to hold the official teaching of the Church responsible for the awkwardness of this amateur theologian; what we must gather above all from the fifth Parable is the uneasy protest of the Christian conscience: the Son of God is not a servant; and also the firm affirmation of his redemptive office and his lordship:

"God created his people, and entrusted them to his Son; and the Son established angels over the people to guard them; and He Himself has washed away their sins with many tears and labours. Having thus washed away the sins of the people, He has shown them the ways of life, giving to them the law He had received from His Father. Thou seest that He is the Lord of the people, having received all power from His Father" (*Simil.*, V, 6, 2-4).

But what we must notice above all is that the points still vague in the fifth Parable are taken up again and firmly treated in the two last, the eighth and the ninth. The seer contemplates an immense Rock, in which a door has recently been hewn:

"What is the rock, and the door?" "This rock and this door, is the Son of God." "How then, O Lord, is the rock old, and the door new?" "Hear and understand, O man who understandest nothing. The Son of God was born before all creation, so that He was the counsellor of His Father in His Creative work. That is why He is old." "But why, O Lord, is the door new?" "Because it is in the last days of the world that He has been manifested; that is why the door is new (and it has been made) in order that those who must be saved shall enter through it into the kingdom of God. . . . None will enter the kingdom of God if he has not received the name of the Son. . . ." (*Simil.*, IX, 12, 1.)

The Son of God, born before all creation, counsellor of His Father in the work of creation, is both rock and door;

"His name is great, infinite, and upholds the whole world";[28] "He manifested Himself" [29] by the Incarnation; He is the door: "He is the only entrance that gives access to the Lord; hence no-one will have access to Him if he goes not through His Son." The highest angels, even, can find access to God only through the Son: "Of these glorious angels not one will have access to God without Him; whosoever has not received His name will not enter into the kingdom of God." (*Simil.*, IX, 12, 6.)

On the rock a tower is built: this is the Church. It is formed of one single stone, and there is no join to be seen; it seems to have been hewn from the rock, and the whole, tower and rock, gives the impression of a monolith (*ibid.*, IX, 9, 7): the Church is one, Christ and the Church are only one Body. And the parable develops, manifesting the indispensable mediation of the Son of God; it concludes by pressing exhortations to martyrdom, fidelity and penance.

It is this deep and sincere Christian faith which made the *Shepherd* in the second century a book dear to very many Christians; and the same character still makes us look upon Hermas as a Christian worthy of sympathy and respect, in spite of the incertitudes and weaknesses in his theology.

§6. PRAYER IN THE PRIMITIVE CHURCH [1]

The Example and Teaching of Christ

The reading of the Gospels and the writings of the apostles have revealed to us the fundamental importance of prayer in the individual life of all Christians and in the social life of the Church. Jesus Christ our leader is, in this as in all things, also our model. It was by prayer that He prepared Himself for the great mysteries and great events in His life: His baptism, the choice of the apostles, the confession of St.

---

[28] *Simil.*, IX, 14, 5: Hermas here repeats *Hebr.* i, 3.
[29] This expression is much more correct than that of "habitation" found in the fifth Parable.
[1] Cf. on prayer and worship in the Antenicene Church, *Histoire du Dogme de la Trinité*, Vol. II, pp. 174-247; Dom Cabrol, *The Prayer of the Early Christians*, London, 1930; Bardy, *L'Eglise à la fin du Ier siècle*, pp. 47-76.

Peter, the Transfiguration, and above all His Passion.[2] It was in prayer that He sought repose and power;[3] it was also by prayer that He desired His apostles to prepare themselves for the great trials and works which awaited them.[4]

This teaching of the Master was not forgotten; prayer was for the apostles their chief and indispensable duty; when the increasing number of the faithful made their task too heavy, they instituted deacons so as to transfer to them a part of their ministry, reserving themselves for "prayer and preaching" (*Acts,* VI, 4). St. Paul asks "incessant prayer" from his faithful (*I Thess.* v, 17); similarly St. Ignatius from the Ephesians (x, 1) and from Polycarp (i, 3).

This prayer of the Christian, the first of his religious duties, and at the same time his consolation and his power, is something so great that God alone can teach it. The apostles understood this: from Judaism they had received a religious teaching, and the custom of prayer; most of them again had been trained in prayer by John the Baptist; and yet they felt that they had everything to learn and when one day they saw Jesus praying, they said to him: "Lord teach us to pray." It was then that Jesus taught them the *Our Father* (*Luke* xi, 1-4); but oral teaching, even that of Christ, was not sufficient; the Christian needed also the interior inspiration of the Holy Spirit: "We know not how to pray as we ought; but the Spirit himself pleadeth in our behalf with unutterable groanings." [5]

This teaching of the Master and the Apostles will enable

---

[2] Prayer at the baptism, *Luke* iii, 21; at the choosing of the apostles, vi, 12; at Cæsarea Philippi, ix, 18; at the Transfiguration, ix, 29; the sacerdotal prayer, *John* xvii; prayer at the Agony in the Garden, *Matt.* xxvi, 39, and parallel verses; prayer on the Cross, *Luke* xxiii, 34, 46.

[3] *Mark* i, 35; *Luke* v, 16.

[4] *Matt.* xxvi, 41; *Mark* xiv, 38; *Luke* xxii, 46.

[5] *Rom.* viii, 26, Westminster version. Père Lagrange thus comments on this text: "This prayer is one which is powerless, which feels its powerlessness but is not ignorant of its aim; a prayer which is already that of the Christian conscious of his end, as is shown by the context. But what can one say to God to touch his heart, how approach Him, and in what dispositions? Jesus had taught this by the *Our Father,* the official prayer of the faithful, but this does not wholly dissipate the difficulty of mental prayer. Wearied by its efforts, and dissatisfied with what it finds to say, the soul says nothing definite, and it is the Spirit who prays within her."

us to understand the prayer of the Church as it is revealed in the writings of the end of the first and the beginning of the second centuries.

Jewish and Christian Prayer

If we consider the matter in general, the first thing we note is that Christian prayer resembles and echoes Jewish prayer in several ways: these resemblances appear in the Gospel canticles, the *Magnificat*, the *Benedictus,* and even in the *Lord's Prayer*.[6]

We find them again in the writings of the Apostolic Fathers, St. Clement, and the *Didache*. There is nothing here which should surprise a Christian: the God of Abraham, Isaac and Jacob is also the Father of Christ; the books of the Old Testament belong to the Church, which is the true Israel. But while the Church appears to Hermas as "the first of creatures" (*Vis.,* II, 4, 1), older than Moses and the patriarchs themselves, she is also the Spouse of Christ, eternally young, and rejuvenating all she touches.

This youthfulness, which the Church receives from the Holy Spirit, appears in her prayer: we feel there a spontaneity, a freshness, and above all a joyful and assured trust which makes the traditional themes vibrate in an entirely new way. Thus, we have in the Eucharistic prayers in the *Didache:*

"We give Thee thanks, O our Father, for the holy vine of David thy servant, which Thou hast made known to us through Jesus, Thy servant.[7] Glory be to Thee for ever! . . . We give Thee thanks, O our Father, for the life and knowledge Thou hast made known to us through Jesus Thy servant. Glory to Thee for ever! Thine is the glory and the power, through Jesus Christ, for ever." (*Didache,* IX, 2-5.)

The blessings the Church receives from God are those asked for by the Synagogue;[8] but they are better understood

---

[6] Cf. *Histoire du Dogme de la Trinité,* Vol. II, p. 177; on the *Our Father,* see *Life and Teaching of Jesus Christ,* Vol. II, pp. 60-78.

[7] Here, as in many of these early documents, Jesus is called παῖς θεοῦ this term signifies both "servant of God" and "Son of God."

[8] Thus, in this eucharistic prayer, the Christian asks "that the Church may be gathered together from the ends of the earth

and more firmly hoped for; the Church relies on the all powerful intercession of the Son of God, and all her prayer is transformed accordingly. This new spirit which animates the Christian soul is felt in the short exclamations of the *Didache;* we feel it also in the long prayer of Clement, and we do not possess for the period we are studying here any liturgical document comparable to this. Half a century later, St. Justin, describing the Sunday liturgy, writes: "When we have finished praying, bread is brought, with wine and water; he who presides sends up to heaven prayers and thanksgiving, according to his ability, and all the people reply by the acclamation 'Amen.' " [9] He who prayed thus did not create his prayer entirely; being full of the Scriptural hymns, he echoed them, as Mary did in the *Magnificat,* and Zachary in the *Benedictus;* but all these traditional themes were enriched by a new inspiration. These improvised prayers, full of Scriptural reminiscences, are our earliest liturgical documents; they were not conserved in books, and most of them have disappeared; those which have survived are all the more precious to us; such is the last prayer of St. Polycarp, transcribed above; such also the great prayer of St. Clement. Towards the end of his letter, the bishop of Rome, after exhorting the faithful at Corinth, concludes his homily, as was his custom, by a prayer:

Prayer of St. Clement

May the Creator of the universe keep intact in the whole world the fixed number of His elect, through His well beloved Son Jesus Christ, through whom He has called us from darkness to light, from ignorance to the knowledge of the glory of His name, so that we may hope in Thy name, the principle whence proceeds every creature.

into thy kingdom"; this is the prayer of the Jews, but transposed by a new hope: what is hoped for is no longer the land of Israel, but heaven.

[9] *Apol.,* I, 67. Similarly, in the Christian meetings of the agapes, at the end of the second century and in the third, those present either sang hymns from memory or improvised them: "Post aquam manualem et lumina, ut quisque de scripturis sanctis vel de proprio ingenio potest, provocatur in medium Deo canere" (Tertullian, *Apol.,* 39). "Sonet psalmos convivium sobrium: et ubi tenax memoria est, vox canora, aggredere hoc munus ex more" (Cyprian, *Ad Donatum,* XVI). Cf. *Histoire du Dogme de la Trinité,* Vol. II, p. 186.

Thou hast opened the eyes of our hearts in order that they may know Thee, the sole Most High in the highest (heavens), the Holy in the midst of holy ones; who humblest the insolence of the proud, who destroyest the imaginations of the nations, who exaltest the humble and humblest the great, who makest rich and makest poor, who killest and savest and makest alive. Sole benefactor of spirits, and God of all flesh; who beholdest the bottom of abysses, who searchest the works of man; help of those who are in danger, saviour of those in despair, Creator and Watcher (Bishop) of all spirits. Who multipliest the nations on the earth, and hast chosen in the midst of all, those who love Thee, through Jesus Christ Thy well beloved Son, by whom Thou hast instructed, sanctified and honoured us.

We pray Thee, O Master, be our help and our support. Save us who are oppressed, take pity on the humble, raise up those who have fallen, show Thyself to those who are in want, heal the sick, bring back those who have wandered from Thy people, feed the hungry, free our prisoners, restore those who languish, console the fearful; let all peoples know that Thou art the only God, that Jesus Christ is Thy Son, that we are Thy people and the sheep of Thy fold.

For Thou by Thy works hast manifested the everlasting constitution of the world. Thou, O Lord, hast created the earth, Thou who art faithful in all generations, just in Thy judgments, wonderful in Thy power and magnificence, Thou who createst with wisdom, and establishest with prudence what Thou hast created, Thou who art good in things visible, and faithful towards those who trust in Thee, merciful and compassionate, forgive us our sins and our injustices, our falls and our wanderings. Reckon not up the sins of Thy servants, but purify us by Thy truth, and direct our steps so that we may walk in holiness of heart and do that which is good and acceptable in Thine eyes and in the eyes of our governors. Yea, Master, make Thy face to shine upon us, so we may enjoy good things in peace; cover us with Thy mighty hand, deliver us from all sin by Thy strong arm, save us from those who hate us unjustly. Give concord and peace to us and to all the inhabitants of the earth, as Thou didst give it to our fathers when they called upon Thee reverently in faith and truth, so that we may be subject to the supreme power and excellence of Thy name, to our governors, and to those who rule us on earth.

Thou, O Master, hast given them the royal power, through Thy magnificent and unspeakable might, so that, knowing the glory and honour which Thou hast given them, we may be subject to them and may not oppose Thy will. Grant them, O Lord, health, peace, concord, stability, so that they may exercise without hindrance the sovereignty Thou hast entrusted to them. For Thou, O Master, heavenly king of ages, givest to the sons of men glory, honour and power over the things of the earth. Direct Thyself, O Lord, their counsel, according to that which is good and acceptable in Thy sight, so that, exercising piously, in peace and meekness, the power Thou hast entrusted to them, they may find Thee propitious.

Thou alone hast the power to do this, and to give us still greater blessings; we praise Thee through the High Priest and Protector of our souls, Jesus Christ, through whom be glory and greatness to Thee, now and from generation to generation, and for ever and ever, Amen (ch. LIX-LXI).

In this prayer, so similar in many features to Jewish prayers, we already perceive the traditional characteristics which will mark the Christian liturgy; [10] we find them also in other parts of this letter, which also have the tone of the primitive liturgy, and which are already related to the liturgies of the fourth century, as for instance to the prayers of the *Apostolic Constitutions.*[11]

This permanence in liturgical characteristics confirms what we said about the composition of these prayers; they were improvised by the bishop, but on a traditional theme, nourished with memories of the psalms, prophets, Gospels, and apostolic writings.

[10] Duchesne, *Origines du culte chrétien*, 1920, p. 55: "It is sufficient to remark that the liturgical language of which St. Clement gives us so early and authoritative an example, and the ritual presented by St. Justin as generally used in Christian assemblies, are altogether similar to those we shall meet with three centuries later, in a time when documents are plentiful. On the contrary, the liturgy described in the *Didache* has all the appearance of an anomaly; it will provide a few features for later compositions, but on the whole it is outside the stream of the general line of development, both for the ritual and for the style."

[11] Such are ch. XX, XXXIII, XXXIV in the letter of Clement; they may be compared with the prayer of thanksgiving found in the liturgy of baptism (*Const. Apost.*, VII, 34) and the anaphora (*ibid.*, VIII, 12, 9 *et seq.*). Cf. *Histoire du Dogme de la Trinité*, Vol. II, pp. 256-260.

Prayers to the Father and to Christ

It is to the Heavenly Father that liturgical prayer is usually addressed: the Church follows in this matter the teaching and example of her Master, as set forth in the *Our Father* and in the sacerdotal prayer of Christ (*John xvii*). This prayer is addressed to the Father in the name of His Son Jesus Christ our Lord, through His intercession, and through His ministry as High Priest.[12] These features are manifest in the prayer of Clement; they similarly appear in most of the documents of this time. But it would be a mistake to see in this liturgical usage an absolute rule, or to regard prayers addressed to Christ as merely late deviations, or alterations of the primitive liturgy. To Christ are addressed the earliest hymns we possess: the morning hymn, and the evening hymn;[13] about the year 113, at the beginning of the second century, Pliny in his letter to Trajan thus describes Christian worship: "The Christians are accustomed to meet together on certain days before dawn, and to sing in alternating ranks hymns in honour of Christ."[14]

We can go still further back, and read once more in the *Apocalypse* the heavenly canticles which are in the epistles of St. Paul echoed by voices on earth:

"The Lamb that was slain is worthy to receive power, and divinity, and wisdom, and strength, and honour, and glory, and benediction" (*Apocalypse*, V, 12).

"Rise thou that sleepest, and arise from the dead, and Christ shall enlighten thee" (*Ephes.*, V, 14).

[12] Cf. *Histoire du Dogme de la Trinité*, Vol. 11, pp. 175 *et seq.*
[13] Cf. *Histoire du Dogme de la Trinité*, Vol. II, pp. 220-222; the morning hymn is the *Gloria in excelsis*, which we sing in the Mass; in its primitive form this is a hymn to Christ. Cf. *Recherches de Science religieuse*, 1923, pp. 322-329; D. Casel, in *Theol. Revue*, 1927, col. 64. The evening hymn in the φῶς ἱλαρὸν: "Joyous light of the holy and immortal glory of the heavenly Father, holy and blessed Jesus Christ. The hour of sunset has come, and seeing the evening star appear, we sing of the Father, Son and Holy Spirit of God. Thou art worthy at all times to be praised by holy voices, O Son of God, who givest life; therefore the world glorifies thee." Cf. E. Smothers, in *Recherches de Science religieuse*, 1929, pp. 266-283.
[14] Pliny the Younger, *Epist.*, X, 96.

> *"Great is the mystery of godliness,*
> *which was manifested in the flesh,*
> *was justified in the spirit,*
> *appeared unto angels,*
> *hath been preached unto the Gentiles,*
> *is believed in the world,*
> *is taken up in glory."*
>
> (*I Tim.*, iii, 16)

The Eucharistic Liturgy

What thus appears in Christian worship as a whole is still more manifest in the heart of the liturgy, that is, in the celebration of the Eucharistic mystery.

It is to the Father that the Eucharistic Sacrifice is offered; the Son of God, Jesus Christ our Lord, is the priest and the victim. The earliest Eucharistic prayers we possess are those found in the *Didache* (IX-X):

"As to the Eucharist, give thanks thus:

"First for the chalice: We give Thee thanks, O our Father, for the holy Vine of David Thy servant, which Thou hast made known to us through Jesus Thy servant. Glory be to Thee for ever!

"For the broken bread: We give Thee thanks, O our Father, for the life and knowledge Thou hast made known to us through Jesus Thy servant. Glory be to Thee for ever.

"As the elements of this bread, scattered upon the mountains, have been gathered together to become one whole, so also may Thy Church be gathered together from the ends of the earth into thy Kingdom. For Thine is the glory and power, through Jesus Christ, for ever.

"After you have been filled, give thanks thus:

"We give Thee thanks, O holy Father, for Thy holy name which Thou hast made to dwell in our hearts, and for the knowledge, faith and immortality which Thou hast revealed to us through Jesus Thy servant. Glory be to Thee for ever.

"Thou, O almighty Master, hast created the universe for the glory of Thy name, and hast given to men food and drink, that they may enjoy them and give Thee thanks; but to us Thou hast given spiritual food and drink, and eternal life through Thy servant. Above all we give Thee thanks because Thou are mighty. Glory be to Thee for ever!

"Remember, O Lord, to deliver Thy Church from all evil and to make it perfect in Thy love. Gather it together from the four winds, this holy Church, into Thy Kingdom which Thou hast prepared for it. For Thine is the power and the glory for ever.

"May grace come, and this world pass away. Hosanna to the God of David. If any one be holy, let him come. If he is not, let him repent. Maranatha! Amen." [15]

In this text, if we leave provisionally on one side the acclamations and the final monitions, we can distinguish two chants, each of three strophes: each of the two first strophes ends in a short doxology: "Glory be to Thee . . . ," and the whole chant by a fuller doxology: "For Thine is the glory . . ." The first chant precedes the communion, the second follows it. These prayers call to mind in more than one feature Jewish prayers, but they are inspired above all by the New Testament, and chiefly by the Johannine and Pauline writings.

These prayers have left little trace in later liturgical tradition. It is quite otherwise with the acclamations and the final monitions. We read, for instance, in the *Apostolic Constitutions*, VIII, 13, 12-14:

"The bishop, addressing the people, says: 'Holy things to the holy!' And all the people reply: 'One only holy, one only Lord, Jesus Christ . . . Hosanna to the Son of David. Blessed is he who cometh in the name of the Lord. God is Lord, and He has appeared amongst us. Hosanna in the highest.' And after that, the bishop communicates, and then the priests and the deacons. . . ."

In this fourth century text we find in a more developed form the same liturgical elements found in the *Didache*: monitions to the faithful, acclamations in honour of the Son of David who comes among his people.

[15] These prayers have often been studied: by the editors of the *Didache*, and also by J. A. Robinson, *Barnabas, Hermas and the Didache*, London, 1920, pp. 94-97; *Histoire du Dogme de la Trinité*, Vol. II, pp. 193-195; Lietzmann, *Messe und Herrenmahl*, pp. 230-238.

The author of the *Didache* ends by saying:

"As to the prophets, let these give thanks as much as they will."

The Eucharistic Liturgy according to St. Justin

Half a century later, a text of an entirely different character makes known to us, not now the eucharistic prayers, but the Christian mystery: the apologist St. Justin, in order to refute pagan calumnies, gives the emperors Marcus Aurelius and Lucius Verus a description of the Mass as Christians celebrated it; he does this on two occasions, explaining first the baptismal liturgy, and then the Sunday Mass. We reproduce here the first text, which is the more explicit:

"LXV. When we have washed the one who has made a profession of faith and who has become one of us, we lead him to the place where are assembled those whom we call our brethren. Together we make fervent prayers for ourselves, for the baptised, and for all others in whatsoever place they may be, in order to obtain, after the knowledge of the truth, the grace to practise virtue and to keep the commandments, that we may arrive at eternal salvation. When the prayers are concluded, we give to each other the kiss of peace. Then one brings to him who presides over the assembly of the brethren, bread, and a cup of wine and water. He takes them, and praises and glorifies the Father of the universe through the name of the Son and the Holy Spirit, and he makes a long thanksgiving ('eucharist') for these good things that we have received from Him. When he has finished the prayers and the thanksgiving, all the people present reply by the acclamation: Amen. 'Amen' signifies in the Hebrew language 'So may it be.' When he who presides has made the thanksgiving, and all the people have replied, the ministers whom we call deacons distribute the consecrated bread and wine to all those present, and they take some to the absent.

"LXVI. We call this food 'eucharist,' and none may partake of it if he believes not in the truth of our doctrine, has not received the washing for the forgiveness of sins and regeneration, and lives not according to the precepts of Christ. For we do not take this food as common bread and common drink, but just as our Saviour Jesus Christ, incarnate by the power of the Word of God, took flesh and blood for our salvation, so the food consecrated by the prayer formed of the words of Christ, this food which is to nourish our blood and our flesh by being assimilated, is the flesh and blood of the incarnate Jesus: such is our teaching. For the apostles, in their memoirs called Gospels, report that Jesus gave them these instructions: he took bread, and having given thanks, said: 'Do this in memory of me, this is my body'; he likewise took the cup, and having given thanks he said: 'This is my blood'; and he gave it to them only. This the evil spirits have imitated by instituting the mysteries of Mithra; for you know, or may know, bread and a cup of water are given in the ceremonies of initiation, and certain formulæ are pronounced."

This description of the baptismal Mass is followed by a chapter dealing with the liturgy of Sunday. It is shorter, but in some details it completes the one we have just read:

"LXVII, 3. On the day called Sunday, all, in town or country, gather together in one and the same place; the memoirs of the apostles and the writings of the prophets are read, as much as the time will permit. When the reader has finished, he who presides gives a discourse, to instruct, and to encourage the imitation of these beautiful teachings. Then we all rise up together and pray. Next, as we have said above, when we have finished praying, bread, wine and water are brought; he who presides sends up to heaven prayers and thanksgivings as much as he is able, and all the people reply by the acclamation: Amen. Then takes place the distribution and partaking of each of the things consecrated, and their sending to the absent by the ministry of the deacons."

This important text suggests to a historian many useful points. What we infer from it in the first place is that the discipline of the secret was not yet enforced: we shall find it at the end of this second century in Tertullian, but Justin shows no knowledge of it. He expounds to the pagans the eucharistic liturgy and the Christian belief in the presence of the body of Christ: this intention to hide nothing is clearly inspired by the desire to refute calumnies, and indeed this exposition was the most effective of apologies.[16]

Origin and Development of this Liturgy

This frank description enables us to reconstitute, at least in its general features, the primitive liturgy. In presence of all the assembled Christians, there were read first "the memoirs of the apostles and the writings of the prophets." The Synagogue service comprised two readings from holy Scripture; the first was taken from the Pentateuch, and the second from the prophets. We find similarly two readings in the Christian liturgy, but one is from the New Testament, and the other from the Old. [17]

In the case of the Jews, these Scriptural readings were followed by a homily; the same takes place in the Christian liturgy. After the homily, all those present rise for common prayer; the letter of St. Clement shows us how the bishop passed from exhortation to prayer, leading all his people.

Readings, homily and prayers together form only a preparatory liturgy. When they are ended, the Eucharist commences: bread, wine and water are brought, then "he who presides sends up to heaven prayers and thanksgivings ('eucharists') as much as he can"; there is as yet no eucharistic form officially adopted by the Church and imposed by her upon bishops and priests; the officiant improvises the form of this prayer, and continues it "as much as he can." [18] At the same time, this eucharistic prayer develops according to a liturgical theme; it

[16] It is evident that the reception of the Eucharist is reserved to believers, as it will be always; Justin says so explicitly (LXVI, 1), and so also the *Didache*, IX, 5. It is supported by the words of the Lord (*Matt.* vii, 6), on which will later be based the law of the secret (Tertullian, *De præscr.*, XLI, 2). But though the pagans have not the right to receive the Eucharist, they have a right to know the rite and the mystery.

[17] Of the New Testament, Justin mentions here only the Gospels; but the epistles were equally read; we see even from the letter of Dionysius of Corinth (cf. *supra*, § 1, n. 6) that the letter of Clement of Rome and that of Soter were read at Corinth during the Sunday office. Of the Old Testament, the prophets were chiefly read by Christians, because they gave a more evident testimony to Christ, but the veneration felt for them did not lead the Pentateuch to be overlooked, or the Psalms.

[18] We have seen a similar expression in the *Didache*, X, 7: "Let the prophets give thanks as much as they wish."

praises the blessings received from God, creation, redemption, and above all the mysteries of the life of Christ; it stresses the Supper, and repeats the words of consecration, which Justin explicitly sets forth; it recalls the death and resurrection of the Lord; it prays for the Church and the faithful; and ends with a doxology. Such is the theme which we shall find developed at the beginning of the third century in the anaphora of St. Hippolytus; that liturgy displays in more than one point the personal impress of its author, but it was not wholly created by him; it was the codification of a previous usage, the terminus of a long tradition.[19]

After the anaphora, the Communion is distributed to those present and carried to the absent. It is at this moment, immediately before the Communion, that we find in many early liturgies the acclamations which we have already read in the *Didache;* we also find, but more rarely, eucharistic prayers expressing the desire of the believer; thus in the *Acts of Thomas:*

"O Jesus, who hast given us the grace of being participants in the Eucharist of Thy holy body and Thy blood, behold we dare to approach Thy Eucharist, and to invoke Thy holy name. Come and communicate unto us." [20]

To these sentiments of adoration and love were often joined, especially from the fourth century, sentiments of reverential fear in presence of the majesty of the eucharistic mystery.[21]

[19] On this anaphora, cf. Lebreton and Zeiller, Bk. III.
[20] *Acts of Thomas,* XLIX. The long eucharistic prayer which follows (ch. L) is clearly of Gnostic origin; the text transcribed above would seem not to come from a Gnostic source (cf. W. Bauer in the collection of *N. T. Apokryphen* of E. Hennecke, 1923, p. 257); but the whole book is too suspect in origin and character to be presented with full assurance as an authentic witness of the Catholic faith.
[21] These sentiments are very marked in St. Cyril of Jerusalem (*Cat. myst.,* V, 4, Migne, *P. G.,* XXXIII, 1112, cf. 1116), and still more in St. John Chrysostom; on the other hand, we do not find them in the Cappadocian Fathers. There is a like difference in the liturgies; these sentiments do not appear in the Anaphora of Serapion, nor in the *Apostolic Constitutions;* on the other hand they are very marked in the liturgy of St. James, somewhat less, but still very noticeable, in that of St. Basil and of St. John

The Baptismal Liturgy

In this passage of St. Justin, we have so far considered the testimony it gives to the eucharistic liturgy, and it is this that gives it its chief interest. But we must also notice the baptismal liturgy; it appears as a solemn rite in which the whole Church takes part. We are no longer in the very beginnings, which the *Didache* showed us: baptism is no longer conferred as it was then, with such means as circumstances permitted; the Church has constructed piscinas for the use of its neophytes; but first of all, before the baptism, there is a profession of faith followed by prayers and fasts in which all the faithful join; [22] then the neophytes "are conducted by us to the place where the water is, and there, in the same way that we ourselves were regenerated, they are regenerated in their turn; for it is in the name of the Father and Master of the universe, and of Jesus Christ our Lord, and of the Holy Spirit that they are then washed in the water." [23]

At the end of this chapter, Justin returns once more to the baptismal initiation. A little later on, St. Irenæus once more sets forth the baptismal rite in his *Demonstration of the Apostolic Preaching:*

"When we are regenerated by the baptism given to us in the name of the three Persons, we are enriched in this second birth with the good things which are in God the Father by means of His Son, with the Holy Spirit. For those who are baptised receive the Spirit of God, who gives them to the Word, that is, to the Son; and the Son takes and offers them to His Father, and the Father communicates to them incorruptibility. Thus without the Spirit one cannot see the Word of God; and without the Son none can arrive at the Father; for the knowledge of the Father is the Son, and the knowledge of the Son of God is obtained by means of the Holy Spirit; but it is the Son who, by office, distributes the Spirit according to the good pleasure of the Father, to those whom the Father wishes, and as the Father wishes.[24]

Chrysostom. Cf. Dom. Connolly, *Fear and Awe attaching to the Eucharistic Service, Texts and Studies,* VIII, pp. 92-97; Nicolas Cabasilas, *Liturgiæ expositio,* 1 (Migne, *P. G.,* CL, 369).

[22] Justin, *Apol.,* I, 61, 2.

[23] *Ibid.,* 3.

[24] *Demonstr.,* ch. vii, cf. ch. iii.

We see from this fine passage that the baptismal formula prescribed by Christ, "baptize in the name of the Father and of the Son and of the Holy Spirit," was not only faithfully repeated, but it planted in the hearts of the faithful belief in the Trinity, and the rite which accompanied the formula again stressed its significance: for the neophyte was washed three times, either by immersion or by infusion.[25]

On coming out of the baptismal piscina, the neophytes were conducted to the assembly of the faithful, and then came common prayers, and the kiss of peace. In the course of the second and third centuries, the catechumenate took shape; the baptismal liturgy, reserved for the vigils of Easter and Pentecost, became more solemn; but already in the first half of the second century its essential features were already fixed, and then more than ever its social bearing was felt. At that time, when persecutions unceasingly threatened the Church and marytrdoms were common, the entrance of the neophyte into the Christian community was a heroic step, and one marked by a fraternal charity the striking fervour of which people loved to recall later on. In the following century, towards the end of a long period of peace, Origen will call up these memories in one of his homilies:

"If we judge things according to truth . . . we must recognise that we are not faithful. Then people were truly faithful, when martyrdom came at our birth (into the Church); when, returning from the cemeteries whither we had accompanied the bodies of the martyrs, we reentered the assemblies, when the whole Church was there, unshakeable, when the catechumens were catechised in the midst of the martyrdoms and deaths of Christians who confessed the truth to the end, and when these catechumens, surmounting these tests, attached themselves without fear to the living God. Then we were aware of having known astonishing and wonderful marvels. Then the faith-

---

[25] The triple infusion is prescribed in the *Didache,* ch. VII. Triple immersion is explicitly attested by Tertullian, *Adv. Praxeam.,* xxvi: "Nec semel, sed ter, ad singula nomina in personas singulas tinguimur." We see also from this chapter that the Monarchian heretics, who had abandoned belief in the Trinity, still had a triple immersion; this proves that they had received this from the custom of the Church, previous to their heresy. Cf. *Histoire du dogme de la Trinité,* Vol. II, pp. 134-141.

ful were few in number, doubtless, but they were really faithful, treading the straight and narrow way which leads to life." [26]

§7. THE APOSTLES' CREED [1]

The study of the baptismal liturgy has shown us that in the history of Christian doctrine and particularly of the dogma of the Trinity, the formulæ and rites of baptism played a most important part: they were the expression and the safeguard of the dogma; this is true especially of the baptismal creed, which we must study more closely.

Profession of Faith in Apostolic Times

Already in apostolic times, neophytes were admitted to baptism only after a profession of faith.[2] Philip the deacon required it already from the Ethiopian eunuch (*Acts* viii, 37); St. Paul required it from all his converts: they had to confess with the mouth that Jesus is Lord, and believe with the heart that God raised Him up from the dead (*Rom.* x, 9); all the candidates for baptism had to accept the traditional catechesis as we find it recalled, for example, in the first epistle to the Corinthians (*I Cor.*, XV, 3 *et seq.*).

The faith proposed by the Church to the neophytes and professed by them was thus the faith of the apostles, which the apostles themselves had received from Christ. This is

---

[26] *Hom. in Jerem.*, IV, 3; ed. Klostermann, p. 25; Migne, *P.G.*, XIII, p. 288-289.

[1] The most detailed study of the history of the Apostles' Creed is that of F. Kattenbusch, *Das Apostolische Symbol*, Leipzig, 1894-1900. The texts are conveniently collected together in A. Hahn, *Bibliothek der Symbole*, Breslau, 1897. Research and hypotheses have been multiplied in recent years. We mention above all J. Haussleiter, *Trinitarischer Glaube und Christusbekenntnis*, Gütersloh, 1920; A. Nussbaymer, *Das Ursymbolum nach der Epideixis des hl. Irenæus und dem Dialog. Justins*, Paderborn, 1921; H. Lietzmann, *Symbolstudien*, articles published in *Zeitschr. f. N. T. Wissensch.*, 1922-1927; Dom B. Capelle, *Le Symbole romain au IIe siècle*, in *Recherches de Théol. anc. et med.*, Vol. II, 1930, pp. 5-20; Lebreton, *Histoire du Dogme de la Trinité*, Vol. II, pp. 141-173; *Les origines du symbole baptismal*, in *Recherches de Science religieuse*, 1930, pp. 97-124.

[2] Cf. *supra*, p. 31.

brought out into full light by Tertullian, in his treatise *De praescriptione contra haereticos*. After transcribing in its entirety the "rule of faith," he adds:

"Such is the rule which Christ instituted—as I will prove —and it can give rise to no questions amongst us other than those raised by heresies and heretics" (ch. xiii).

A little later he links up this baptismal creed with the formula of baptism, and shows that this teaching of Christ was entrusted by him to the apostles, who in their turn taught it to the Church; thus is assured the chain of tradition which links us through the Church to the apostles, through the apostles to Christ, and through Christ to God.[3]

We cannot infer from this that this teaching communicated by Christ to the apostles must, according to Tertullian, consist in the formula of the Creed, but it remains true that this Christian and apostolic faith has its "rule" in the baptismal creed, and that this creed is based on the baptismal formula which Christ prescribed; this is what Tertullian himself teaches when, speaking of the replies given by the neophyte to the baptismal questions, he writes: "We reply by a formula somewhat longer than that which the Lord gave us in the Gospel" (*De Corona,* iii).

We have here not only theological theses of great importance, but also some fruitful historical statements. The Christian liturgy was determined by the initiative of Christ; the whole anaphora is based on the narrative of the Institution and on the words of the Lord, "This is My body . . . this is My blood . . . do this in memory of Me." Similarly the baptismal liturgy is determined by the commandment of Jesus: "Go, teach all nations, baptizing them in the name of the

[3] "One of the apostles having been expelled, He commanded the eleven others . . . to go and teach the nations and to baptize them in the name of the Father, Son and the Holy Spirit. . . . It was in Judea that they first established the faith in Jesus Christ and founded churches; then they set out across the world, and announced to the nations the same doctrine and the same faith" (XX, 3-4). "It is clear that every doctrine which is in agreement with that of these churches, mothers and sources of the faith, must be regarded as true, since it evidently contains that which these churches received from the apostles, the apostles from Christ, and Christ from God" (XXI, 4).

Father, and of the Son, and of the Holy Ghost." By repeating these words over the head of the baptized person, the Church consecrates him to the God whom Jesus Christ has revealed to us; she at the same time calls upon the neophyte to consecrate himself to God, and to make an act of faith in Him.

The Baptismal Creed

For a long time, until after the middle of the second century, we shall not as yet find a liturgical formula imposed authoritatively in the name of the Church: this conclusion, to which we are led by the study of the eucharistic liturgy, is also suggested to us by the study of the baptismal liturgy, and in particular of the Creed; but at the same time we note in the Creed as in the anaphora, through the accidental variations of a still plastic formula, the affirmation of the same dogma: the Creed, basing itself on the baptismal formula, confesses God in three Persons, Father, Son and Holy Spirit. The earliest forms of the Creed are very short; the *Epistle of the Apostles,* a Christian apocryphal work written about 180, gives us this formula:

> I believe in the Father Almighty,
> in Jesus Christ our Saviour,
> and in the Holy Spirit, the Paraclete;
> in the Holy Church, in the forgiveness of sins.[4]

The papyrus of Der-Balizeh, which contains an Egyptian ritual of the end of the second century, presents the following text:

> I believe in God the Father Almighty,
> and in His only Son Our Lord Jesus Christ,
> and in the Holy Spirit;
> in the resurrection of the flesh, in the holy Catholic Church.[5]

About the same date, or a little later, we find more developed texts, as for instance, this of St. Irenæus:

> The Church, although spread throughout the universe as far as the ends of the earth, has received from the apostles

[4] Cf. C. Schmidt, *Gespräche Jesu mit seinen Jüngern,* p. 32; cf. p. 400.
[5] Cf. B. Capelle, *art. cit.,* p. 6.

and their disciples the faith in one God, the Father Almighty, who made heaven and earth and the seas, and all that is in them; and in one only Christ Jesus, the Son of God, who was incarnate for our salvation; and in one Holy Spirit, who through the prophets announced the dispensation, the coming, the virginal birth, the passion, the resurrection from the dead, and the bodily ascension into heaven of the well beloved Christ Jesus Our Lord, and His second coming, when in the heavens He will appear at the right hand of the Father, to restore all things and to raise up all flesh and all humanity, in order that before Christ Jesus Our Lord, God, Saviour and King, every knee may bend in heaven, hell, on earth, and every tongue confess Him, and He may give to all a just judgment. . . .[6]

This statement is not a literal transcription but a brief commentary on the Creed; at the same time it must be noted that this commentary is wholly formed of traditional formulæ which will remain living in tradition.[7]

Before appearing here in Irenæus, these expressions were familiar to Barnabas, and Justin; they will be more familiar still to Hippolytus and Tertullian; we shall find them again in the *Apostolic Constitutions*, the Creeds of Antioch, Cæsarea, Jerusalem and Sirmium. We see by this example how liturgical usage came to be formed, and how in turn it reacted on theological literature, passing on to it its formulæ and giving a priestly and solemn character to its style.

These precisions which tend to determine still further the formula of faith will multiply in the course of the centuries; to the denials of heresy the Church will oppose the professions of faith in her Creeds; against Arius, Nestorius, Eutyches, and all the teachers of error she will define ever more and more explicitly the dogmas she sets forth to her faithful. This is apparent to us already in the second century in Tertullian, Irenæus, and in the first years of the century, in Ignatius of Antioch:

Shut your ears, then, to the speech of those who do not speak to you of Jesus Christ, born of the race of David,

[6] *Adv. hær.*, I, 10, 2, Cf. *Demonstr.*, c. VI, quoted and commented on in *Histoire du Dogme de la Trinité*, Vol. II, p. 152, and *Recherches de Science Religieuse*, 1930, p. 102.
[7] Cf. Lietzmann, *Zeitschr. f. N. T. Wiss.*, XXVI (1927), p. 93.

born of Mary, who was really generated, really ate and drank, really suffered persecution under Pontius Pilate, was really crucified and died, in the sight of heaven, earth, and the lower regions; who was really raised up from the dead. . . .[8]

We find in this fragment some formulæ already traditional, and which are echoed in the majority of the Creeds, in particular the passion, dated under Pontius Pilate, the crucifixion, death, and resurrection. Ignatius had to oppose those who taught Docetism; he set against them these great facts of the life of Christ, and stressed with energy their reality.

These progressive precisions of the Creed affect Christology above all: to the profession of faith in the Trinity is added the profession of faith in the principal mysteries of the life of Christ.[9]

The Roman Creed

If we wish to sum up this account, and to separate it from the hypotheses and discussions which weigh it down, we can reduce it to these main points. After the formulæ of faith of the apostolic age, we find at Rome from the first half of the second century a baptismal creed professing faith in God the Father Almighty, in Jesus Christ His Son, and in the Holy Spirit; the mention of the Holy Spirit was followed by those of the Holy Church and the resurrection of the flesh.

This brief formula, similar to those we have mentioned above,[10] is enriched from the time of St. Justin with a profession of faith in the principal mysteries of the life of Christ. The Christological formulæ, joined sometimes to the third

---

[8] *Trall,* IX; cf. *Smyrn.,* I; *Magn.* XI.
[9] This Christology has not the same place in the different creeds of the second century: in the text of Irenæus quoted above (*Hær.,* I, 10, 2) it is joined to the third article of the Creed, which has as its subject the Holy Spirit; so also in St. Justin, *Apol.* I, LXI, 10-13. On the other hand, in the *Demonstration* of St. Irenæus, c. vi, it occupies in the second article the place which it will henceforth retain in the Creed. From this fact it is not unreasonably inferred that the Christological formulæ, first of all isolated, took their definitive place in the Trinitarian symbol only towards the end of the second century. Cf. *Histoire du Dogme de la Trinité,* Vol. II, pp. 160 *et seq., Recherches de Science Religieuse,* 1930, p. 107 *et seq.*
[10] Cf. *supra,* pp. 172-174.

article,[11] will find their definitive place in the second article, as is natural. Thus from the end of the second century or the first years of the third, the Creed will be subject only to a few literary retouches of little or no importance. [12]

In this progressive elaboration of the baptismal creed, the part played by the Church of Rome was decisive; [13] it was she above all who assured throughout the whole Christian world that unanimity of faith which St. Irenæus attested towards the end of the second century with such force:

> "It is this preaching that the Church has received, this faith, as we have said; and although she is scattered through the whole world, she keeps it carefully, as if she dwelt in one single house, and she believes it unanimously, as if she had but one soul and one heart, and with perfect accord she preaches it, teaches it, and transmits it, as though she had only one mouth. Doubtless the languages on the surface of the world are different, but the force of tradition is one and the same. The churches founded in the Germanies have not another faith or another tradition; nor the

---

[11] As we have seen from the texts of Justin and Irenæus, this position is due to the mention of the prophecies: to the prophetic Spirit is joined all these mysteries which it foretold.

[12] Cf. Dom Capelle, *Rech.*, p. 19. The same author, speaking of the texts of Tertullian and Hippolytus, reconstitutes thus the Roman creed of the last years of the second century (*Revue bénédictine,* 1927, p. 39):

> "I believe in one God almighty, creator of all things,
> "And in Christ Jesus, the Son of God, born of the Holy Spirit and of the Virgin Mary, crucified under Pontius Pilate, dead and buried; raised from the dead the third day; ascended into heaven; seated at the right hand of the Father; who will come to judge the living and the dead;
> "And in the Holy Spirit, the Holy Church, the resurrection of the flesh."

For some details, this reconstitution is conjectural: thus the omission of the word "Father" in the first article seems insufficiently guaranteed in view of the texts of Tertullian (*De bapt.,* VI, *Adv. Prax.,* II) and of Hippolytus (Capelle, p. 36). On the other hand, the omission of "the forgiveness of sins" in the third article seems well established (p. 42).

[13] Cf. Kattenbusch, *op. cit.,* Vol. I, p. 80 (dependence of the other Western creeds); Vol. I, p. 380 *et seq.* (dependence of the Eastern creeds).

churches founded amongst the Iberians, or the Celts, or in the East, or in Egypt, or in Lybia, or in the centre of the world; but just as the sun, that creature of God, is one and the same in all the world, so also the preaching of the truth shines everywhere and enlightens all men who wish to come to know it" (*Adv. hær.*, I, 10, 2).

The Rule of Faith

What assures this uniformity in the teaching of the Church is above all the living magisterium which conserves, transmits and develops the deposit received from Christ and the apostles; but this living magisterium utilises the Creed in order to express its faith and to give it the official formulation which maintains all its force, which opposes it to error, and which determines for all people and all times its immutable doctrine. When the Arian heresy will arise, the Church gathered together in council at Nicæa will define its faith in a Creed; she will not create it entirely; she will base herself on a baptismal Creed, contenting herself with adding to it some new precisions aimed at the new heresy.

During the three centuries which precede Nicæa, there was no universal council; the Church had nevertheless to conquer many heresies: Gnosticism, Marcionism, Monarchianism, Modalism; it opposed to these not conciliar definitions, but the baptismal creed, the solemn expression of the apostolic faith. This faith, sworn to by the Christian at baptism, is his most precious treasure, and at the same time his pasword, or *tessera,* which will lead to his being recognised everywhere as a son of the Catholic Church, and as one of Christ's faithful. He may, like St. Irenæus, be born and grow up at Smyrna, live in Rome, and evangelise the Gauls: he will find everywhere the same faith, and will be everywhere illumined by the same sun of God.

Chapter 6

Ecclesiastical Organisation in the First Two Centuries [1]

IN THE CONDITIONS, apparently so precarious, in which the Church found itself in the Roman Empire in the first two centuries, what was its organisation?

§1. THE PRIMITIVE CHURCH

Charity and Fraternity

The Church is an organic collectivity, and not a mere juxtaposition of men thinking and acting in the same way on certain points regarded by them as fundamental; there is a bond uniting them which makes them a society with an externally visible organisation.

Yet in the very earliest days, this organisation shows itself only in a few somewhat ill-defined features. The Church. the society of the friends of Christ, that is, of those who love Him and are loved by Him, and who for love of Him love one another, form above all a brotherhood and a "charity,"

[1] Bibliography. Besides the works indicated in the General Bibliography, one may consult for the matters treated in this chapter: A. Michiels, *L'origine de l'épiscopat*, Louvain, 1900; C. De Smedt, *L'organisation des églises chrétiennes jusq'au milieu du IIIe siècle*, 1er partie, in *Revue des questions historiques*, 1888, pp. 329-384; J. Zeiller, *La conception de l'Eglise aux quatre premiers siècles*, in *Revue d'histoire ecclés.*, Vol. XXIX, 1933, pp. 571-585 and 827-848; Bartoli, *The Primitive Church and the Primacy of Rome*, London, 1909; F. Mourret, *La Papauté* (*Bibliothèque des Sciences religieuses*, Paris, 1929); E. Caspar, *Die römische Bischofsliste*, in *Schriften den Königsberger Gelehrten Gesellschaft Geisteswissenschaftliche Klasse*, 2 Jahr. Heft 4, 1926, and *Geschichte des Papsttums*, Vol. I, Tübingen, 1930, the theories in which are discussed below: F. X. Seppelt, *Der Aufsteig des Papsttums. Geschichte der Päpste des von Anfangen bis zum Regierungsantritt Gregors des Grossen*, Leipzig, 1931; J. Turmel, *Histoire du Dogme de la Papauté des origines à la fin du IVe siècle*, Paris, 1908.

ἀλάπη. This is the term of St. Ignatius of Antioch,[2] who was
indeed a man consumed by the love of God and of men's
souls for God's sake. This charity is inseparable from unity:
if this unity does not yet find its explicit expression in certain
organs having its maintenance and manifestation for their
special function, primitive Christianity has nevertheless a passion for deep unity, inseparable in fact from the existence of
a hierarchy;[3] this ἀγάπη is a consensus, the realisation itself
of the *sint unum* which is the object of the prayer of Christ
in the Gospel of St. John.[4]

The sense, will, and consciousness of this unity shine forth
in the letters of St. Ignatius, which make us realise so well
that all the churches are but one, and that all Christians make
only one single body, or better, one soul. But this unity is
not merely imposed by a commandment. It remains essentially based on charity, it is the fruit of the union of those
who love one another, as well as one of the reasons for this
love; they love one another because they are all one, and they
are one because they love one another, Christ being the bond
of this unity and the centre of this love.

Unity

Being one single body throughout the world in which they
are scattered, not a federation of distinct groups but the one
society of Christ's faithful spread in many places, they constitute one single whole in each place. The Christian community
in each city—for Christianity shows itself as a religion of
cities and not one of corporations—appears as one whole
which is not at first divisible into various sections. "From the
first generation, wherever it was established, and for instance
in a great city such as Antioch or Rome, Christianity did not
constitute synagogues distinct from one another, as," it seems,
at least in the absence of proof, and in spite of certain contrary theories,[5] "the synagogues of the Jews were in Rome,
nor did it constitute autonomous colleges, such as the pagan
collegia. It had as its meeting place the house of some particular Christian. All the Christians of the city, however great
it may have been, formed one single confraternity or ἐκκγησία,

[2] *Epistola ad Romanos, inscr.*
[3] On the infant church as a hierarchical society, as shown in the
Gospels, Acts and St. Paul cf. above, pp. 35 *et seq.*
[4] xvii, 11.
[5] Cf. Lebreton and Zeiller, Bk. I, pp. 29-30.

which bore the name of this city. A cult like that of Mithra developed by cells or brotherhoods, dividing up regularly when the number of the devotees of the god increased: the law of Christianity, a law which was constant long before the principle of the monarchical episcopate was everywhere in force, was that there is only one church in each city, and similarly, that no church in the world is isolated from the others." [6]

Nevertheless, each church lived its own life, without any regular intervention by the action of directing centres through clearly defined organs. Intercommunion for a long time manifested itself above all by the exchange of letters, just as, in the quite primitive time, the great founders of churches, Peter, Paul or John, had assured the nascent tradition and the unity of minds by their letters to so many churches in Asia, Macedonia, Greece or Italy. The letters of Clement of Rome, Ignatius of Antioch, Polycarp of Smyrna, and of the Church of Lyons after the tragedy of 177, played a similar part in the general life of the Church.

§2. THE EPISCOPATE AND THE PRESBYTERATE

The Origins of the Episcopate

But each community, however simple it may have been in constitution in the primitive period, had from the first the essential elements of a real organisation. A council of presbyters or elders governed it, subordinated, in the apostolic period, to the apostle-founder, or his representatives, who were at first itinerant.[1] The fixation of this superior authority is the beginning of the episcopate such as we know it. This is distinctly found quite early in many places. It is evident at Jerusalem from the beginning in the episcopate of James;[2] we find it in Crete with Titus, Paul's disciple, shortly afterwards;[3] the letters of Ignatius show it in existence at Antioch about the year 100;[4] nothing shows that it did not exist at Rome already in the time of the first successors of Peter.

[6] P. Batiffol, *L'Eglise naissante et le catholicisme,* 1st edn., Paris, 1909, pp. 41-42.
[1] Lebreton and Zeiller, Bk. I, pp. 29-30.
[2] *Ibid.,* pp. 306-07.
[3] *Epist. ad Titum,* i, 5.
[4] Cf. *supra.*

Collegiate or Unitary Episcopate

The collegiate organisation of ecclesiastical government which characterised most of the known churches in primitive times did not, then, exclude the unity of the directing authority. Some have thought that towards the end of the first century Roman Christianity was still governed according to the collegiate system, for when the letter of St. Clement was written to the Church of Corinth in the reign of Domitian, its writer seems to appear therein rather as the chief mandatory of the Church of Rome, in the name of which the epistle is sent, rather than as its head properly so called. The collegiate character, if not of the episcopate itself, at least of the ecclesiastical organisation of Rome in early times, may seem to be confirmed by the tradition registered in the *Liber pontificalis,* according to which the two persons usually presented as the first successors of Peter, Linus and Anacletus, began to preside over the destinies of the Roman Church already in his lifetime. But this tradition is perhaps not anterior to the third century, and even if well founded, it would follow also from it that there was in the college itself a definite hierarchy, for Peter the apostle and his coadjutors could obviously not be put on the same plane as the others. After Peter, the college of presbyters still had a head, and the great reputation enjoyed by Clement makes it impossible to doubt that if he wrote the letter to the Corinthians, it was not merely as secretary to the Church, as has too easily been inferred from a slightly later work, the *Shepherd* of Hermas,[5] but as its best qualified representative. The early episcopal lists of Rome, moreover, make no difference between the first representatives of the Roman Church and those of the time when the existence of the monarchical episcopate admits of no question. Moreover, a college must always have a president, and it is easily understandable that there was a swift passage from an apparently plural episcopate to a unitary one.

One might indeed think to find an attestation of the existence of the unitary episcopate in the letter of St. Clement itself, for it borrows from the Greek version of the Old Testa-

---

[5] The *Shepherd* (*Vis.*, II, 4, 3) says that it was Clement's office to correspond with the other churches. There is nothing here which would reduce him necessarily to the functions of a secretary; inter-ecclesiastical relations are the province of the head of a church.

ment the significant terms ἀρχιερεύς and ἱερεύς, and seems to apply these to two kinds of dignitaries, who would be none other than the governors of the Christian communities, the bishop, ἐπίσκοπος and the priests, πρεσβύτεροι. But some question whether Clement had in mind in these passages any hierarchy other than the Mosaic one. Even so, this is figurative of the new. But the distinction between the bishop and the presbyteral body, even if not made in works such as the letter of Clement or the *Shepherd* of Hermas, is affirmed in a most striking way almost at the same time in the letters of St. Ignatius of Antioch to the churches of Asia. It is incontestably the monarchical episcopate that these letters proclaim, with a clearness which leaves nothing to be desired, as existing in the greatest metropolis of the East. And they do not speak of it as a new institution, or one which met with any difficulties or opposition in its introduction. The *Muratorian Fragment*, about 150, speaks of Pius the brother of Hermas who wrote the *Shepherd,* as the one bishop of the Church of Rome, and moreover, an ecclesiastical organisation similar to that of Antioch appears in the course of the second century, sooner or later in very different countries, and hence there is reason to believe that if this ecclesiastical organisation did not exist everywhere as such from the beginning, at least it was not something fundamentally unlike the collegiate organisation, and that the latter, under a different appearance, already contained the germ of the future development, from which this naturally and very quickly arose.

It has indeed been suggested that the monarchical episcopate was not really founded until after the middle of the second century, and that its development was connected with the general movement of reaction in the Church against Marcionism,[6] and that the Church only then defined against this heresy its dogmas, its Scriptural canon, and even its hierarchy, concentrating this in the episcopal authority. The theory makes light of the testimony of Ignatius, and requires the inauthenticity of the Ignatian letters. But these letters say nothing of Marcion and the resulting controversy, and the episcopate is represented in them as in possession: how then

[6] On the exaggerations of the "Pan-Marcionism" of some contemporary writers, see Book III. One of the most recent refutations, dealing essentially with the formation of the Scriptural canon, is that of Père Lagrange, *Saint Paul ou Marcion,* in *Revue Biblique,* pp. 5-30.

can they be explained by the anti-Marcionite controversy, or as a defence of an institution which they do not represent as being contested?

The truth is rather, as we have already said, that the explicit distinction between the presbyteral college, and its head the bishop, was made more or less rapidly in different places; towards the middle of the second century it was an accomplished fact almost everywhere.

The Question of Alexandria

An apparent exception is presented by the Church of Alexandria, where, until about the middle of the third century, the bishop would seem to have been really only the *primus inter pares* in the presbyteral body, the members of which consecrated him. The testimony of the patriarch Eutyches seems definite in this respect.[7] It would follow from this that the Church of Alexandria retained the primitive regime longer than others, and that the distinction between the presbyteral college and its head was less marked than it became subsequently.[8] This peculiarity might be explained by the fact that, until the third century, there was no other bishop in Egypt besides that of Alexandria. Demetrius (189-232), was the first to establish others, for he set up three outside the metropolis. Until then, the sole bishop of Egypt, who had his seat of Alexandria, could not have been consecrated by other members of an episcopate which he alone represented; he would seem to have been consecrated by the co-participants of the apostolic authority residing in the college, the members of which had more power than simple priests have today, while those of the bishop were less exclusively concentrated in his person. Things would no longer be the same after Demetrius. A memory of this situation would seem to exist in a passage in the fourth century treatise of uncertain authorship called the *Ambrosiaster*, which mentions the right to confirm, *consignare*, as possessed by the priests of Egypt in default of the bishop.[9]

Similarly the period, vague in duration, in which in Rome also the distinction between the bishop and the presbyteral

---

[7] Migne, *P. G.*, CXI, 982.
[8] Thus Timothy, to whom St. Paul entrusted the church of Ephesus, received the imposition of hands of the college of presbyters (*I Tim.*, iv, 14).
[9] *Ambrosiaster*, Eph. 4, 11 *et seq.*

college would seem to have been less explicit than it was later on, might correspond to the period in which there was no other bishop in Italy besides that of Rome, i.e., down to the middle of the second century. When other episcopal sees were instituted, the holder of one of them consecrated the bishop of Rome, and such would be the origin of the traditional custom by which a newly elected pope, if not already a bishop, is even to-day consecrated by the bishop of Ostia, the first of the suburbican bishops of Rome.[10]

But in reality, how many conjectures are involved in all this! The text of the *Ambrosiaster* has not much weight, for the instances of priests invested with the power to confirm are not rare. The testimony of the patriarch Eutyches is very late, seeing that it belongs only to the tenth century. St. Jerome, much closer to the facts, who also speaks in a letter of the office of the priests in the nomination of the bishop of Alexandria, does not explain whether he is referring to the election or the consecration. Finally, Origen, a compatriot and contemporary of Demetrius, and therefore also of the change of discipline said to have taken place in the mode of consecration of the Alexandrian bishop, makes no allusion whatever to it in his homilies at Cæsarea on the duties and privileges of bishops.[11] It is quite possible, in fine, that the later tradition has here confused election with consecration.

From the moment when the episcopate as we know it was organised everywhere, the bishop appears universally as the authentic head of a church; he is its pastor *par excellence,* its essential priest, without whom the liturgy cannot be celebrated in its integrity, its guide in the faith, its director in discipline, its administrator in the matter of its collective interests, and its representative to those outside.

Priests

The presbyteral college, from which the bishop is not in early days always explicitly distinguished, is composed of the priests, $\pi\rho\epsilon\sigma\beta\acute{\upsilon}\tau\epsilon\rho\omicron\iota$, or elders. These form the bishop's council, and help him in his liturgical and teaching functions; they take his place when necessary, and particularly when the see is vacant.

[10] On all this cf. K. Mueller, *Kleine Beiträge zur alten Kirchengeschichte,* in *Zeitschrift für neutestamentliche Wissenschaft,* Vol. XXVIII, 1929, pp. 273-305.

[11] *In Num., Hom.* 22. Cf. also *Contra Celsum,* VIII, 75.

In all the churches at the head of which we see in the course of the second century a bishop in action, he seems to be almost everything, and the office of the priests is not, so far as we can judge, comparable with what it becomes later on, except in large Christian communities or where the ineluctable law of the division of labour calls for a more positive collaboration by them.

Certain texts even give the impression that the second order of collaborators of the bishop, inferior in dignity to the priests, namely, the deacons, διάκονοι, servants, had then, if not more real authority, at least a more effective ministry.[12] The priests will have more importance when the extension of the Christian communities will bring about their division into sections which will be called parishes, παροικίαι, at the head of which certain priests will be placed.

§3. THE OTHER ECCLESIASTICAL ORDERS

The Deacons

The diaconate, the third rank in ecclesiastical order, clearly goes back to the apostolic age. We have seen that it was instituted by the Apostles themselves when, according to the account in the *Acts* (vi, 2 *et seq.*) they chose the seven who were to "serve tables," διακονεῖν τραπέζαις and laid hands on them. Very soon the care of the poor, which had so greatly preoccupied the Church from its birth, was also entrusted to them.

Hence we get the two fold ministry of deacons in the first centuries: they were the active liturgical auxiliaries of the Church, distributing the Eucharist and conferring baptism with the authorisation of the bishop, and assisting the latter in his administration, particularly in seeing to the interests of the community. This explains why, at a time when practically the whole of the priesthood properly so called was

12 St. Ignatius, in his letter to the church of the Magnesians, VI, 1, in a symbolical interpretation of the ecclesiastical hierarchy, says that the bishop presides in place of God, the priests in place of the college of the apostles, and the deacons are charged with the ministry of Jesus Christ. The *Didascalia Apostolorum* (see Book III) attributes an absolute right to the portion of the oblations not distributed to the faithful to the bishop and the deacons only.

still concentrated in the bishop, the diaconate stood out in greater relief than the priesthood.

Inferior orders were to be created later on, in order to relieve the deacons of a certain number of functions of lesser importance. But they were completely organised only in the third century.

Deaconesses

On the other hand, we note the early disappearance of an institution the existence of which is clear in apostolic times, that of deaconesses, mentioned in the epistle to the Romans (xvi, i), who are probably not distinct from the widows referred to in *I Tim.* (v, 3 *et seq.*), although there must have also been some who were virgins: they devoted themselves to the care of the sick, and the unfortunate, and to the education of children.

They are mentioned still in the letter of Pliny, who tells Trajan that he had put two *ministræ* to the torture, to get confessions from them.

Doctors

Certain Churches, amongst them the greatest such as Rome and Alexandria, also had teachers or *didascaloi,* who devoted themselves to religious teaching. The Acts of the Apostles (xiii, 1) and the epistles of St. Paul (*I Cor.* xiii, 28-31; *Ephes.* iv, 11-12) already mention them. The *Shepherd* of Hermas refers several times to the activity of the teachers in the Roman community towards the middle of the second century. St. Justin the philosopher and other personages taught about the same time. But in their schools a teaching was given for which the ecclesiastical authority did not take the responsibility, though it certainly did not disinterest itself in it. The Roman schools of the second century were in fact only private institutions, due to personal initiatives. It is not till a little later that we find an ecclesiastical school functioning at Alexandria. This was an advanced school of catechetics whose mission it was to teach the truths of the faith, not merely to children, but to adult and educated converts, and placed as it was under the direct control of the Church, it became an official institution.[1]

[1] On the *didascaloi,* cf. *infra,* pp. 250 *et seq.,* and Lebreton and Zeiller, Bk. III.

Prophets

The Primitive Church had also known "prophets," whom
St. Paul treated with honour; the *Acts* mention the daughters
of Philip as having received the gift of prophecy. But already
the *Didache* seems to mistrust the prophets: they were itinerant preachers, destined to disappear fairly soon, inasmuch
as they doubled the existing hierarchy, and the nature of their
ministry involved the risk of opening their ranks to persons
of unequal worth. Thus, although the *Didache,* while warning
readers against the false prophets, displays a great veneration
for those inspired by the Spirit of God, and although the
Shepherd of Hermas puts prophets above priests,[2] they very
quickly ceased to play a recognized part. Montanism was in
the second half of the second century an attempt to restore
the reign of prophets in the Church; in spite of its local success in Asia and some sympathy elsewhere, mainly in Africa,
it collapsed in the presence of the firm resistance of the
hierarchy.[3]

Clergy and Laity

The bishop, the presbyteral college and the deacons, then,
alone constituted the clergy properly so called, forming in
each church a group separate from the rest of the faithful.
The separation is not so sharp as it will be later between lay-
folk and clerics,[4] but the distinction is already shown by the
exercise of functions to which in fact not all can aspire. They
call for a certain number of particular qualities in those who
desire them. The pastoral epistles (*II Tim.* iii, 21-23; *Titus*
i, 5-9) already excluded those with two wives, i.e., who had
married more than once. According to the *Didascalia Apostolorum,* the episcopate could be received only by those fifty
years old, and the priesthood only by those who were thirty.
On the other hand, there was no thought in the first two
centuries of the obligation of celibacy. The preferences of
St. Paul (*I Cor.* vii, 7, 32-34) for this state are manifest, and
he might have appealed to the words of Jesus Himself (*Matt.*
xix, 12) about spiritual eunuchs. But the esteem for con-

[2] *Visio,* III, 1, 8.
[3] Cf. Bk. III.
[4] The expression ἄνθρωπος γαικός is already found in the letter of
St. Clement (XI, 5).

tinence, however real it may have been in the primitive epoch, did not go so far as to impose it even on those who aspired to holy orders. A married man could receive them without being obliged to renounce conjugal life. On the other hand, quite early—for the practice was established by the third century—ordination deprived one who was then celibate of the right to marry subsequently, at least unless he renounced the exercise of ecclesiastical functions. But from the second century the state of virginity was in high honour in the Church,[5] and it is not surprising that the idea spread of calling to the priesthood by preference those Christians who were disposed to keep to this state and who were regarded as more perfect.

Choosing Clerics; Bishops Elected by the Churches

The choice of the first clerics belonged almost exclusively to the Apostles, and the choice of their successors and of new ecclesiastical recruits to the successors of the Apostles. But the opinion of the ordinary faithful was not without its influence upon this choice, and after the death of the first heads of communities, the latter designated their new pastors. In other words, the bishops were elected by the Churches, but they were usually proposed by the clergy of the episcopal city, and it was for the Christian people then to confirm their choice. The transmission of the episcopal character took place only by the consecration of the new elect by a bishop already in office, allowing for the possibility of survivals of the collegiate episcopate which would explain episcopal consecrations made by a presbyteral body like that of Alexandria, if the existence of such a usage were proved.

§4. ECCLESIASTICAL GEOGRAPHY

Were the forms of religious life and ecclesiastical organisation we have just described found wherever Christians existed?

Episcopal Sees

The answer is in the affirmative, generally speaking, but there were exceptions. Very small Christian nuclei could not constitute themselves into communities possessing all the organs found in more important communities. And in par-

[5] Cf. St. Justin, *Apologia*, I, 15; Athenagoras, *Legatio pro Christianis*, 33; Minucius Felix, *Octavianus*, 31.

ticular, there could not be as many bishops as there were Christian centres.

From the fourth century, the almost general rule will apparently be that to each *civitas* in the Empire in which the faith is solidly established there will correspond an episcopal see. In the second century Christian penetration was not sufficiently advanced to bring this about, and there are reasons for thinking that in a country like Gaul, for example —apart from Narbonne—there was, until the third century, no episcopal see other than that of Lyons, whereas according to the martyrological traditions, the Gospel had been previously preached and received beyond the Gallic metropolis in a degree surpassing that of the ecclesiastical dioceses of the later epoch. For no other bishopric is mentioned then, and other sees seem from the episcopal lists not to go back before the third century. This state of things lasted perhaps longer than is sometimes allowed;[1] it was the most probable in the second century.

The Future Metropolises

At a time when not every city possessed a bishop, the grouping of bishops into ecclesiastical provinces such as it would be later on did not yet exist. But geographical proximity and common traditions already established a natural solidarity between sees in the same region, and we can thus speak of an Asiatic Church, formed by the various Churches of this province, which comprised numerous episcopal cities like Ephesus, Smyrna or Sardis.

It is probable that already in the groups thus constituted, the more venerable antiquity of a particular Church, and sometimes its apostolic foundation, itself not altogether unconnected with the previous importance of the city, gave it a particular prestige and thereby also a particular authority. This was the case with Ephesus, Antioch and Alexandria.

[1] We shall return in Book III to this question of the Gallic sees before the middle of the third century. It has been the subject of an interesting discussion between Mgr. Duchesne, *Fastes épiscopaux de l'ancienne Gaule,* Vol. I, pp. 29-59, and Harnack, *Mission und Ausbreitung des Christentums,* 2nd edn., Vol. II, pp. 373-397.

§5. THE ROMAN CHURCH

The Roman Church in the 1st Century

Still more did the Church of Rome enjoy from the first a special position. Because it was the centre of the Greco-Latin world, Rome had attracted the head of the apostolic college and also the Apostle *par excellence* of the Gentiles. Inasmuch as Rome was the last residence of Peter, hallowed for ever by his martyrdom and that of Paul, and occupied the incomparable place of the capital city, whatever sentiments some Christians may have entertained concerning the Empire itself, the Roman Church appears as the senior member of the great Christian family from its first manifestation in history after the deaths of Peter and Paul, although in fact other Churches may have been older. In the Apostolic period, and so long as James the Lord's brother, who presided over the destinies of the Christian community at Jerusalem, was alive, this latter church, although it never exercised any special authority after the departure of Peter, remained nevertheless the Mother Church, venerated and assisted by the others. On all sides collections were made to give help to its members, who had voluntarily deprived themselves of their possessions by the communal system instituted in the enthusiasm of the first days. But that lasted only for a time. After the catastrophe of A.D. 70, Jerusalem temporarily ceased to exist. The Church which continued that which had been in the Holy City rapidly became isolated in the particularism of the Jewish Christians, and the churches as a whole soon ceased to look towards her. Rome quite naturally came to inherit to the full this spiritual succession, as a more vigorous branch substitutes its strength for that of a trunk which the sap no longer nourishes.

Thus the history of the Church of Rome very quickly overflows its own boundaries, and either by its spontaneous action or by reason of the recourse had to her, she becomes very closely concerned in the happenings in the Church universal.

St. Clement

We see this almost at once after the death of St. Peter. His immediate successors Linus and Anacletus, if they were not, as certain traditions seem to indicate,[1] merely his auxiliaries, did not in any case stand out in much relief; Linus is honoured as a martyr, but we do not know his title to this veneration. But we feel ourselves in the presence of a person of some importance when we come to the one who may be regarded as the real successor of Peter, St. Clement,[2] whose intervention in the ecclesiastical affairs of another Christian community, that of Corinth, and the almost canonical character attributed thereupon to the letter written by him on this occasion, show clearly the prestige and authority of his church.

Let it suffice to recall briefly the facts already set forth.

The community at Corinth, the most important, apparently, at that time in Roman Greece, of which this famous city was the metropolis, was disturbed by serious internal disagreements in the reign of Domitian: some members of the presbyteral college, appointed by the Apostles themselves, were set at nought by a party of young people with a readiness which even gave some scandal to those outside.

The Church of Rome, acting as though from its origin it had been conscious of a mission which, as the sequel shows, was not denied, considered it its duty to make its voice heard. It had itself hardly emerged from a difficult time—for we know that it had been hard pressed towards the end of the reign of Domitian, when about the year 95 it sent to the Church of Corinth three of its members, Claudius Ephebus, Valerius Bito and Fortunatus, to make representations, and to take a letter from Clement, written in Greek, then the language of the Church, recommending fraternal charity and respect for authority.

This letter is truly a noteworthy document, very Roman in character, in which we perceive a kindly Christianity, in no wise hostile to the society in which it is developing, a valuable example of "the wise and positive spirit which ever since those far-off times has animated Roman piety." [3] It is strange that some modern writers see here nothing more than a reflection of the Jewish mentality.[4] Speaking of the evil

---

[1] Cf. *supra*, p. 179.

[2] On the personality of Clement, cf. *supra*, p. 82.

[3] L. Duchesne, *Hist. anc. de l'Eglise*, Vol. I, p. 221.

[4] Bousset, *Kyrios Christos*, Göttingen, 1st edn., 1913; 2nd edn., 1921, pp. 291 *et seq.* Cf. *supra*, ch. 5, § 1, n. 23.

effects of indiscipline, and the value of obedience, Clement
sets forth the ecclesiastical ministry as coming from the
Apostles and Christ, and therefore as having the right to be
obeyed. Consequently, the guilty faithful of Corinth ought to
repent, and certain of them should depart, if peace should
require it. "Is there amongst you someone generous, compassionate, and filled with charity? Let such a one say: 'If I am
the cause of the sedition . . . I will leave the country, I will
go wherever it is desired . . . but let the flock of Christ live
in peace with its constituted presbyters!' He who will act
thus will gain great glory in Christ, and he will be well
received everywhere." [5] The Church will pray for these re-
pentant Christians, and Clement thereupon utters a prayer in
which we may see "a specimen of the way in which the leaders of the Christian assemblies developed at that time the
theme of the eucharistic prayer." [6] The letter ends with a
last exhortation, and salutations.[7]

There is no indication at all that this Roman initiative gave
rise to any discontent or surprise at Corinth. True, we do not
know how the Corinthian crisis was settled. But the success
of Clement's initiative is shown by the fame of his letter, for
it was put by its recipients with the books read together with
the Scriptures in the Sunday assemblies.

The Testimony of St. Ignatius of Antioch

Shortly afterwards, the pre-eminence of the Roman Church
was proclaimed, as we have already seen,[8] by St. Ignatius of
Antioch. In a letter he addressed in August, 107, to the
Roman Church, he calls it "president of the charity" or
"brotherhood," προκαθημένη τῆς ἀγάπης,[9] and this name
"agape" was at that time a synonym for the Christian union,
or in other words, the Church itself.[10] This presidency was

[5] 54.

[6] L. Duchesne, *ibid.*, p. 222.

[7] The best editions of the *Prima Clementis,* thus named to distin-
guish it from a second apocryphal letter, are those of Lightfoot,
Apostolic Fathers, Part I, London, 1890, and of Funk, *Patres
Apostolici,* Vol. I, Tübingen, 1901. Cf. *supra,* ch. 5, § 1, n. 4.

[8] Cf. above, pp. 121-22.

[9] *Rom., inscr.* On the sense of these words, see Lelong's edn. in
Les Pères Apostoliques, III, Paris, 1910, pp. 54-5.

[10] The translation of προκαθημένη τῆς ἀγάπης as "which presides
over charity," i.e., which is superior by its work of charity, is,
although in harmony with the facts, to be rejected. Προκαημένη

no mere honorary one: Ignatius adds that Rome, which heard the very words of the Apostles Peter and Paul, has the right to guide the other churches in the faith: "You have never deceived anyone; you have taught others; I desire that all that you prescribe by your teaching may remain incontested."[11]

The Testimony of St. Irenæus

The end of the second century echoed its beginning, the West echoed the East, Irenæus, Bishop of Lyons echoed Ignatius of Antioch when, in his *Adversus hæreses*, written under the pontificate of Pope Eleutherius (175-189) he attributed to the Roman Church a superior pre-eminence, *pontentior principalitas*, which he likewise connected with its foundation by the Apostles Peter and Paul, and by reason of which the other churches ought to be in agreement with it, *convenire*.[12]

The Epitaph of Abercius

Lastly, let us add that a well known text, the epitaph of Abercius, Bishop of Hierapolis in Phrygia Salutaris, under Marcus Aurelius, also gives, in the form of a symbolism which has given rise to many discussions but the sense of which seems now to be beyond question, a witness to the majesty of the Roman Church, the Queen of the Christian world.[13]

---

requires a concrete complement, designating a place or a collectivity. And we know besides that St. Ignatius currently uses ἀγάπη in the sense of ἐκκλησία (cf. *Trall.*, XIII, i; *Phil.*, XI, 2).

[11] *Rom.*, III, 1.

[12] *Adv. hær.*, III, 3, 2 (Migne, *P. G.*, VII, 848-849). [On the interpretation of this passage see Fortescue, *Early Papacy*, London, 1920, pp. 55-7. More detailed discussion in *Dictionnaire de Théologie Catholique*, s.v. Irenée.—Tr.]

[13] "I am the disciple of a holy shepherd, who feeds his flocks of sheep on the mountains and in the plains, who has great eyes whose vision extends everywhere. It is he who taught me the Scriptures worthy of belief. It is he who sent me to Rome to contemplate the royal majesty, and to see a queen in golden vestments and golden sandals." The text of the epitaph, with a summary of the discussion it has aroused, and the literature of the subject down to 1907 will be found in the article *Abercius* in the *Dictionnaire d'archéologie chrétienne* of Dom Cabrol. [Text, translation and photograph of the grave stone are given in S.P.C.K.'s *Texts for Students*, No. 11.—Tr.]

Nevertheless, apart from the striking intervention of St. Clement in the affairs of Corinth, the Church of Rome, from the end of the first century to the end of the second, remained like others, modest in its external action, and of the majority of its heads, from St. Clement to Pope Victor, the contemporary of Irenæus, we know very little.

The Roman Pontiffs as Guardians of Doctrine and as Heads of the Church

But that would certainly not be a sufficient reason to deny that the Roman Church had heads at that time. We have said above that the possible survival, perhaps more apparent than real, of the collegiate episcopate during a time difficult to determine, would not contradict it.[14] On the other hand, a rather strange theory has been advanced in connection with the Roman episcopal lists by a recent historian of the Papacy, Erich Caspar. Before the publication of the first volume of a *Geschichte des Papsttums*[15] he had written a work entitled *Die ältere römische Bischofliste*[16] in which he maintained that the Roman episcopal list, conserved with more or less important variations in catalogues such as the Philocalian and Liberian and the Chronicle of Eusebius, is the list not so much of heads of the Roman Church as of personages regarded as the guardians of the authentic tradition, whose names could be opposed to those of the heretics; going back as far as St. Peter, they would oppose the innovators by the antiquity of the true doctrine as taught by the Apostles.

This is attractive if it be regarded as an affirmation of the essentially doctrinal character of the ecclesiastical magisterium, but hardly an acceptable thesis if it implies a dissociation of the governing authority and the teaching authority: the list of the popes of the first two centuries would in that case be, not a list of heads of the Church, but of leaders of thought, or hardly more. But those who represented doctrinal tradition had thereby doctrinal authority also, and authority as such could not exist apart from it.

[14] Cf. *supra,* pp. 180-82.
[15] Vol. I: *Römische Kirche und Imperium romanum,* Tübingen, 1930.
[16] In *Schriften der Königsberger gelehrten Gesellschaft,* Jahr 2, 1926, Heft 4.

Chapter 7

The Various Churches in the Second Century [1]

[1] Bibliography. On the churches of the various parts of the Christian world, consult: F. Lanzoni, *Le origini delle diocesi antiche d'Italia* (*Studi e testi*, 35), Rome, 1923, 2nd edn. under the title: *Le diocesi d'Italia dalle origini al principio del secolo VII*, 2 vols., Faenza, 1927; F. Savio, *Gli antichi vescovi d'Italia dalle origini al 1300 descritti per regioni. La Lombardia*, 1st part, Bergamo, 1898, 2nd part, 1929 and 1932; F. Ughelli, *Italia sancta*, Re-edited by J. Colegi, 10 vols., Venice, 1717-22; S. A. Morcelli, *Africa cristiana*, 3 vols., Brizen, 1816-17; P. Monceaux, *Histoire littéraire de l'Afrique chrétienne depuis les origines jusqu'à l'invasion arabe*, 7 vols. so far, Paris, 1901-23; Dom A. Leclercq, *L'Afrique chrétienne*, 2 vols., Paris, 1904, 2nd edn. of Vol. I; A. Audollent, *Carthage romaine*, Paris, 1901; A. Toulotte, *Géographie de l'Afrique chrétienne*, 4 vols., Rennes-Paris, 1892 (1); Montreuil-sur-Mer, 1894 (II and III); Rennes-Paris, 1894 (XIV); J. Mesnage, *L'Afrique chrétienne, Evêchés et ruines antiques d'après les manuscrits de Mgr. Toulotte*, Paris, 1912; E. Le Blant, *Inscriptions chrétiennes de la Gaule*, 2 vols., Paris, 1856-65; *Nouveau recueil des inscriptions chrétiennes de la Gaule*, Paris, 1892; *Gallia christiana*, by Dom Denis de Sainte-Marthe and the Benedictines of St. Maur, 13 vols., Paris, 1715-85, completed by B. Hauréau, 3 vols., Paris, 1856, 1860 and 1865; the 13 first volumes reprinted by Dom Piolin, 1870-5; Mgr. L. Duchesne, *Fastes épiscopaux de la Gaule*, 3 vols., Paris, 1894, 2nd edn., 1907, 1910 and 1915; T. Scott Holmes, *Origin and Development of the Christian Church in Gaul during the first six centuries of the Christian Era*, London, 1911; C. Jullian, *Histoire de la Gaule*, Vol. IV; *Le gouvernement de Rome*, Paris, 1914 (ch. xi is devoted to the Christians in Gaul); J. Zeiller, *Les origines chrétiennes de la Gaule*, in *Revue d'histoire de l'Eglise de France*, Vol. XII, 1926, pp. 16-34; Dom. L. Gougoud, *Les chrétiennes celtiques*, Paris, 1911; Huerner, *Inscriptiones Hispaniæ christianæ*, Berlin, 1871, Supplement, 1900; L. Garcia Villada, *Historia ecclesiastica de Espana*, I, *El cristianesimo durante la dominacion romana*, Madrid, 1929, 2 vols.; Huerner, *Inscriptiones Britanniæ christianæ*, London and Berlin, 1876; Dom H. Leclercq, *L'Espagne chrétienne*, Paris, 1900; Le Quien, *Oriens christianus*, 3 vols., Paris, 1740; V. Chapot, *La province romaine d'Asie*, Paris, 1904; ch. vii deals with the Christian

§1. THE ROMAN CHURCH

The Episcopal Succession in Rome established from Apostolic Times

HOWEVER LITTLE may be our knowledge of the history of the popes of the first two centuries, we know more of the Roman episcopate than of that of any other Church, for the Roman Church alone has its episcopal success established without a gap from its apostolic founders.

The Popes of the First Century

But its chronology remains uncertain. A catalogue, the first form of which may go back to the time of Pope Eleutherius,[2] who was a contemporary of the Emperor Commodus, and who died in 189, gives, if St. Peter was really martyred in 64, a total of 125 years for the pontificates of his first twelve successors.

We have already had occasion to say[3] that the first two, Linus and Anacletus, are almost unknown; they were perhaps first the auxiliaries of Peter in the government of the Roman Church, and the transposition to the time of Peter of the twelve years of episcopate attributed to each of them might be the origin of the tradition of the twenty-five years of the Roman episcopate of the Prince of the Apostles. St. Clement, the first successor of Peter who is well known, was a contemporary of Domitian.

---

church; H. Grégoire, *Recueil des Inscriptions grecques chrétiennes d'Asie Mineure,* in course of publication, Paris, 1922; Heckel, *Die Kirche von Agypten, Ihre Anfänge, ihre Organisation und ihre Entwicklung, bis zur Zeit des Nicenum,* Strassburg, 1918; G. Hanotaux, *Histoire de la nation égyptienne,* Vol. III, 2nd part, *L'Egypte romaine,* by V. Chapot, and 3rd part, *L'Egypte chrétienne et byzantine,* by C. Diehl, Paris, 1933; F. J. A. Hort, *Judaistic Christianity,* London, 1894.

[2] The list of Roman bishops is given by St. Irenæus in the third book of his treatise *Against Heresies.* It is reproduced by Eusebius, *Hist. Eccles.,* V, 6, 1. But it did not indicate the length of each pontificate. On the various catalogues, cf. the article *Listes episcopales* in the *Dictionnaire d'Archéologie chrétienne.*

[3] Cf. *supra,* pp. 180, 189-90.

The Popes of the Second Century

Next come Evaristus, Alexander, Xystus and Telesphorus, almost all bearers of Greek names, contemporaries of the emperors Nerva, Trajan and Hadrian. Telesphorus alone is known, because of his martyrdom under the reign of Hadrian.[4] Hyginus and Pius, the latter mentioned in the *Muratorian Fragment* about 150, perished under Antoninus.[5]

Anicetus, who succeeded Pius, received in 154 a visit from the illustrious bishop of Smyrna, St. Polycarp. Soter next, under Marcus Aurelius, may have heard in Rome the story of the prodigy of the Thundering Legion.[6] He was replaced by the old deacon of his predecessor, Eleutherius, who became pope before the death of Marcus Aurelius and received the letter from Dionysius of Corinth to the Church of Rome which forms one of the links in the chain of testimonies concerning the Roman apostolate of St. Peter;[7] Eleutherius received also a visit from Irenæus, the envoy of the Church of Lyons,[8] illustrious then because of its martyrs, and whence the Gospel was to spread over a whole portion of Gaul; he was requested to define his position in the matter of Montanism.[9] His pontificate ended only in 189, nine years after the coming of Commodus to the throne.

But it was only his successor, Pope Victor, who saw the pardon granted by the emperor to those condemned to the Sardinian mines, and the precarious but unquestionable improvement in the relations between the Church and the Empire which marked the reign of the last of the Antonines.

§2. THE OTHER CHURCHES IN THE WEST

The Churches of Italy

Besides Rome, several Christian communities in Italy have left traces of their existence before the end of the second century.

[4] Cf. *supra*, p. 88.
[5] Cf. *supra*, p. 91.
[6] Cf. *supra*, pp. 96-97.
[7] Eusebius, *Hist. Eccles.*, II, 25, 8, and IV, 23, 9. Cf. *Lebreton* and Zeiller, Bk. I, pp. 292-94.
[8] Eusebius, *Hist. Eccles.*, V, 4, 2.
[9] Cf. Book III.

We have already spoken of those of Puteoli and of Pompeii, known already in the first century.[1] Christian cemeteries have been discovered at Naples and elsewhere which may go back to the second century. But only two episcopal sees, other than Rome, can claim such great antiquity, and these are Milan and Ravenna.

The seventh bishop of Milan, Mirocles, was present at the synods of Rome and Arles in 313 and 314, and the twelfth bishop of Ravenna took part in the Council of Sardica in 343, and hence the respective founders of these two churches, or at least their first titular bishops, must have lived between 150 and 200. The traditions concerning an apostolate of St. Barnabas at Milan belong to the sphere of legend, like that which makes St. Apollinaris, the Apostle of Ravenna, a disciple of St. Peter.

Also, we know hardly anything more about the history of these Churches before the fourth century besides the fact of their existence and the names of the pastors who ruled them. We must add, however, so far as Ravenna is concerned, that its Christian community arose in the port of Classe, as is shown by the first episcopal tombs which are at some distance from the town. Here Orientals were numerous;[2] and here, as in many other places, they evidently provided Christian propaganda with its first agents and its first recruits. But as to the progress which it then made, or its penetration into other parts of Italian territory before the third century, we are so far unable to say anything. In fact, until that time, the history of the Church in Italy reduces itself practically to the history of the Roman Church.

Africa

In Africa before this date we know only of the martyrdom of the Scillitans and what the catacombs of Hadrumetum suggest concerning a Christian life which must have begun a long time previously.[3] But the writings of Tertullian, which are a little later in date, show African Christianity occupying already such a position in the time of the Severi that it must

[1] Cf. *supra,* p. 51.
[2] On these beginnings of the sees of Milan and Ravenna, cf. F. Lanzoni, *Le origini delle diocesi antiche d'Italia* (*Studi e testi,* 35, Rome, 1923), pp. 452-75 and 543-60.
[3] Cf. pp. 58-59, 98-99.

have counted for something before the end of the Antonines.

Spain and Gaul

In Spain the position is obscure, as we have said. In Gaul, a very old inscription preserved at Marseilles, and which seems to allude to martyrs,[4] might well constitute a positive testimony to the diffusion of Christianity on the coasts of Provence before the foundation of the Church of Lyons. On this church the martyrs in the persecution of Marcus Aurelius bestow an incomparable splendour in the middle of the second century. St. Irenæus, successor to St. Pothinus, will bring it a new glory.[5] But from Lyons we know little as to the progress of the Gospel and Christian life in Gaul down to the period of the Severi.[6]

Britain

Of Roman Britain[7] we know nothing in this period, and the same remark applies to the Illyrian countries. But it is otherwise with the Mediterranean East.

§3. THE CHURCHES OF THE EAST

Greece

We have enumerated above[1] the already numerous churches which have left proofs of their existence in Greece in the first and second centuries. Eusebius has handed on the illustrious name of the first bishop of one of these, Dionysius the Areopagite, the convert of St. Paul, who was put at the head of the Christian community of Athens.[2]

As to their internal life, we know the famous episode which caused the intervention of Clement of Rome at Corinth in the last years of the first century.[3] Some seventy years later, we find at the head of this same Church of Corinth a

---

[4] Inscription called the Volusian, *C.I.L.*, XII, 480.
[5] Cf. Book III.
[6] Cf. O. Hirschfeld, *Zur Geschichte des Christentums in Lugdunum vor Constantin* (*Sitzungsberichte* of the Berlin Academy, 1895, pp. 381-409) and Book III.
[7] The origins of British Christianity are discussed in Book III.
[1] Cf. pp. 55-56.
[2] Eusebius, *Hist. Eccles.*, IV, 25.
[3] Cf. pp. 189-91.

very prominent personage, Dionysius, who had succeeded a bishop named Primus. Dionysius was consulted from all sides, and his letters were so well thought of that they were collected together.[4] This collection contains amongst others the letter to the Church of Rome, the importance of which we have already pointed out,[5] another to the Church of Sparta, and another to the Church of Athens, which had just passed through a serious crisis. Following the persecution which had removed the bishop Publius in the reign of Marcus Aurelius, the Christians of Athens had almost abandoned their faith; but their new bishop, Quadratus, brought them back once more to the straight path.

Two other Hellenic Christian communities, both in Crete, appear also in the correspondence of Dionysius of Corinth: that of Knossos, which had for its bishop Pinytos, an ascetic, and that of Gortyna, whose bishop was called Philip.

These testimonies are all the more valuable because we know little otherwise concerning Christian Greece in the second century. Indeed, it seems that at this time, as in the following century, its history was hardly so full as that of Greek Asia. Perhaps Christianity made slower progress there; it would not be surprising that its propaganda found greater difficulty in overcoming resistance in a country in which the lower classes were most fully penetrated by the traditions of the old Mediterranean polytheism, and whose upper classes were most inclined to rationalistic criticism. Even so, Christian Greece produced in the second century besides Dionysius of Corinth, two apologists,[6] the Athenian Marcianus Aristides, and Athenagoras, perhaps of the same town.[7]

Asia Minor

Asia Minor was more speedily and more thoroughly won to the new faith. The testimony of Pliny the Younger concerning Bithynia in the time of Trajan was repeated half a century later under the pen of Lucian, through whom we learn of the anger of the famous pseudo-prophet Alexander

[4] Eusebius, *Hist. Eccles.*, XVIII, 23.
[5] Cf. Lebreton and Zeiller, Bk. I, pp. 291-92.
[6] Cf. *infra*, ch. 9.
[7] The Athenian origin of Athenagoras is indicated only by Philip of Sidon, whose statement is too late to call for an unreserved acceptance. [But the title of the *Apology* states that Athenagoras was "an Athenian, Christian philosopher."—Tr.]

of Abonouteiches at the great number of Christians in Pontus.[8]

Some illustrious personages shed the light of their martyr-dom or of their activity as theologians or as preachers on the Asiatic Churches in the second century. Let it suffice to mention the names, most of them already met with, or to appear later on, of St. Polycarp of Smyrna, Papias of Hierapolis, Melito of Sardis, the apologists Quadratus, Apollinaris and Miltiades, Ammias of Philadelphia, Papirius the successor of Polycarp, Sagaris of Laodicea, Thraseas, bishop of Eumenia in Phrygia, martyred at Smyrna.

Syria and Palestine

To the south of Asia Minor, Syria occupied a position in the front rank in the Church until the second century. It was at Antioch that Christianity had freed itself from Judaism. We might almost say that the Church became truly what it ought to be only on the day when Paul, joining with Barnabas, the founder of the community at Antioch, organised with him the first distant mission, and when the supreme authorities in the Apostolic college, Peter, John and James, the brother of the Lord, accepted their view and admitted the recruits from the Gentiles without imposing circumcision upon them. The temporary establishment of St. Peter at Antioch confirmed the new state of things. In order to take his place when his own apostolate called him elsewhere, he left there Evodius,[9] who had as his successor St. Ignatius.

Syria from that time, like the Palestinian communities which are naturally grouped with it, figured prominently in the universal Church, with its martyrs, its bishops and its writers.

Aelia Capitolina, the Roman city built in Hadrian's time on the ruins of Jerusalem, had very soon a group of believers mainly of Gentile origin;[10] they had in the middle of the second century a bishop named Marcus;[11] one of his successors, Narcissus, was celebrated in the time of Commodus because of his longevity, his miracles and his sanctity. But whereas the first Christian Church of Jerusalem had always been regarded as the Mother Church, that of Aelia had from its commencement neither particular prerogative nor prestige,

[8] *Alexander seu Pseudomantis*, 38.
[9] Eusebius, *Chronicon*, ann. 43; *Hist. Eccles.*, III, 22.
[10] Cf. Bk. I, p. 315.
[11] Eusebius, *Chronicon*, ann. 135.

and when later on there was established in the Church the provisional organisation which raised the metropolises above ordinary bishoprics, its bishop depended for some time on that of the civil metropolis of the province, Cæsarea in Palestine.

Palestine, like Syria, could boast of illustrious martyrs. St. Simeon of Jerusalem and St. Ignatius of Antioch had laid down their lives out of fidelity to Christ almost at the same time. In the second century, Palestinian Christianity had above all to suffer from the Jews, instigated by Bar Kokhba under Hadrian (132-5).[12]

But it is by the work of religious teaching on the part of several of their members, clerical and lay, that the Syro-Palestinian Churches left most traces in history in the second century: not to mention the unknown authors of the *Didache* and the *Epistle of Barnabas,* the origin of which is uncertain —it might be Egyptian—Ariston of Pella, St. Justin, born at Flavia Neapolis in Samaria, from whence he went to Rome, Tatian, Theophilus of Antioch and Hegesippus all bear their witness.[13]

Egypt

Christian Egypt was also to shine particularly in the theological domain, and from the second half of the second century, the Catechetical School of Alexandria, destined to become so famous, had begun to function. We know less about the other aspects of the history of the Church in Egypt at the same time. We can only say that Christianity made rapid progress there, for from the beginning of the following century we find it spread over a great part of the valley of the Nile.

§4. THE JUDEO-CHRISTIAN CHURCH

The Christian Community of Pella

There was one ethnic group which retained a character all its own in the Church of the first two centuries: this was that of the Christians who had come from Judaism, known as Judeo-Christians. We know[1] that some of the faithful of

[12] Cf. *supra,* pp. 83, 89.
[13] Cf. ch. 9.
[1] Cf. Lebreton and Zeiller, Bk. I, p. 313.

Judea who had constituted the community at Jerusalem had taken refuge at Pella in the course of the war which ended in the destruction of the Holy City.[2] But neither this separation nor the disappearance of the Temple were able to break their links with Judaism, and they continued to unite with the practice of the religion of Christ that of a certain number of ancient observances, which they reverently maintained.

Characteristics of the Judeo-Christian Church

This Christian community was, however, not able to retain the prestige possessed by that of Jerusalem: governed by James, the Lord's brother, until the Sanhedrin had him stoned in 62, and next by Simeon, another near relative of Jesus, the Mother Church had attracted the regard and consideration of all the others. When the sale of the possessions of its first members with a view to the common use of the proceeds soon rendered its material existence difficult, alms poured into it; if the Roman *plebs,* unaccustomed to work and fed by the care of its rulers, lived on the rest of the world, compelled to feed it, this mother of the Churches lived mostly on the charity of the others, but they were free offerings, and it was thought natural to send them.

The situation changed after 70, when Simeon, in presence of the imminent prospect of the ruin of Jerusalem, headed the exodus of his flock towards Pella.

Pella could not claim the prestige of the Holy City, and the particularism of its little Church tended speedily to isolate it. Some few of its members returned, it is true, to Jerusalem, which did not remain a pure desert after 70.[3] It was only after the repression of Bar Kokhba that the history of the old Jerusalem came to a definite end. But the reconstruction

[2] Eusebius, *Hist. Eccles.,* III, 5.
[3] St. Epiphanius, *On weights and measures amongst the Jews,* 14-15, ed. Dindorf, IV, 17, says that the fugitives returned from Pella, and that there was once more a small Christian community at Jerusalem, where St. Simeon certainly seems to have been martyred. According to Eusebius, *Chronicon,* ann. 131, this community would seem to have had a certain importance in the time of Hadrian. Cf. Schlatter, *Die Kirche Jerusalem von* 70-130, Gütersloh, 1898, who has utilised rabbinic texts on this subject, and J. Jeremias, *Golgotha,* in ΑΓΓΕΛΟΣ, *Archiv fur neutestamentliche Zeitgeschichte und Kulturkunde,* Beihefte, Leipzig, 1926.

of the city under the name of Aelia Capitolina by Hadrian was far from bringing about a general return, the Emperor having forbidden Jews to stay there, and so the Jewish Christians had under these circumstances to keep away. But it is possible, nevertheless, that their pacific spirit, which kept them outside the insurrection, in spite of the assaults of the revolutionaries, and which was calculated to tranquillize the Roman authority, won for some the authorisation to return, or to remain in their ancient city. But the majority remained outside. Some migrated to Kokhaba in Transjordania, to Nazareth in Galilee, and even to Berea (Aleppo) in Northern Syria.[4]

The spirit of these communities continued with its particular characteristics. The representatives of the family of Christ were always held in honour among them. The sons of Jude, the Lord's brother, who according to the historian of the Judeo-Christian communities, Hegesippus,[5] had had to appear before Domitian, "presided then over the churches"; perhaps one of them succeeded to Simeon, martyred under Trajan. In the third century there were still in the Judeo-Christian centres some of these Δεσπόσυνοι, members of the Lord's family, regarded with great respect.[6]

The Judeo-Christians had their own Gospel, which received the name of the *Gospel according to the Hebrews*. It was related mainly to that of St. Matthew, but differed from it in some ways.[7]

The Judeo-Christian Church, which soon appeared somewhat singular in the group of churches, ended by occupying a border-line position. Thus almost immediately after the death of James, the Lord's brother, a section which was more Judaistic, to the point of claiming to impose the legal observances even on converts from paganism, had opposed to Simeon a rival named Tebuthis: "He began in the people," says Hegesippus,[8] "the work of corruption arising from the seven Jewish sects to which he himself belonged." But the other part of the Judeo-Christians came also to be regarded as a sect, that of the Ebionites, from which it had neverthe-

---

[4] Epiphanius, *Hær.*, XXIX, 7.
[5] Cf. Bk. I, pp. 313-14.
[6] Eusebius, *Hist. Eccles.*, I, 7; III, 19 and 20.
[7] On this Gospel, cf. Harnack, *Chronologie*, p. 631, and James, *Apocryphal New Testament*.
[8] Quoted in Eusebius, *Hist. Eccles.*, IV, 22, 5.

less been quite distinct at the beginning of the second century;[9] the name of "Ebionites" took the place or was added to that of "Nazarenes," formerly used to designate the Judeo-Christians. This name "Ebionite," which meant "poor," became theirs, either because they were really poor, in accordance with the tradition of the old community of Jerusalem, or else they themselves took this name because of the merit attributed to poverty in the Gospel. But some ecclesiastical writers speak of a certain Ebion as their founder.[10] Whatever may have been the origin of the word, their designation by a particular term making them Christians apart was not unreasonable; the survival amongst them of the Judaism of the early times in a backward state eventually made them a veritable sect. Using only one gospel, and rejecting the epistles of St. Paul, who was in their eyes an apostate from Judaism, a part of them came to repudiate in addition the belief in the virginal conception of the Lord, and towards the latter part of the second century they already appeared as separated from the great Church.[11]

They gradually grew less in numbers. They existed still as a distinct group in the fourth century, when several Fathers of the Church speak of them in not very favourable terms.[12] They were regarded with curiosity by scholars such as St. Jerome, or students of heresies such as St. Epiphanius, but none regarded their Church as quite pure in doctrine. Yet a certain reunion seems to have taken place between them and the Great Church, and there was doubtless some fusion in the end, "but by individual action. None of the Judeo-Christian communities entered as such"[13] into the ecclesiastical system of the East. It is possible on the other hand that some portions may have been re-absorbed by Judaism.

"Thus ended Judeo-Christianity, obscurely and miserably.

[9] Cf. Bk. I, pp. 313-14, and *supra,* pp. 83-84, for the circumstances of the martyrdom of Simeon, a victim of heretics, amongst whom the Ebionites must have had their place.
[10] Cf. Tertullian, *Liber de carne Christi,* c. 14; Eusebius, *Hist. Eccles.,* III, 27; Epiphanius, *Contra hæreses,* Hær., XXX.
[11] Cf. Origen, *In Johannem,* I, 1.
[12] Cf. St. Augustine, *Contra Faustum,* XIX, 4, 17; *Contra Cresconium,* I, 31; St. Jerome, *Epist. ad August.,* 89; Epiphanius, *Hæreses,* XXIX, who regards them frankly as heretics.
[13] Duchesne, *Hist. anc. de l'Eglise,* Vol. I, pp. 127-8.

The Church, in the measure in which it developed in the Greco-Roman world, had left its cradle behind it. It had had to emancipate itself from Judeo-Christianity, just as it had to do from Judaism itself." [14]

[14] *Ibid.*, p. 128.

Chapter 8

Christian Life in the First Two Centuries [1]

THE CHARACTERISTICS of various Churches may differ, but the Christian life is one in its essence, and the same signs reveal the Christian everywhere.

§1. CHRISTIANS AND ORDINARY LIFE

Christians Share in Civil Life

Their name distinguishes Christians sufficiently for them to appear not to be like all the world, yet it did not make them strangers in the city, although some have maintained this.

---

[1] Bibliography. Besides the works mentioned in the General Bibliography and those cited in the notes to the preceding chapter, the following may be consulted: G. Bardy, *L'Eglise à la fin du Ier siècle,* Paris, 1932; J. Lebreton, *La vie chrétienne au Ier siècle de l'Eglise,* Paris, 1932; C. Guignebert, *Tertullien, Etude sur ses sentiments à l'égard de l'Empire et de la société civile,* Paris, 1901; G. Boissier, *La fin du paganisme,* I, Paris, 1913, 5th edn., Paris, 1907; Martin-Doisy, *Histoire de la charité chrétienne pendant les six premiers siècles,* Paris, 1848; F. Allard, *Les esclaves chrétiens depuis les premiers temps de l'Eglise jusqu'à la fin de la domination romaine en Occident,* 5th edn., Paris, 1914; *Dix leçons sur le martyre,* Paris, 1893; H. Delehaye, *Martyr et confesseur,* in *Analecta Bollandiana,* Vol. XXXIX, 1921, pp. 20-49 and 50-64; *Les origines du culte des martyrs,* 2nd edn., Brussels, 1933; A. Harnack, *Der Vorwurf des Atheismus in den drei ersten christlichen Jahrhunderten,* Leipzig, 1905; C. M. Kaufmann, *Handbuch der christlichen Archeologie,* Paderborn, 1905, and *Handbuch der christlichen Epigraphik,* Freiburg in Bresgau, 1917; P. de Labriolle, *La réaction paienne, Etude sur la polémique antichrétienne du Ier au VIe siècle,* Paris, 1934; Dom H. Leclercq, *Manuel d'archéologie chrétienne,* Paris, 1907, 2 vols.; O. Marucchi, *Manuale di Archeologia cristiana,* 4th edn. revised by G. Belvederi, Rome, 1933; *Le catacombe romane,* posthumous work published by E. Josi, Rome, 1933; J. Martigny, *Dictionnaire des Antiquités chrétiennes,* 3rd edn., Paris, 1889; J. Wilpert, *Die Malereien der Katakomben Roms,* Vol. I, Text, Vol. II, Plates, Freiburg in Bresgau, 1903, and *I sarcofagi cristiani antichi,* 2 vols. in 4 (text and plates), Rome, 1929-32.

The author of the valuable work of the end of the second century, the *Letter to Diognetus*,[2] insists[3] that Christians do not differ from their contemporaries either in vesture or in housing or in food, although the interdiction of things strangled and of the blood of animals, derived from the Jews, may have persisted in some communities until this time;[4] in all these matters which concern earthly life, they conform themselves to the customs of their countries. Tertullian, who began to write at the end of the second century, and who describes Christian life as the contemporaries of the last of the Antonines would have seen it, says in his *Apologeticus*, written about 195, addressing the pagans:[5] "We others, Christians, do not live apart from this world; we like you frequent the forum, the baths, the workshops, the shops, the markets, the public places; we follow the professions of sailor, soldier, planter, merchant, we put at your service our labour and our industry."

A typical detail in the martyrological history of the second century confirms these statements of Tertullian: the letter of the Church of Lyons concerning the persecution of 177 narrates that when the population, roused against the Christians, began to molest them in all kinds of ways pending the intervention of the authorities, they expelled them from the baths and the forum, which proves that they had not deserted the public places.

Christians Did Not Object to Military Service

The episode of the Thundering Legion,[6] even if religious enthusiasm had transformed it into an imaginary miracle due to the prayers of Christian soldiers, would even so suffice to prove the existence of Christians in the armies in the Antonine period. After all, had not St. Clement in his letter to the Corinthians in the preceding century spoken of "our legions" and of "our generals," from the standpoint of a Roman?

[2] Cf. *infra*, pp. 242-45.
[3] V. 1, 4.
[4] One of the martyrs of Lyons answers the accusation of cannibalism made against Christians by saying that it is strange to accuse of eating human beings those who abstain even from the blood of animals (Eusebius, *Hist. Eccles.*, V, 24).
[5] *Apol.*, 42.
[6] Cf. *supra*, pp. 96-97.

Tertullian also confirms that the Christian faith did not exclude the calling of a soldier. His own mind may have changed on this point, and the opposite idea and the conduct it leads to will find its disciples. But until the end of the second century, a "conscientious objection" against bearing arms is no more a theme of discussion in literature than it is a current fact in Christian practice.

§2. CHRISTIANS AND SOCIAL LIFE

Christians and the Life of the Ancient City

Nevertheless, the disagreement which might arise between the duty of the believer and certain obligations of the citizen was the difficult point in the situation of Christians in the city. The close union in the ancient State between civic activity and religious acts unacceptable to those who adored the one God, or of customs which the Gospel morality reproved, such as the combats in the circus, compelled the Christians to renounce a part of social life; it put them in a certain measure on the boundaries of the city. This was a moral semi-secession, incontestable and inevitable, which may have been aggravated by the apocalyptic tendencies of some inclined to prophesy, if not to desire or to prepare for the more or less proximate collapse of the ancient order. But the legitimate authorities of the Church and the most qualified representatives of Christian thought in the first two centuries did not at all stand for this extremism. Only it must be said that for Christians preoccupations of a terrestrial order went to the background, and that there existed among them, in degrees varying according to individual temperaments, a relative lack of interest in social matters, which might well prove a difficulty one day.

But in the second century their number was relatively too small for this partial abstentionism to have much effect, although it already deprived the Roman State of the active concourse of some of its best subjects, in limited domains.

Christian Asceticism

But on the other hand, the Christians made up for this civic failing by providing the example of a conduct better calculated than that of other men to give to human life all its dignity, which is that of a life according to the spirit. For as the *Letter to Diognetus* says again,[1] Christians live in the flesh, but not according to the flesh. If they avoid spectacles, combats of gladiators and wild beasts, and all the distractions of a similar nature which seem so natural to pagan society, it is because of the cruelty or immodesty of such things and all the disorders inseparable from them.[2]

Christians also showed themselves indifferent to the advantages of riches, or at least they refused to enjoy them selfishly: the good things of the earth are only a means for heaping up better treasure in heaven, and they spend them liberally in the service of those deprived of them. "We who once loved gain," St. Justin in his First Apology,[3] "now distribute all we possess, and give to all the needy." Thus Christians condemned unnecessary expenditure, renouncing splendour and luxury in dress, although doubtless some of them allowed themselves a certain licence in this matter. Tertullian[4] criticises the liking, excessive in his view, that too many Christian women retain for the care of the person and the choice of dresses. Rigorists like him go as far as to forbid the use of flowers in the hair, as well as in the ornamentation of tombs.[5]

Circumspection in the personal use of the goods of the world, and also in moral conduct: these are two characteristics distinctive of the true Christian. Alone amongst all the religions, Christianity, maintaining inexorably the law of the apostolic assembly of Jerusalem, has always regarded sexual relations outside marriage as a grave fault. There were even amongst a few a tendency to condemn second marriages. Nevertheless, St. Paul had not only tolerated these, but recommended them for young widows: "I will that the younger should marry, bear children, be mistresses of families, give no occasion to the adversary to speak evil." [6] But the Church did not view a second marriage with a very favourable eye, and she made it an impediment for the reception of holy orders.

[1] V, 8, 9.
[2] Cf. Tertullian, *De spectaculis.*
[3] I, 14.
[4] *De cultu feminarum.*
[5] Tertullian, *De corona militis.* Cf. Minutius Felix, *Octavius,* 12, 38; Clement of Alexandria, *Pædagogus,* II, 8.
[6] *I Tim.,* v, 14.

§3. CHRISTIAN PRACTICES

Prayer

Pure in their morals, and using earthly goods only for the satisfying of their essential needs and for the benefit of their neighbours, if they really lived according to the Gospel ideal, Christians also gave a large place in their daily life to prayer. Apart from worship properly so called, which was celebrated in common,[1] the faithful Christian, in accordance with the Gospel precept,[2] prayed to his heavenly Father in secret. Following the Master, Tertullian recommends the use of the *Lord's Prayer*.[3] The Psalter was also utilised as a prayer book. Prayer was made more particularly in the morning and evening, as also at the third, sixth, and ninth hour (9 A.M., noon and 3 P.M.). This is the origin of the offices of Prime, Terce, Sext, None and Vespers.[4] We must also pray, says Tertullian, before meals and before a bath.[5]

Fasts

The Christian who unites his soul to God in prayer also mortifies his body, the appetites of which endanger this union. He gives himself to penance as well as to prayer. Fasting, the practice of which associates him with the voluntary mortification of Christ in the desert, is the chief ascetical practice.[6]

In the first two centuries, the faithful fasted twice a week, on Wednesdays, perhaps in reparation for the treason of Judas, and on Fridays, in memory of the Passion; these fasts were called stational, from the Latin word "statio," which designated the guarding by soldiers of a military post. To the stational fast there began to be added towards the end of the second century a paschal fast, mentioned by St. Irenæus, which extended to the days immediately preceding the feast of Easter, and particularly Good Friday and Holy Saturday; the fast of forty days in Lent will be a later extension of this

[1] Cf. *supra*, ch. 1.
[2] *Matt.* vi, 6.
[3] *De Oratione.*
[4] *Ibid.*
[5] *Ibid.*
[6] Cf. Hermas, *Shepherd*; Tertullian, *De jejunio;* Clement of Alexandria, *Strom.*, VII, 14.

practice. These fasts consisted in abstention from all food and even all drink until the ninth hour, that is, until the middle of the afternoon.

Charity

Mortified in his personal life in memory of Christ and to keep in check the ever dangerous pressure of his lower passions, the Christian worthy of this name sought only the good of his neighbour.

Each member of the community was at the service of all, and the fulfilling of this duty of charity went from almsgiving, which prevented death from hunger, to encouragement to martyrdom. The Christians of Lyons gave amongst others a very moving example of this.[7] Such mutual love struck the pagans: "See how they love one another," they said,[8] and this is perhaps among the various traits of Christian life, and in spite of all the prejudices which slandered it, the one which was most perceptible, and which people could not help admiring. The chief argument put forward by the apologists of the first centuries in favour of Christianity is, in fine, the exemplary conduct of its followers.

A pure life, a solid piety, a perfect loyalty, and a boundless charity have perhaps done more for the extension of the reign of the Gospel than the most eloquent discourses intended to convert the pagans.

§4. CHRISTIANITY AND HUMANITY

Christianity and Slavery

This unique charity renewed the relations between men to such a degree that it began by a radical transformation of a social institution which seemed to be inherent in ancient society, but the principle of which was nevertheless incompatible with the spirit of Christianity, so that the latter was bound to lead to its disappearance by the extension of its domination. We refer to slavery. St. Paul had already said in the beginning[1] that in the Church there is "neither bond nor free," any more than one can distinguish before God the Jew from the Greek, or man from woman. Physiological,

---

[7] Cf. *supra*, pp. 93-96.
[8] Tertullian, *Apologeticus*, 39, 7.
[1] *Gal.* iii, 28.

ethnical and juridical distinctions may continue to exist between human beings; but morally they fade away, and all, being equally children of God and "clothed with Christ," [2] "form now only one person in Jesus Christ," and those who had ceased to belong to themselves by reason of their social condition as slaves, recover their liberty in order to give themselves, like the others, to Jesus Christ, who has made them free in making them His. In the eyes of the Church there are no slaves in reality, for the person of a man cannot belong to another man, and it was this ownership of man by man that constituted slavery.

Nevertheless, in the political and social sphere, the Church did not begin by condemning an institution which she found established, and which as a system of social and economic organisation seemed then quite natural, if not necessary, to almost all the world.

Some Stoic philosophers, rising to a conception hitherto unknown of the value of human personality and of the natural equality of all may well have thought and said that slavery was opposed to them, but these were only theoretical views. Christianity said less, but it spoke in a different tone, [3] and it did more. There was no condemnation for long centuries of the institution, but an implicit denial of its basis, in the doctrine of the divine sonship as St. Paul formulated it. Together with a *de facto* acceptance of the existing social regime there was brought into being a moral system which undermined its basis. In ancient law, the slave, not being a complete person, could not exercise personal prerogatives: the slave, for instance, could not contract a veritable marriage, and the caprice of his master could break up his union. The Church did not sanction such an inferiority, and condemned such abuses of power. Furthermore, she made such an appeal to a charity which, for a true Christian, has all the exigencies of justice, that the master, in his relations with the slave, will renounce the exercise of rights which hitherto had constituted

[2] *Gal.* iii, 27.
[3] ". . . Let us contrast the doctrine of the Stoics, for instance, with Christian morality. They proclaim themselves citizens of the world, and they add that all men are brothers, having come from the same God. The words were almost the same, but they did not find the same echo, because they had not been spoken in the same tone" (H. Bergson, *Les deux sources de la morale et de la religion,* Paris, 1932, p. 58).

STOICS on SLAVERY

him the veritable master of a person, and not merely of his services.

The slave of a Christian master was doubtless compelled, unlike a servant of our days, to remain in his service; he might receive orders from him, or even a severe treatment, which domestic service has known even down to a time near our own, but even so he was a man, towards whom the master had duties higher and more imperious than those dictated by his own interests or those of the city.[4] The day would come when the pressure of this sentiment of the obligation of a master towards one whom circumstances had made subject to him would be so strong that it would bring about the slave's enfranchisement.[5] Enfranchisement multiplied in the last ages of the Roman Empire. Earlier on it was only a counsel and more rare. But this counsel was given very soon, or at least it corresponded to the implicit desire of the Christian spirit.

In any case, both masters and slaves were reminded from the commencement that they ought never to forget in their mutual relations that they are children of the same God, but to fulfil their reciprocal duties one to the other: careful service and submission on the one hand, and kindness on the other. St. Peter, it is true, exhorts the slaves of evil masters—doubtless pagan masters—to a higher virtue: "What glory is it if committing sin and being buffeted for it, you endure? But if doing well you suffer patiently, this is thankworthy before God." [6]

[4] "There are institutions the fruits of which are modified by the very fact that their spirit is improved. Slavery in the house of Pliny or in that of a Christian was similar only in name to slavery in the house of Epaphroditus or of Vedius Pollio. The legal position had not changed: the slave remained theoretically the property of his master, but for the former he was a possession that was prized and protected; he remained for the others a possession, which one used and enjoyed." (O. Lemarié, *Précis d'une sociologie,* Paris, 1933, pp. 91-2.)

[5] "How could the new conception fail eventually to react on the institution itself, to lessen its abuses, and finally to dissolve it? The breathing of a new spirit into a society renders all its rules flexible, and predisposes it to modify their tenor. This first reform, wholly moral, is in fine a change in the inmost recesses of individual wills. Morals are changed before laws" (*ibid.,* p. 92).

[6] *I Pet.,* ii, 20.

The Epistle to Philemon

We also see St. Paul intervening, with great delicacy, but also with a calm assurance of being heard, in order to obtain the pardon of a slave, Onesimus, who had fled from the house of his master Philemon, a Christian of Colossæ, and had taken refuge near the Apostle, who had converted him. "Perhaps," writes Paul, "Onesimus therefore departed for a season from thee, that thou mightest receive him again for ever, not now as a slave, but instead of a slave, a most dear brother, especially to me, but how much more to thee both in the flesh and in the Lord? . . . Trusting in thy obedience I have written to thee, knowing that thou wilt also do more than I say." [7]

That was an exceptional case, or at least one relatively rare. But the prestige which surrounded the little slave Blandina in the midst of the martyrs of Lyons, and as we shall see later, the sentiments of the Carthaginian matron Perpetua for her slave Felicitas[8] bear eloquent witness to the fact that the Church was unaware of any distinction between master and slave in spiritual matters. "Both received from her the same means of personal sanctification, saw opening before them the same possibility of ecclesiastical honours, and underwent the same penances for their sins." [9] The attitude of the Church towards slavery, like the exquisite and magistral note of St. Paul to Philemon, show what was in fact the powerful action of the Gospel which, regenerating men's souls and proclaiming the universal brotherhood of all men in Jesus Christ, created a new society without overturning social institutions.

This universalism is again one of the characteristics of the Christian conception. It was to extend to the whole world: it embraces all humanity, and the immense domain of the Roman Empire was itself transcended. The Church was made for all the earth, whence its name Catholic, which we find already in St. Ignatius[10] about the year 100.

[7] *Philemon*, i, 15-21.
[8] See Book III.
[9] Funk-Hemmer, *Histoire de l'Eglise*, Vol. I, p. 312.
[10] Ad *Smyrn.*, VIII, 2.

§5. THE PAGAN ATTITUDE TOWARDS CHRISTIANITY

Pagan Hostility

Such is the Christian ideal, in all its grandeur—an ideal evidently, and one which will not be realised by all those who aim at it. Christians, even at a time very close to the "primitive fervour," had their faults, and the earliest writings of Christian literature blame their weaknesses. Christians nevertheless gave to pagans an example of a life surpassing that which usually characterised nature left to itself, good enough for them to notice it, and either to admire it or else to be disturbed by it.

The Accusations by the Populace

"See how Christians love one another," they said; and on more than one occasion, when public calamities happened, they were able to see that Christian charity put itself at the service of all, whether believers, indifferent, or opponents. But principles of living in some respects so new, and which were in so great a contrast with the easy characteristics of current morality as well as contrary to the customs of social conformity, could not fail to lead to an unfavourable reaction on the part of pagan society.

Not only did political authority condemn Christians as men who did not worship the gods of the Empire, and the higher and cultivated classes tend to despise them as groups in which the lower classes predominated and in which culture and refinement were not preponderant, but also the mass of the people, in spite of their admiring wonder provoked by the spectacle of a superhuman charity or of unheard of heroism, suspected almost inevitably, those who followed a life apart, separated from the common religion, of faults and vices, and even of secret crimes, and from suspicion to belief and then on to accusation, the passage was easy.

Atheism, since Christians did not render the homage due by all to the gods of Rome; magic, since they celebrated ceremonies which were known little or not at all; and cannibalism, and by extension, child murder, arising perhaps out of a wrong idea people had of the communion in the Body of Christ; scandalous indecencies again, for that is a charge easily hurled against those whose lives one does not like; such were the current imputations, combined moreover with less dangerous criticisms affecting the cultural practices attributed to Christians through unexpected confusions, such as the supposed adoration of a god with an ass's head—an ancient calumny of which the Jews had been the first victims and which was now revived against the Christians.[1] Who has not heard of the famous *graffito* of the Palatine, a chance inscription traced perhaps at the beginning of the Antonine era, by a sorry jester and representing one crucified with an ass's head, accompanied by the words: "Alexamenos adores his god"? To which the Christian thus teased by a fellow disciple of the imperial pedagogium replies with this tranquil affirmation of his faith: "Alexamenos fidelis." [2]

The Prejudices of the Intellectuals

Educated people entertained less inexact ideas about Christianity. Even so we know only too well the readiness with which men and women of the world at all times will believe the most unlikely stories about people who profess ideas which do not square with their own.

But, apart from excessive partiality or credulity, the sentiment entertained on the whole in the high social circles in the Empire in the second century concerning the Christians, most of whom were of humble condition, in spite of the existence of converts from higher levels, and without any claim to intellectual elegance, was one of contempt, tempered sometimes with a little pity, sometimes also with astonishment, like that which Marcus Aurelius felt in view of their desire for martyrdom.[3]

The *literati*, orators or philosophers in high repute under the Antonines, many of whom attained to honours, a Herod

[1] On this, cf. P. de Labriolle, *La réaction paienne*, Paris, 1934, pp. 193-9, which gives more complete data on the question. Complementary indications in C. Cecchelli, *Noterelle sul cristianesimo africano* (Estratto dal volume 'Studi dedicati alla memoria di Paolo Ubaldi'; Pubblicazioni del' Universita cattolica del Sacro Cuore, Ser. V: Scienze storiche, Vol. XVI, Milan, 1937), pp. 197-9.
[2] This very precious relic is conserved in the Kircher Museum in Rome. Bibliography on the subject in *Dictionnaire d'archéologie chrétienne* of Dom Cabrol and Dom Leclercq, Vol. I, p. 2041 et seq.
[3] Marcus Aurelius, *Meditations*, XI, 3.

Atticus, a Fronto, a Claudius Severus, were also very ill disposed.

The polemic of Celsus, known to us by the refutation which Origen wrote of his pamphlet [4] in the next century, reflects in a way very instructive for posterity the complex sentiments entertained for a long time in the circles of imperial society with regard to Christians, sentiments in which a lack of understanding of the spiritual realities of the Christian life play a large part. Celsus especially criticises Christianity as being "a barbarous and absurd doctrine, suitable for people without culture," [5] and as finding most of its recruits from people of that kind.

Contempt on the part of the aristocracy of mind if not of birth certainly occupies a large place in this anti-Christian prejudice. To this is to be added that of the philosophers, for whom the Christian beliefs lower the Divinity, or are against reason. But Celsus also criticises Christians because "they separate themselves from other men, despise the law, customs, and culture of the society in which they live," [6] as also knowledge itself. Far from allowing that the improvement in individual morality is in the last analysis good for the State, he sees in the Christian "chimera" only a public danger, for it attacks on points regarded as vital the social edifice, and "the civilisation to which it remains deeply attached." [7] The numerous pagans who, animated with the same spirit as Celsus, continued to put the State, "the defender of the national traditions, and administrator of material goods, in the first place in their preoccupations" [8] could not agree with an affirmation of the superiority of the invisible world over the visible. Such a doctrine was to them unhealthy and even seditious.

It is not to be wondered at, then, that being thus in agreement with a public opinion inspired by mistrust, contempt, or open hostility, the severe legislation which denied to Christians the right to exist and held over their heads a constant threat of death maintained itself so long.

[4] *Contra Celsum.*
[5] P. de Labriolle, *La réaction païenne*, p. 112.
[6] *Ibid.*, p. 118.
[7] *Ibid.*, p. 168.
[8] *Ibid.*, p. 169.

§6. MARTYRDOM

The Frequency of Martyrdom

This explains also why Christians were always thinking of a possible martyrdom, and why we find among them a voluntary preparation for its calm or even joyful acceptance, and amongst many a positive desire for it. These characteristics constituted a definite feature of the life of the Church of the first centuries, and one which was none the less disconcerting to those outside, as it still is for many in our own day.

But in point of fact, during these two first centuries in which, by virtue of the principles of the Neronian decree as interpreted by Trajan, persecution was never more than temporary and sporadic, though in periods of greater frequency and length, martyrdom was not the lot of the majority of the disciples of Christ. Nero made a veritable massacre at Rome; the executions in Bithynia, in spite of the natural moderation and kindness of Pliny the Younger, made numerous victims, in proportion to the great number of conversions which had taken place in that region; apostasies were likewise not rare there. Lastly, the reign of Marcus Aurelius and the first years of Commodus undeniably constituted a particularly severe phase in the history of the development of Christianity, for in it we see hatred and severities increased against members of the Church in Asia, Greece, Italy, Gaul, and Africa. But apart from these critical moments, though the danger never ceased for Christ's faithful, surrounded as they were by an atmosphere of hatred or suspicion, and threatened by an implacable law, yet the passage from hostile intentions to acts which set the law in motion took place only occasionally.

The Number of the Martyrs

Were the martyrs in fact very numerous or not? This has been much discussed. For the first two centuries, when the Church lived under the sign of the Neronian *Non licet,* applied in the sense of Trajan's commentary, and did not suffer from general persecutions but only sporadic attacks many times repeated, the reply to the question is particularly difficult.

Out of the total number of martyrs attested by documents of relatively good standing, such as the *Hieronymian Martyrology,* it is not possible for us to say which ones belonged to these two centuries, for many of them are of unknown or uncertain date. The *Passions* which, for the most part, deal with martyrs appearing in the *Martyrology*, provide only a weak supplement for the historical information contained in the latter, as there is so much in them that has nothing to do with history.

On the other hand, it is at least to be supposed that everywhere there were some Christians who perished for the faith, from the time of Nero to that of Commodus, though their names have not come down to us. We may add that if we could count up all the martyrs, which would certainly be most helpful, this absolute figure would possess its complete significance only if it were accompanied by a relative figure, that is, if we could evaluate the proportion of the martyrs in relation to the total number of Christians. But this figure remains equally beyond our knowledge, and moreover it happily never ceased to vary, since we can affirm—and it is the only affirmation we can make here—that it was ever increasing.

Even so, very different estimates have been given. There is evidently a strong dose of rhetoric in the oft quoted passage in the *Apologeticus* of Tertullian: [1] "We are of yesterday, and we fill your cities, your islands, fortified towns, country towns, centres of meeting, camps, tribes, classes of public attendants, the palace, the Senate, the forum; we leave you only the Temples. If we were to withdraw from amongst you, you would be aghast at your solitude." To this has been opposed another statement, made later by Origen, who seems to say that Christians were very insignificant in the midst of the tens of millions of men who peopled the Empire, πάνυ ὀλίγοι. [2]

We also get the impression, when reading the history of the martyrs of Lyons, for instance, of a little flock lost in a great hostile multitude. But how many of the Christians of Lyons were seized by the authorities and sent to their death? The Church of Lyons continued to exist, for it shortly afterwards addressed letters to those in Rome and Asia; a new bishop, Irenæus, took over its government, and the Christian life continued in the capital of the Gauls. It had therefore taken deeper and wider root there than one would be tempted to infer from the account of the persecution.

Moreover, the same Origen who wrote πάνυ ὀλίγοι also uses

[1] 37.
[2] *Contra Celsum,* VIII, 69.

in another place in the same treatise *Contra Celsum,* the contrary expression, οὐκ ὀλίγοι [3] and Tacitus had already called the Christians of Rome *multitudo ingens.*[4] The singularly rapid progress of Christianity in some regions, as in at least a part of the Asiatic provinces, cannot be doubted, since unbiased pagans such as Pliny the Younger testified to it,[5] and the declarations of Tertullian himself in his *Apologeticus* would have seemed to his readers somewhat of a mockery if the Christians in the western provinces of which he spoke from experience, namely, Italy and Africa, had been only a handful of men.

But the martyrs? We have seen that they shed their blood in all the countries of the Empire, intermittently, without doubt, sometimes in this place only, sometimes in that. At the same time, every imperial kingdom, or almost every one, and every province had its own. And at times, as under Marcus Aurelius, we find some in so many different places that we might almost think that there was then a generalised persecution, even though this was not really the case. All these groups of distinct martyrs together form a total which demands respect.

Besides, it is no mere conjecture that there were also a number, perhaps a large number, of unknown victims. What liturgical, literary or lapidary text has conserved the name of a single one of the martyrs of Bithynia under Trajan? "How many times already has an archeologist not deciphered on a piece of marble sticking in the earth the names of martyrs that no parchment has conserved?"[6] De Rossi wrote sixty years ago: "The more I continue the study of history and of the monuments of the centuries of persecution, the more I am persuaded that the number is very great of martyrs whose names have not come down to us, and whose anniversaries are not indicated even in the rich and ancient compilation of the *Hieronymian Martyrology.*"[7] The ancient inscriptions themselves allude to these anonymous heroes, whose names are known to God, *quorum nomina Deus scit.*

Lastly, this strong sentiment of expectant martyrdom, in

---

[3] I, 26.
[4] Cf. *supra,* p. 65.
[5] Cf. *supra,* pp. 85-86.
[6] Paul Allard, *Histoire des persécutions pendant les deux premiers siècles,* 3rd edn., Paris, 1903, p. 477.
[7] *Bollettino di archeologia cristiana,* 1875, p. 179.

which the Christian generations of the first centuries lived, could be explained only if the threat of death, following on denunciations which were at all time possible, had not only overshadowed them but also had over and over again been realised. This is perhaps the most decisive argument in favour of the thesis of the great number of the martyrs, that is, of a relatively very high proportion of Christians compelled to choose between confessing Christ and saving their lives. And that before this terrible choice, confessors were in a great majority over apostates, is a natural inference from accounts such as the Letter of the Church of Lyons on the persecution of 177. The letter of Pliny to Trajan certainly gives a different impression; without saying anything precise as to the respective number of the fearless and the weak amongst the crowd of accused persons brought before his tribunal, he says explicitly that he had succeeded in persuading many to return to the ancient religion, though this does not prevent him from expressing regret at the number of condemnations, still too numerous in his view, which he had had to pronounce. We may believe that the proportion of apostasies in the course of the first centuries and in the various parts of the Roman Empire was so much the higher as the Christian community put to the test was itself more numerous; there is generally more active energy and persevering courage in minorities.

§7. THE VOLUNTARY EFFACEMENT OF CHRISTIANS

Christians Compelled to Lead a Retired Life by Pagan Hostility

The constant threat under which they lived during the first centuries certainly had its effect in the voluntary partial withdrawal of Christians from the social life of the time. Causes and effects then, as often, reacted on one another.

Cut off by their beliefs and the precepts they obeyed from a certain number of practices inseparable from public or private life, the Christians appeared to be suspect; this suspicion involved their condemnation by public opinion and the law; this condemnation ended by relegating them to the borders of Society, for sometimes it caused their expulsion, as we see in the popular movements which expelled them from public places, and at others they themselves sought to separate and withdraw themselves from inquiries or dangerous curiosity.

Nevertheless Christians Were Still Found Everywhere

Yet that is only one aspect of things, which may have seemed more striking at certain moments. The reality is often more complex and more resilient than the principles which seem to govern it; and we should be mistaken were we to picture the Christians as reduced to live like hunted animals, and the pagans as always ready to fall upon them.

If Christians were found even close to the throne, in the Palace and the Senate, amongst the representatives of the most prominent families and amongst the philosophers who taught in the Forum, such as the Flavian princes, Apollonius, Justin, and many others, the periods of respite for the various groups of faithful must have lasted for some time, and further, it is clear not only that people did not on every occasion seek for an opportunity to denounce them, but also that the authorities themselves, knowing over and over again the position of various individuals, intentionally shut their eyes to this.

This *de facto* toleration was accompanied by attitudes which were the exact opposite of a lack of interest in Society and public matters. If Apollonius sat in the Senate, if Justin argued in the Forum, and if other disciples of Christ sat in the municipal curiæ, they evidently did not live as strangers to their city and their times. The statement of Tertullian as to the presence of Christians in all the spheres of general activity thus seems to be confirmed by a certain number of facts.

It remains true, nevertheless, that the rigour of the laws, the hostility of the crowds, or the sarcasms of the upper classes were constantly directed against men whose religion, which admitted no compromise on its doctrine and morality, kept them apart from their fellow citizens. In presence of the ever-threatening danger of an outburst of hatred and violence, and in spite of the acceptance in advance of marytrdom, which the most ardent went so far as to desire, but which the religious authority would not allow to be voluntarily brought about by provocative acts capable of leading to an unhappy increase in official measures against Christianity, it was necessary, if not always to dissimulate, at least not to advertise oneself. In particular, for reasons also of reverence towards the sacred mysteries, it became the custom not to celebrate religious services except when free from indiscreet curiosity.

§8. THE CATACOMBS

Christian Worship in Private

Thus is explained the organisation by Christians of a part of their existence, at least in some places, away from the light, which they must nevertheless have loved like other men. They consented to spend underground the time they devoted to honouring God, so as to keep to themselves, and in periods of greater danger they spent more time there. But we must avoid a serious misunderstanding here: the usage made by Christians of catacombs at Rome and several other places, at Naples,[1] and Sicily,[2] in Tuscany,[3] in Africa,[4] at Alexandria,[5] and in Asia Minor[6] was not at first due to a care for personal safety on the part of people who no longer dared to live in daylight, and it was only progressively that such use became frequent at Rome, if not almost habitual in times of crisis.

Christians had used private houses as their first places of worship, and apart from exceptional cases they were able to continue peacefully until the time of the great persecutions. The fairly numerous conversions among the aristocracy, particularly in Rome, resulted relatively quickly in their putting at the disposition of the Church some of their great houses

[1] The catacombs of Naples are among the largest which have been explored, after those of Rome. There are those of St. Vitus, St. Gaudiosus, St. Severus, St. Euphebus, and St. Januarius. In the last mentioned, in addition to numerous inscriptions, paintings have been discovered some of which go back perhaps to the second century. Cf. Schultze, *Die Katakomben von S. Gennaro,* Jena, 1877, and *Bollettino di archeologia cristiana,* 1871, pp. 37-8 and 155-8, the account of the latest excavations by A. Bellucci, *Atti del III Congresso internazionale di Archeologia cristiana,* Rome, 1934, p. 327 *et seq.,* and above all H. Achelis, *Die Katakomben von Neapel,* Leipzig, 1936.

[2] Chiefly at Syracuse, where the catacombs are still more extensive than those of Naples.

[3] Cf. the nomenclature of the Italian catacombs other than those of Rome, in the *Dictionnaire d'archéologie chrétienne,* Vol. II, 1910, col. 2443-5.

[4] On the catacombs of Hadrumtemum, cf. *supra,* p. 58, n. 26.

[5] *Dictionnaire d'archéologie chrétienne,* Vol. II, col. 2442-3.

[6] *Ibid.,* col. 2442.

which, with the atrium, peristyle and long chamber called the tablinum, lent themselves very well to the carrying out of the Christian rites. Penitents could there be separated, as well as catechumens from the faithful; if it was thought desirable, one side could be reserved for men and another for women, and the clergy could be installed in the *alæ* or wings. The use of private houses as places of worship lasted until after the second century, but other places were then also utilised.

The Origin of Catacombs as Cemeteries

The Christian catacombs, which go back to the beginnings of the Church, were not always used for this purpose of worship. They were at first cemeteries.

Christians, who like the Jews always buried their dead and did not cremate them, had two kinds of cemeteries: those in the open air, usually in the East and in Africa, and subterranean cemeteries, which are found above all in the other Western provinces; these were given the name of crypts, *hypogea* or catacombs. This last term, used especially for underground cemeteries of Rome, which were by far the largest of all, originated in one of them, situated in the neighbourhood of the actual Church of St. Sebastian, a few miles to the south-east of Rome, near to a depression in the ground which had caused it to be named in the Greek language, the official language of the Roman Church until the end of the second century, κατὰ κύμβην, that is, in Latin, *ad catacumbas*. This underground cemetery "of the catacomb" was the only one opened in the Middle Ages, and its name was extended to all the others when these began to be rediscovered in the period that opens with the fifteenth century.[7]

[7] The first methodic explorer of the catacombs in modern times was Bosio, in the seventeenth century. His researches were continued in the second half of the nineteenth century by J. B. de Rossi, whose *Roma Sotterranea cristiana* (2 vols. and 2 vols. of plates, Rome, 1864-7) is still the chief work on the Roman catacombs. An abridged adaptation was published in English by J. Spencer Northcote and W. B. Brownlow in 1879. More recently, several volumes of popular information on the catacombs have been published: A. Perate, *L'Archéologie chrétienne* (the study of the Catacombs forms only a part of this), Paris, 1892; M. Besnier, *Les catacombes de Rome*, Paris, 1909; H. Chéramy, *Les catacombes romaines,* Paris, 1932; J. P. Kirsch, *Le catacombe romane,* Rome, 1933. The important works of Mgr. Wilpert on the paintings in the catacombs and on the sarcophagi, a certain

The usage of underground cemeteries was not peculiar to Christians. The Egyptians and Phœnicians had already adopted it, and they had been copied by the Jews. In Italy, the Etruscans, whose eastern origin seems to be more and more clear, had left not far away from Rome numerous necropolises which in their deep caves and neatly hewn passages resembled small catacombs. Lastly, in Rome itself, where the practice of cremation was neither primitive nor general, and where certain families had retained or returned to the practice of burial, there existed some sepulchres which recalled on a smaller scale those of the East; such was the tomb of the Scipios. And the Jews, a large colony of whom had settled in Rome even before the Empire, also had underground burial places which were still more important.

It is not surprising that the Christians of Rome, whose first nucleus had been recruited from amongst the Jews, followed the same usages, and that those of Campania or Sicily did the same. But the Christian catacombs, especially at Naples, Syracuse and Rome, speedily attained to a much greater extension: in Rome, or rather round about it, for the ancient cemeteries were outside the cities, there was a veritable underground city, *Roma sotterranea,* which gradually grew larger, a city of the dead which began at the walls of the living city, and extended away into the country to limits which we shall probably never know completely.

This extraordinary extension is explained both by the state of the Christians and by their faith. Christians, who believed firmly in the resurrection, had learnt from St. Paul that the body which is to rise again will be a spiritual body, compared to which the body of our earthly life is, as he himself says, like the seed as compared with the future plant. But nevertheless they had a profound respect for the remains of the dead. Such was the origin of the cult of relics, as also of the custom of going to pray near the dead, to meet at their tombs, and even to celebrate a sacred repast there. This was, it is true, merely the continuance of the pagan rite of the funeral banquet, which also implied a belief in another life. Thus Chris-

---

number of which belong to them, are mentioned in the bibliography to this chapter.

Several reviews in various languages published by the different national groups of Friends of the Catacombs give information nowadays on the discoveries and researches which are always being made in the catacombs of Rome and other places.

tians possessed a first motive for frequenting their cemeteries, namely, to meet together there and celebrate rites.

The Catacombs become Places of Worship

The insecurity in which they lived, which was at least relative, and sometimes terrible, provided them with another. The friendly houses in which they met in the first period to celebrate divine service doubtless ensured a secrecy which seemed sufficient at first, and also safeguarded those taking part. But though respect for private property was great in Rome, it had to give way to the requests of the public authority. Arrests could be made even in private dwellings.

Amongst the private properties, some were especially sacred, namely, the burial properties. The respect with which Roman law surrounded the dead has received a new proof in the rescript of Augustus, reproduced in a Palestinian inscription recently published,[8] which lays down very severe penalties against the violators of tombs. Now, tombs were, at Rome and many other places at the beginning of Christian history, family properties: great families put their funeral grounds at the disposition of their brethren. The latter knew that not only would their dead be free from profanation there, but also that they themselves would, so to speak, be protected there by the dead. Thus when the Christians descended into the catacombs to celebrate their religious rites, this was not at first in order to hide themselves, although the catacombs provided a material shelter, but it was both to honour their dead and to put themselves under their protection, which their sepulchres legally offered them, as a moral rather than a material shelter.

Development of the Catacombs

Hence the great development of the catacombs, which soon underwent a tremendous extension.

Their use must have begun from the very first days of Roman Christianity, if we are to believe the tradition according to which St. Peter himself exercised his ministry in the Ostrian cemetery, near the present Church of St. Agnes outside the Walls, on the Via Nomentana.[9] We may, it is true,

---

[8] Cf. Lebreton and Zeiller, Bk. I, ch. 4, § 2, n. 27.
[9] Tradition transmitted in a fourth century *Passion*, the *Acta Marcelli*.

wonder whether, before they were disturbed, the Christians really adopted the cemeteries as meeting places. But even if the words of Peter did not resound in its galleries, the Ostrian cemetery is undeniably very ancient. The neighbouring catacomb, that of St. Priscilla, on the Via Salaria, the origins of which are linked with the mausoleum of the Acilii Glabriones, likewise goes back to the earliest Christian times.[10]

But others again have a no less venerable past: the Vatican crypt, in which were buried not only St. Peter, but many of his successors down to the end of the second century; the cemetery of Commodilla, on the Ostian Way, in which St. Paul was buried; the cemetery called that of Domitilla, from Flavia Domitilla, niece of Domitian,[11] on the Via Ardeatina; the crypts of Lucina on the Appian Way, put perhaps at the disposition of the young Church by the illustrious convert made by her in the time of Nero from among the high Roman aristocracy, Pomponia Græcina, and which were the starting point of the cemetery of Callistus, the official cemetery of the Roman Church in the third century, where numerous popes were buried. The cemetery of Prætextatus was utilised in the second century, and the body of a son of St. Felicitas, martyred under Marcus Aurelius, was placed there. Perhaps the first Christian tombs in the catacomb of St. Sebastian are not much less ancient.

§9. THE ART OF THE CATACOMBS

The Decoration of the Catacombs

Christians did not content themselves with depositing their dead in tombs, *loculi*, hollowed out from the walls of the long galleries of the catacombs, and framed sometimes in an arcade, *arcosolium*, under which a *mensa* or altar table enabled the Holy Sacrifice to be offered: the catacombs became veritable places of worship, and efforts were made to adorn them.

[10] The identification of the cemetery "where Peter baptized," *ubi Petrus baptizabat, ad nymphas sancti Petri*, with the very ancient catacomb of Priscilla, proposed by O. Marucchi, has not received much support. Cf. J. Zeiller, *A propos de l'inscription damasienne de Saint-Sebastien*, in *Bulletin des Amis des Catacombes romaines*, 1933, pp. 272-7.

[11] Cf. *supra*, pp. 76-77.

The paintings with which they were gradually covered count amongst the most precious sources of information left to us by Christian antiquity on the faith and religious life of the first ages of the Church.[1]

Purely Decorative Paintings

At first, these paintings were purely decorative. The pagans, Egyptians, and Greeks, Etruscans and Romans, decorated the underground chambers in which their dead rested. The Jews themselves, so opposed to pictorial ornamentation, set to work at Rome to enliven with paintings the caves of their catacombs. It seemed quite natural for Christians to do the same, and as the decorative motifs of the pagan tombs were much the same as those of their houses, so also was it at first with the Christians. The decorative artists of the houses of the great Roman families which created the first Christian cemeteries were called upon to decorate the catacombs, and they introduced there the then traditional motifs, inherited from Greek art, which we find in many houses at Pompeii, graceful and symmetrical lines, birds, flowers and vases, forming very pleasant wholes, but with nothing specifically Christian.

The same may be said of another kind of painting, full of interest moreover, and equally ancient, portraits and scenes from real life, such as the famous portrait of the fossor Diogenes, or a picture of the distribution of wheat to the people, executed in the catacomb of Domitilla for the college or corporation of the employés of the *annona,* that is, of the victualling service. In another part of the same cemetery we see the Tiber market, at the foot of the Aventine Hill, but also Christ and the Apostles, in one and the same decoration. Were the artists who executed these works Christians? We cannot say so definitely. But at any rate the inspiration which guided them was at least respectful towards the Christian faith.

Religious Paintings

The paintings of the catacombs soon manifested a more religious inspiration, and the Christian crypts began to reflect

[1] The chief work on the paintings in the catacombs is that by Mgr. Wilpert, *Die Malereien der Katakomben Roms.* We must also mention, concerning the origins of Christian art, W. Elliger, *Zur Entstehung und frühen Entwicklung der altchristlichen Bildskunst,* Leipzig, 1934.

the ideas of the first Chrstians: the religious art, truly original, which arose in the catacombs, came from the piety of
the faithful. But this piety, though deep and tender, remained for a long time discreet and, as it were, restrained;
during the first centuries it expressed itself only with a pious
and perhaps timid reserve and in a veiled manner; it ab-
stained from setting forth always clearly the mysteries with
which it dealt, and just as Christ had given a great part of
his teaching in the form of parables, which were in fact trans-
parent, so also it expressed itself by symbols, derived in part
from traditions anterior to Christianity.

It is thus that in the second century, and still more in the
third, Jesus was personified sometimes by the figure of the
Good Shepherd, carrying, like the Creophore Hermes, a lamb
on his shoulders, at other times by Orpheus, the ideal singer,
who had descended to the lower regions and had returned
thence. The lamb, who represented first of all the believer,
the soul saved by Christ and led to paradise, soon became the
divine victim, in accordance with the two evangelical symbols:
"Behold the Lamb of God," and "Feed my lambs" (*John* i,
20 and xxi, 15).

Another symbol is the *Orante,* a female figure which, with
its eye upturned towards heaven and its arms raised, seems
to implore mercy from God or to thank Him for His benefits;
its symbolises also the human soul praying or entering into
a blessed immortality, and it remains the most constant and
the most traditional representation.

Numerous other representations, always connected with
the work of salvation, were in use in the decoration of the
catacombs: some, still borrowed from pagan symbolism, like
the peacock, the emblem of immortality; the phœnix, the emblem of the resurrection; and the dove, the bird of the goddess of love but now the emblem either of the Holy Spirit or
else of the soul; others again ingenious Christian inventions:
the dolphin curled round a trident, a deliberate transformation of the cross or *Tau,* under which is also hidden the sign
of the Redemption; the fish, whose name in Greek with its
five letters forms the acrostic Jesus Christ, Son of God,
Saviour; and again the ship, a figure of the Church, and the
lighthouse which guides the ship to the harbour, and the
anchor, which expresses Christian hope.

Lastly, in addition to symbolic figures, Christian art very
soon shows traces of a veritable religious iconography. This

primitive art did not confine itself to the one theme of hope in the future life, as though it had the essentially funerary character which was wrongly attributed to it at first. "A more careful interpretation of the paintings in the Roman catacombs as a whole had modified this point of view. From the end of the second century, in the cemetery of Callistus, the Chamber of the Sacraments presents themes which funerary symbolism no longer suffices to explain: what are figured are the essential doctrines of Christianity. . . . Already in the second century the figures appear which are destined to become the very centre of religious iconography: that of Christ and that of the Virgin." [2] Christ here is no longer the Christianised Orpheus or the Good Shepherd of the allegorical paintings; in the cemetery of St. Prætextatus, in which we see him healing the woman with an issue of blood, He has the appearance of a young beardless man with curly hair, clothed in a tunic over which is thrown a pallium enveloping the left arm, leaving the right arm free, and with bare feet.

The figure of the Virgin is fixed equally early. "A celebrated painting in the cemetery of St. Priscilla, which may go back to the middle of the second century, shows the Virgin seated, carrying on her knees the Infant Jesus. . . . Before her a man standing up and draped in a pallium is drawing a star. This scene has been interpreted as a representation of the prophecy of Isaias (ix, 2), who compares the coming of the Messias to the rising of a star." [3]

Other themes in the decoration of the catacombs, directed also towards the religious instruction of the living rather than towards the solace or the commemoration of the souls of the dead, Biblical or evangelical episodes, or illustrations of sacramental doctrine, will become frequent, especially a little later on. But already in the end of the first century we can see in the gallery of the Flavians in the cemetery of Domitilla, Daniel in the den of lions, which we find again in the next century in the crypt of Lucina; and in the Capella Græca in the cemetery of Priscilla besides Daniel we have the history of Noel and the sacrifice of Abraham. The history of Adam and Eve painted on the vault of the vestibule of the cemetery of St. Januarius in Naples is of no less antiquity. The same is true of the baptism of Christ in the crypt of Lucina,

---

[2] L. Bréhier, *L'art chrétien*, 2nd edn., Paris, 1928, pp. 27 and 40.
[3] *Ibid.*, p. 40.

the resurrection of Lazarus in the Capella Græca, the meeting between Jesus and the Samaritan woman, and the healing of the woman with an issue of blood at St. Prætextatus; and the twofold miracle of the marriage at Cana and the multiplication of the loaves, prefiguring the Eucharist, in a catacomb at Alexandria.[4]

The Sarcophagi

Lastly although the reproduction of the human figure in stone was at first forbidden amongst Christians, as in Judaism, and because of a similar aversion for idolatry, the sarcophagi which were put in the underground caves of the catacombs were finally ornamented with bas reliefs. But the first examples of this Christian sculpture are not met with before the third century. Until then the Christians, reduced like all the world to utilising commercial models from pagan workshops, contented themselves with a plain ornamentation, usually of simple strigils. Very exceptionally they accepted sometimes an Orpheus or an Aaron, or even a Ulysses, attached to the mast of his vessel so as not to give way to the call of the sirens, in which we might see an allegory of the temptation.[5]

As for a Christian architecture, there was no question of such then, for the only places of worship were private houses or the catacombs.

§10. CHRISTIAN ECONOMY

The Contributions of the Faithful to the Material Life of the Church

During the first two centuries, the Church had for its upkeep only what the faithful put at her disposition. The Christian cemeteries remained private property, which their own-

[4] A German scholar, P. Styger, in a quite recent work, *Die römischen Katakomben,* Berlin, 1933, thinks it possible to give a much later date for a number of Christian cemeteries in Rome. These would go back only to the third, or more often only to the fourth century, and he thinks that many of their paintings, such as the Eucharistic Banquet, are only the representations of pagan scenes, without religious signification. But that seems to run counter to the evidence.

[5] Cf. J. Wilpert, *I sarcofagi cristiani antichi,* Vol. I, Rome, 1929, pp. 1*-2*.

ers opened to their brethren living or dead. There was as yet no ecclesiastical ownership of property. But we may suppose that it was not the same in the case of goods of other kinds and of money. From the first, the Christian communities had their charitable treasury, filled by the offerings of the faithful. The *Didache* and the *Didascalia* mention the custom, possibly peculiar to the East, of taking to the Church and putting into the hands of the bishop the first fruits of the harvest. The *Didascalia* speaks of tithes. This contribution, which was subsequently to become obligatory, was first of all vountary, and it does not seem to have been general even in the third century, much less in the second.

The End of the Second Century Marks the End of an Epoch in the History of the Church

But in the history of ecclesiastical property, as in that of the condition of Christians in the Roman Empire, the end of the second century is also the end of an epoch. The reign of the last of the Antonines was marked, for the first time since Nero, by an act of toleration towards the Church, although the previous legislation was not withdrawn. With the Severian dynasty, other initiatives will be taken, which will modify the regime to which the Church is subject. The relations between the Church, which does not cease to make progress, and the Empire, which goes through a deep internal crisis, will be different in the third century from what they were in the second.

Chapter 9

Christian Apologetics in the Second Century [1]

§1. THE ORIGINS OF CHRISTIAN APOLOGETICS

APOLOGETICS, understood in its widest sense, is as old as Christianity; from the first, those who came to preach the good news did their best to prove its truth and answer the objections made against it. Many of the discourses of Christ, especially those He pronounced at Jerusalem and which are reported by St. John, are apologetical; as also are those of St. Peter, St. Stephen, and St. Paul, which we read in the *Acts*. Amongst the writings of the apostolic age, the *Epistle of Barnabas* has a plainly apologetic character. But it was above all in the course of the second century that this class of literature developed, and this calls for a special study.

The Pagan Calumnies

The history of the persecutions suffices to make us realise the necessity of an apologetic effort. Christianity, spreading throughout the Empire, met everywhere with hostility, not only on the part of the authorities, but also that of public opinion. Already in the persecution under Nero, the Christians were regarded by the populace as wretched people who deserved the worst punishments. In the *Acts of St. Polycarp* we find the populace taking the initiative in the measures against the bishop; when he appeared, they called for his

[1] Bibliography. Editions: Dom Maran, 1742, edition reproduced in Migne's *Patrologia Græca*, VI; J. C. T. de Otto, *Corpus apologetarum christianorum sæculi secundi*, Jena, 1847-72, 9 vols. Literary studies: A. Puech, *Les Apologistes grecs du IIe siècle de notre ère*, Paris, 1912; A. Puech, *Histoire de la Littérature grecque chrétienne*, Paris, 1928, Vol. II, pp. 109-234. Theological studies: J. Tixeront, *La théologie anténicéenne*, Paris, 1905, pp. 221-46; J. Lebreton, *Histoire du Dogme de la Trinité*, Vol. II, Paris, 1928, pp. 395-516. Dictionaries: E. Goodspeed, *Index Apologeticus*, Leipzig, 1912. Bibliographical indications special to each author will be given in the course of the chapter.

death; a similar spectacle took place at Lyons in 177. This hatred had its origin in the calumnies spread everywhere, and which for a long time were blindly believed.[2] The deadly and ever-present danger of denunciation compelled the Christians to hide themselves and to conceal from hostile eyes their meetings and their mysteries; but this very reserve caused mistrust; all kinds of suspicion were entertained about them. It was said that in the eucharistic supper a child was butchered in order to drink his blood, and that in the agapes they gave themselves up under cover of darkness to all sorts of disorders; even the terms "brothers" and "sisters" evoked in the pagan imagination the idea of incestuous unions. Minucius Felix in the first part of his *Octavius* sets out to reproduce these accusations, basing himself perhaps on Fronto; this indictment is too long to be given here in its entirety, but it will be useful to give some of its points. We must remember that the pagan into whose mouth Minucius puts his words belongs to the best Roman society and is speaking to Christian friends:

"How can we witness without pain the attacks against the gods made by this miserable, unlawful and fanatical faction? They collect from the scum of the populace ignorant and credulous folk and make them fellow-conspirators; in their nocturnal meetings, after solemn fasts and unnatural repasts, they bind themselves together, not by an oath but by a sacrilege; they are a race which hides itself, and flies from the light, silent in public, loquacious in their retreats. . . . They recognise each other by secret signs, and love each other almost before knowing each other; they are united together by a religion of debauchery, they all call one another brother and sister. . . . It is said that by some unheard-of-folly they adore the head of a filthy animal (of an ass): a fine religion, and one well worthy of them! . . . Their rites of initiation are as detestable as they are known. A child covered with flour, to deceive the uninstructed, is presented to the one to be initiated; the latter, seeing only a floury mass, and thinking

[2] These calumnies, which are reproduced in all the literature of this period, have often been set forth, e.g., by H. Leclercq, article *Accusations contre les chrétiens,* in *Dictionnaire d'Archéologie chrétienne;* Harnack, *Mission und Ausbreitung,* pp. 513 et seq.

his blows harmless, strikes the unseen child and kills him. And then these wicked people greedily drink his blood; they unite themselves together by this sacrifice, and bind each other mutually to silence by complicity in this crime" (*Octavius,* VIII, 3).

These calumnies seem to us foolish as they are odious, but in the second century they were spread everywhere, even in the most cultivated circles, and there was no apologist who did not have to refute them.

Anti-Christian Literature

The pagan literature of the second century enables us to follow the progess of this anti-Christian propaganda; by contrast it marks the stages of the Christian conquest penetrating gradually all the classes of greco-roman society and there encountering an opposition which became more violent every day. The Christian Church in its beginnings was recruited above all from the lower classes: "See your vocation, brethren, that there are not many wise according to the flesh, not many mighty, not many noble" (*I Cor.* i, 26). The little flock kept this appearance for a long time; at the end of the second century again, Christians recognised it and pagans urged it against them.[3] Nevertheless from this date educated circles had been reached by Christian propaganda: this penetration became evident in the reign of Hadrian, and much more so in the second half of the second century.

Pagan literature, which had long adopted a contemptuous attitude, began then to be alarmed: we find about 120 references in Epictetus, then in Marcus Aurelius, Galen, and Aelius Aristides.[4] From the reign of Marcus Aurelius we get organised attacks: that of Fronto, the tutor to the emperor;[5] in 167 Lucian published his *Peregrinus,* in which he attacked mainly the Cynics, but also the Christians;[6] about 178 Celsus

---

[3] Minucius, *Octavius,* V. viii, xii; Celsus, *apud* Origen, I, 27; III, 18, 44; VIII, 75.
[4] Cf. Harnack, *Mission,* pp. 254 *et seq.,* 517; P. de Labriolle, *La réaction paienne, Etude sur la polémique antichrétienne du Ier au VIe siècle,* Paris, 1934.
[5] Cf. P. de Labriolle, *op. cit.,* pp. 87-94.
[6] Cf. Zahn, *Ignatius,* pp. 517-28.

composed his *True Discourse;* [7] and all these writers were only the advance guard; behind them the historian sees an army of controversialists: Porphyry, Hierocles, Julian, and hosts of others. The fight continued without respite: it is still going on around us.

Against all these calumnies and attacks, Christians had to defend themselves; they felt the fearful weight of public opinion against them, but they felt also the tremendous force of a pure doctrine and a holy life. And they did not confine themselves to defence; they attacked the immorality and the superstitions of the pagans.

Jewish Apologists and Pagan Controversialists

In this task they had had forerunners; the Jews first of all who had also defended monotheism and attacked idolatry. [8] Amongst the pagans themselves the apologists could find many criticisms of idolatry and superstitions, to be utilised in their polemic. [9] Thus this polemic is the least original and least solid part in the work of the apologists; but on the contrary, their defence of Christianity is directly based on life; this is what gives it its persuasive force and, to a historian, constitutes the value of its testimony. The first Christian writers felt that they were despised by the educated world around them; but they were aware that they possessed a force which was worth more than all literature, namely, life. "Non eloquimur magna, sed vivimus." [10]

[7] The work has perished, but we find in Origen the whole process of reasoning, and even a great part of the text of Celsus. Cf. on Celsus P. de Labriolle, *op. cit.,* pp. 111-169. On this conflict between the apologists and educated people, cf. *Histoire du Dogme de la Trinité,* Vol. II, pp. 396-400.
[8] Cf. M. Friedlander, *Geschichte der Jüd. Apologetik als Vorgeschichte des Christentums,* Zurich, 1903; in this very full work the most interesting features are taken from Philo and Josephus; for instance, p. 289, Philo, *De Cherubim;* pp. 154 *et seq.*: the contrast between the religious festivals of the Jews and those of the pagans.
[9] J. Geffcken devoted himself especially to seek out these pagan sources in the work he has written on Aristides and Athenagoras: *Zwei griech. Apologeten,* Leipzig, 1907; a learned study, but marred by the author's antipathy against the Christian apologists.
[10] These words are from Minucius Felix (*Octav.,* XXXVIII, 6); they were repeated by St. Cyprian, *De bono patientiæ,* III.

Apologetic of the Martyrs

The martyrs, when called to appear before their judges, endeavoured always to defend before them the cause for which they were to die. Jesus Himself had done the same before Pilate, Stephen before the Sanhedrin, and Paul before Festus; the *Acts* of the martyrs show that these great examples were duly followed. But this apologetic, powerful because of the testimony which guaranteed it, could scarcely be developed: the judge usually cut short these words of the prisoner[11] and moreover circumstances did not permit long speeches. It was therefore opportune and even necessary to compose works which could make known to well disposed pagans the Christian life and teaching. These expositions are of great value for the historian: he finds, for instance, in Aristides, in the *Letter to Diognetus,* or the *Apology* of Justin, excellent descriptions of Christian customs; Justin introduces him into the intimacy of liturgical assemblies, and there he is able to follow all the ceremonies of baptism and the Eucharist.[12] The sincerity of these pages is evident. At the same time, the desire to gain attention and sympathy is not without danger, especially in the exposition of the Christian doctrine: in order to render it, if not acceptable, at least intelligible to the pagans, there will occasionally be a temptation to modify it somewhat; we know how in Josephus the desire to defend Judaism in pagan eyes led more than once to altering its sense, by transforming the Pharisees into Stoics, the Sadducees into Epicureans, etc. The Christian apologists were more circumspect and more sincere, but they were exposed to the same danger, and the historian must bear this in mind.[13]

The Apologies, Their Destination and Their Object

Several of these apologies are addressed to the emperors; it certainly seems that this was not a mere conventional

[11] Thus in the *Acts* of Justin, the Scillitan martyrs, etc., Apollonius had a certain amount of freedom to expound his belief, and he profited by it; but he was a Roman senator, interrogated by the prætor, and treated by him with consideration which ordinary Christians did not receive.

[12] These descriptions of the Christian liturgy have been reproduced and studied above, pp. 164 *et seq.*

[13] Cf. *infra,* p. 267, and *Histoire du Dogme de la Trinité,* Vol. II, pp. 400 *et seq.*

formula, but that the writers of these books had in fact a hope, which may indeed seem chimerical to us, to be read by the emperors, to gain their attention and even their sympathy for Christianity. This desire enables us to understand the effort made by Justin above all in his second Apology, to set forth in Stoic language the Christian theology of the Word, and to make himself thus the more easily understood by the Emperor Marcus Aurelius; [14] hence also in the apology of Athenagoras the delicate flatteries addressed to Marcus Aurelius and Commodus; [15] these first apologists did not adopt towards the emperors the attitude of Tertullian; in the midst of persecution they believed in the reconciliation of Church and Empire, and worked for it.

Nevertheless, though this official audience was really in view, it was above all the public in general that was to be enlightened. The apologists had come from its ranks, they knew its prejudices and also its miseries, they wished to help it to become Christian, and realised what light and power they could bring to it; that is why they lay so much stress on the holiness of Christian morals, and the moral transformation which comes from Christianity.[16] In this great pagan populace, apologists after Justin single out the philosophic and educated public, and endeavour to reach it. They themselves have so long and so laboriously sought for religious

---

[14] Cf. *Histoire du Dogme de la Trinité*, Vol. II, p. 437 and note 2.

[15] Cf. Puech, *Les apologistes grecs*, p. 5: "When Justin asked the emperors to give the official stamp to his Apology (II, 14), he did not think in his simple mind that such a request was absolutely chimerical, however bold it may have seemed. . . . Why should Athenagoras have multiplied as he did his delicate flatteries of Marcus Aurelius and Commodus, and why should he have insisted on their justice, their enlightened mind, their philosophy, if he had not had some hope of being read, if not by them, at least by some of the magistrates who persecuted in their name? For such dreams to be abandoned, and for Tertullian to write that the very idea of a Christian Cæsar or of an imperial Christian was an absurdity (*Apol.*, XXI, 24), a progressive disillusionment was required. Not Quadratus or Aristides, not Justin or Athenagoras could have given that trenchant statement of an inexorable conflict; however dark may have been the horizon in their day, their ideas were less proud and more confident."

[16] Just, *Apol.*, I, xiv, 2; *Aristides*, XV, xvii; *Athenagoras*, XI, xxxiii; *Theophilus*, III, ix-xv; *Minucius Felix*, xxxviii; *Diognetus*, vi.

truth; now they have passed from darkness to this wonderful light; they are aware that they possess a truth which the most exalted minds around them had sought but had failed to find; they realise through their personal experience how precious and indispensable this revelation would be to so many troubled minds, and they set it forth to them. This presentation may sometimes seem somewhat clumsy, but too much will not be made of this: it is not the talent of the writer which constitutes the value of these works, but the moral value of the witness; from this standpoint most of them[17] still draw the attention of the reader and please him.

Quadratus

The earliest apologist we know of is Quadratus. He addressed an *Apology* to Hadrian (117-38); we possess of it only a fragment of a few lines, transmitted to us by Eusebius.[18]

Aristides

In the same chapter, Eusebius[19] mentions an apology by Aristides. This work, addressed to Antoninus,[20] was long unknown; it has been rediscovered, in whole or in part, first in

---

[17] All of course are not on the same level: one cannot compare Justin with his pupil Tatian, whose defection followed so soon after his *Apology*, which already contained indications of it; but Tatian is an exception in this group of early apologists; the others, so far as we know, remained faithful to the Church.

[18] *Hist. Eccles.*, IV, iii, 2: "The works of our Saviour have always lasted, for they were real: the sick He cured and the dead He raised were not seen merely on the day of their cure or resurrection, but also subsequently; they continued to live during the earthly life of the Saviour, and even after his death they lived a considerable time, so that some of them have continued until our own time."

[19] IV, iii, 3. Eusebius seems however not to have read it: he is mistaken in saying that it was addressed to Hadrian.

[20] Antoninus reigned from 138 to 161; in 147 he associated Marcus Aurelius in the government; the apology of Justin will be addressed to the two emperors; that of Aristides, addressed to Antoninus alone, is therefore previous to 147; this date is moreover confirmed by the description of the Christian life, which seems to indicate a relatively peaceful period, and also by the mention made (viii, 7) of great famines; this last fact seems a reference to the reign of Hadrian (cf. Spart., *Had.*, 21).

an Armenian translation, then in Syriac, and lastly in its
original text, in the Lives of SS. Barlaam and Joasaph, in
which a Byzantine hagiographer had inserted it.[21]

Aristides begins his work with an exposition of belief in
God; a high and pure theodicy, but one which stays on the
ground of natural philosophy.[22] Then, setting out to explain
the religious beliefs of humanity, he distinguishes four races
of men: the Greeks, the barbarians, the Jews and the Christians. This leads him to describe the Christian life, which he
does in a beautiful and affecting way: [23]

> "Christians are nearer than other people to the truth.
> For they know God and believe in Him, Creator of heaven
> and earth, in whom are all things and from whom are all
> things; who has no other god as companion; from whom
> they have received these commandments which they have
> graven in their minds and which they keep in the hope of
> the world to come.
>
> Because of that, they commit no adultery or fornication;
> they bear no false witness; they deny not the deposits they
> have received; they covet not that which is not theirs; they
> honour their father and mother; they do good to their
> neighbour, and when they judge they judge justly. They

[21] An Armenian fragment was discovered in 1878 by the Mechi-
tarists of Venice; the Syrian translation in 1889 by Rendel Harris
in the monastery of St. Catherine on Sinai; J. A. Robinson, associated with the publication of this Syrian text, recognised the
original in the Lives of Barlaam and Joasaph, ch. 26 and 27
(Migne, *P.G.*, XCVI, 1108-24); this Greek text had indeed been
fairly freely translated by the hagiographer; the comparison with
the Syriac reveals notable omissions in it. The *editio princeps,* by
Robinson and Harris, appeared in 1891 in *Texts and Studies,* I, 1,
Cambridge; 2nd edn. without change in 1892. Ed. Hennecke,
Texte und Untersuchungen, IV, 3, 1893; De Geffcken, 1907. A
fair-sized portion found in the Oxyrhynchus papyrus has enabled
the chief lacuna in the Greek text to be filled. This fragment was
published by H. J. M. Milne in *Journal of Theological Studies*
XXV (1923), pp. 73-7; it is translated above.
[22] This philosophy owes much to Stoicism, and also resembles
Philo closely.
[23] This picture, which the Syriac version contains in its entirety,
was shortened by the Greek hagiographer; the papyrus mentioned
above contains the whole of the Greek text except the first lines,
and confirms the testimony of the Syriac version.

adore no idols in human form; whatever they wish not that others do to them they do not to anyone; they eat no food offered to idols because it is impure.

Those who injure them they succour and make their friends; they do good to their enemies; their daughters are pure and are virgins, and avoid prostitution; the men abstain from all unlawful alliances and from all impurity; the women are similarly chaste, in the hope of the great reward in the next world; as for their slaves, if they have any, and their children, they persuade them to become Christians because of the love they have for them, and when they have joined them they call them simply brethren. They adore no strange gods; they are gentle, good, modest, sincere; they love one another; they do not despise the widow, they save the orphan, he who has gives without murmuring to him who has not. When they see strangers, they make them enter into their houses and rejoice at it, recognising them as true brethren, for they call brethren not those who are so according to the flesh, but those who are so according to the spirit.

When a poor man dies, if they know of it, they contribute according to their means to his funeral; if they learn that some are persecuted or put in prison or condemned for the name of Christ, they put their alms in common and send them what they need, and if possible they deliver them; and if there is a slave or a poor man (to be helped) they fast two or three days, and the food which they had prepared for themselves is sent to him, for they consider that they rejoice themselves just as they have been called to joy.[24]

They observe carefully the commandments of God, living holily and justly as the Lord God has instructed them; they give Him thanks every morning and at all hours, for all food and drink and all other goods. And if a pious man dies amongst them they rejoice, they give thanks, they pray for him, and they accompany him as if he were setting out on a journey. And if a child is born to one of them, they give thanks to God, and if the baby dies they give thanks still more for that he has departed without sin. And if a man dies in sin they weep as for one who is gone to receive his punishment.

[24] These two lines are lacking in the Syriac; Milne corrects κεκλησθαι into κεκλῆμένοι (art. cit., p. 76).

Such are, O king, their laws. What good things they should receive from God they ask from Him, and thus they go through this world until the end of time, because God has subjected all to them. Therefore they are grateful to Him; it is for them that the whole universe has been made, and the creation."

We have purposely translated this beautiful passage here; [25] it is a precious document. Doubtless it has not the literary charm of the *Epistle to Diognetus;* its style is without art, its composition loose and embarrassed; but beneath its somewhat awkward simplicity the Christian life appears pure and sincere, as the Christians made a point of practising it. Tending towards the great reward which God promises them in the other world, they strive to live here below without sin, in joy and gratitude towards God, and in charity towards man. This last feature is particularly striking: in this pagan world "without affection, without mercy" (*Rom.* i, 31), what a revelation and what an attraction is this spectacle of a life so full of affection and devotion! [26] Lastly, let us note its first lines: these reveal the source of this very holy life: if Christians live thus it is because they "know God and believe in Him." [27]

The Letter to Diognetus

To this early *Apology* we must join a document the date of which cannot be exactly determined, but which belongs without doubt to the end of the second century, or perhaps

[25] We have translated it from the Greek text of the papyrus; in more than one point the Syriac, which the translators have generally followed, glosses it fairly freely.

[26] But to realise this programme there had to be, especially in the rich, a wonderful fervour; if this enthusiasm died down, it was quickly felt that this duty of assistance was a heavy burden; it is this weakness which was condemned by Hermas, *Shepherd,* Parable ix, 20, 2.

[27] Cf. Puech, *Apologistes,* p. 43: "The best propaganda was the purity and charity of the primitive churches. The best apology was the depicting without rhetoric of these sweet and innocent virtues. We feel ourselves still very close to the apostolic age; we understand that primitive Christianity appears less as a new doctrine than as a new way of spiritual life, and a tremendous hope; and there is so little egotism in this way of speaking of oneself that Aristides succeeded in the most difficult thing in the world: the praise of oneself without surprising anyone."

to the beginning of the third: the *Letter to Diognetus*.[28] In order to answer the questions of his correspondent, Diognetus, the unknown author of this little work explains what Christianity is, what are its titles, and why it has appeared so late. The Christian life is described in a page which won the admiration of Renan[29] and of which Tillemont already praised the "magnificent and eloquent style." [30] In the construction of the work, with its parallel and antithetical members, we recognise the influence of St. Paul; [31] we find it still more in the exposition of God's plan, suffering for a long

[28] This epistle was found in one single manuscript, the *Argentoratensis*, 9, of the thirteenth or fourteenth century, burnt with the library of Strassburg on August 24th, 1870. It was put under the name of Justin, together with the *Discourse to the Greeks*. There is a lacuna at the end of chapter 7 and at the end of chapter 10, in the conclusion; chapters 11 and 12 are not authentic. This opusculum is found in the editions of the Apostolic Fathers, or in collections of the apologists.

[29] *Marc-Aurèle*, p. 424. He who could not forgive Christians for having been persecuted by Marcus Aurelius sees nevertheless in the author "an eloquent anonymous but fairly good writer, who reminds us at times of Celsus and Lucian": two unexpected comparisons, which are made mainly for the sake of contrast. For the rest, Renan recovers himself very soon, and after transcribing chapters 5 and 6, he draws from them an argument against the Christians: "When a society of men takes up such an attitude in the midst of the great society, when it becomes in the State a republic apart, even if composed of angels, it is a plague . . ." (p. 428).

[30] *Mémoires*, II, p. 371. Cf. Puech, *Apologistes*, p. 255.

[31] See for instance ch. V: ". . . They (the Christians) live on earth, but are citizens of heaven. . . . They love everyone, and they are persecuted by everyone. They are despised and condemned and put to death, and this ensures their life. They are poor, and they enrich others. They lack all things, and superabound. They are covered with insults, and by insult they attain glory. They are calumniated, and a moment later they are proclaimed to be just. When harmed, they bless; they answer insult by respect. Doing only good, they are punished like malefactors; when punished they rejoice, as if life were bestowed on them. . . ." (Puech., p. 255). Cf. *II Cor.* vi, 9-10: ("We are regarded) as deceivers, and yet true; as unknown, and yet known; as dying, and behold we live; as chastised, and not killed; as sorrowful, yet always rejoicing; as needy, yet enriching many; as having nothing, and possessing all things."

time the injustice of men, and repairing it finally by the incarnation of His Son:

> "God . . . conceived a great and ineffable thought, and communicated it only to His Son. While He kept and hid His wise design in mystery, He seemed to forget and to neglect us. When He revealed by His beloved Son and discovered what He had prepared from the beginning, He gave us all things at the same time. . . . Having therefore disposed all things in Himself in union with His Son, He left us to walk as we wished until the present time, in a disordered manner, led on by our pleasures and our passions; not at all that He rejoiced at our faults, but because He bore with them; not that He took pleasure in times past, those times of injustice, but because He was preparing the present time, the time of justice, in order that, having been convinced in the past by our own works that we do not deserve life, we might be judged worthy of it now through the goodness of God, and that having shown that of ourselves we are incapable of entering into the Kingdom of God, we might become capable of it by the power of God. When our injustice was complete, and it had been conclusively proved that the reward in store for it was punishment and death, then came the moment which God had reserved in order to manifest His goodness and His power." [32]

We have here the reply of the apologist to one of the questions put by Diognetus: why did Christianity appear so late? What the author had said before (VII, 2) about the Word sent into the hearts of men seemed to prepare for another solution, that which Justin loved to develop: [33] our apologist has left it on one side, and to this difficult question he knows only the answer of St. Paul: "All have sinned, and do need the glory of God. Being justified freely by His grace, through the redemption that is in Christ Jesus. Whom God hath proposed to be a propitiation, through faith in His blood, to the shewing of His justice, for the remission of former sins, through the forbearance of God, for the shewing of His justice in this time, that He Himself may be just,

[32] Ch. viii and ix (Puech, p. 258).
[33] Cf. *infra*, p. 257.

and the justifier of him who is of the faith of Jesus Christ." [34]
This Paulinism is worthy of note in view of the circumstances and the date.[35]

We note on the other hand that, though the apologist
speaks of the incarnation of the Word, he does not name
Jesus Christ, and says nothing of His life, His miracles, His
passion and resurrection. This silence is not peculiar to our
author; most of the apologists follow a similar course, reserving doubtless to a later Christian instruction all the
Gospel teaching. St. Justin departs from this reserve: while
the other apologists stop on the threshold, he enters into the
sanctuary of faith and takes his reader with him; for this
reason and many others he deserves a specially careful study;
it is he above all who will show us not only by his teaching
but by the history of his conversion and by his martyrdom,
what could be the place and work of an apologist in the
second century.

§2. ST. JUSTIN [1]

Life of St. Justin

Of all the Greek apologists, St. Justin is by far the best
known. Quadratus and Aristides are nothing more than
names; Athenagoras and St. Theophilus do not appear much
in their works; Tatian is less in the shadow, but he is known

---

[34] *Rom.* iii, 23-26; cf. viii, 32; *Ephes.* i, 7; *I Tim.* ii, 6.

[35] We do not find it elsewhere in the group of apologists; and in
the second century, in the Catholic Church, we can hardly recognise this Pauline influence except in Irenæus. But it would be an
abuse of language to call the author of our epistle for this reason
"a Catholic Marcion," as has been done by Harnack, in his preface to his edition of the Apostolic Fathers, p. 152.

[1] Editions: Dom P. Maran, Paris, 1742, reproduced in Migne,
Patrologia Græca, VI; Otto, *Corpus apologetarum sæculi secundi,*
I-V, Jena, 1875-1881; L. Pautigny, *Justin, Apologies,* Paris, 1904;
G. Archambault, *Justin, Dialogue avec Tryphon,* Paris, 1909, 2
vols. Chief studies: A. Puech, *Les apologistes grecs.,* pp. 46-147;
Histoire de la littérature grecque chrétienne, Vol. II, pp. 131-70;
G. Bardy, art. *Justin* in *Dict. de Théol. Cath.,* especially cols.
2242-62; J. Lebreton, *Histoire du Dogme de la Trinité,* Vol. II,
pp. 405-84, and in Cayré, *Manual of Patrology,* Engl. tr., pp. 114
et seq. A more complete bibliography will be found in these
works.

as a restless spirit who after defending the Church became the leader of a sect. Justin on the contrary is revealed in his works; he crowned his life by martyrdom, and his confession is known to us by authentic *Acts;* his friends and disciples, especially St. Irenæus, have testified to his merits and helped us to appreciate his importance. Not only is Justin one of the best known Christians of the second century, but also his apologetic work is the most complete that this period has left to us: the two *Apologies* addressed to the emperors are completed by the *Dialogue with Trypho;* besides the controversy with the pagans we can study the controversy with the Jews, and see in this way not only another side of Christian apologetic, but also another point of view on Christianity.

"Justin, son of Priscos, son of Baccheios, of Flavia Neopolis in Palestinian Syria"; that is how he presents himself in the first line of his *Apology*. He was therefore born of pagan parents, in a pagan city, but in a country which retained many vestiges of its Jewish past, and many memories. Justin left Palestine and went to stay some time at Ephesus; that is where he places his dialogue with Trypho; he dates it in the time of the war of Bar Kokhba (132-5); he was then a Christian; his conversion thus goes back at the latest to about the year 130.

His Conversion

The motives of this conversion have been set forth by Justin himself: in the first pages of his *Dialogue* he narrates his philosophical Odyssey: pressed by the desire to know God, he put himself first of all in the school of a Stoic; but very soon he found that his master "knew nothing about God, and even maintained that this knowledge was not at all necessary." A Peripatetic gladly welcomed him, but very soon asked him for honoraria; a Pythagorean required as an indispensable preparation the study of music, astronomy and geometry. A Platonist who then came upon the scene, fascinated the young man: by considering incorporeal things and contemplating the ideas, Justin thought himself quite ready to attain to the vision of God. But one day when he was walking by the side of the sea, he met a mysterious old man who destroyed his illusions and showed him that the human soul cannot attain by its own powers to the contemplation of God, but that it must be led thereto by the prophets.

Clearly we must not regard this famous page as an autobiography: there is here, as in the recollections of Goethe, "poetry and truth," [2] all in it is not "truth," but also all is not "poetry"; the experiences of Justin are presented as an Odyssey through all the schools of philosophy in order to show their weakness, and to lead the reader to the Christian revelation. But the efforts made by the young Justin cannot be denied; this frequentation of the philosophers who had fascinated him for awhile had not left him merely with the memory of lost illusions; he understood, having once shared it, the enthusiasm of these philosophers, and especially of the Platonists, for the contemplation of the ideal world; he rejected their claim to attain to God by ecstasy, but he did not despise their aims or their endeavours.[3] From the first line of the *Dialogue*, Justin presents himself under their mantle; that is not a disguise, serving to draw to Christianity the Jew Trypho or others; Justin remains a philosopher, but the philosophy he professes has been learnt by him from Christ and the prophets, who in turn received it from God:

"That which we teach, after learning it from Christ and the prophets who preceded him, is the only true doctrine, and more ancient than that of all your writers, and if we ask you to accept it, it is not because it resembles the latter, but because it is true" (*Apol.*, I, xxiii, 1).

[2] This is the title which Zahn has given to his study of these chapters: *Dichtung und Wahrheit* in Justin's *Dialog.*, in *Zeitschrift für Kirchengesch.*, Vol. VIII, 1885-6, pp. 37-66.
[3] Engelhardt (*Das Christentum Justin des Martyrers*, Erlangen, 1878), and still more Aubé (*Saint Justin philosophe et martyr*, Paris, 1861) regarded Justin as a half-converted philosopher who continued to teach within the Church Platonist and Stoic speculations. This is most unfair to Justin. Without going so far as that, P. Pfættisch (*Der Einfluss Platos auf die Theologie Justins*, Paderborn, 1910) thinks that his theology was seriously affected by his Platonist formation; but this thesis also is an exaggerated one. Justin quite realised the fundamental lack of power in Platonism to elevate the soul to the contemplation of God, and the indispensable necessity of the Christian revelation in order to attain to it. It remains true that on some important questions such as those of the transcendence of God and the generation of the Word, he sometimes allows his theology, anxious to utilise Greek philosophy for apologetic ends, to be drawn on to the ground of his opponents. Cf. *Histoire du Dogme de la Trinité*, Vol. II, pp. 422-8, 449, 452-5.

The ascendancy of religious truth was revealed to Justin
not only by the theology of the prophets, but also by the life
of the Christians. This other aspect of his conversion and of
his apologetic is hidden in the *Dialogue*, but is brought out in
the *Apologies*:

> "I myself, when I was a disciple of Plato, hearing the
> accusations made against the Christians, and seeing them
> fearless in face of death and of what men dread, I said to
> myself that it was impossible that they should be spending
> their lives in sin and in the love of pleasure" (*Apol.*, II,
> xxii, 1).

These autobiographical fragments complete each other:
the *Apologies* show us Justin convinced by the sanctity of
Christian morals (*Apol.*, I, xiv), the *Dialogue* presents him
as persuaded by the divine truth of Christian doctrine. These
are the two great proofs which convinced him, and which he
utilises in his turn in order to convert the Jews and the
pagans.

St. Justin in Rome

Justin lived at Ephesus apparently for a fairly long time.
He went to Rome on two occasions, as he later on tells the
prefect of Rome in the interrogatory which preceded his
martyrdom; he lived "near to the Baths of Timotheus, with
a man named Martin." There he had his school; six of his
disciples were arrested and condemned at the same time as
himself, about 165, by the prefect Rusticus, their names were
Chariton, Carito, Evelpistus, Hierax, Pæon and Liberianus.
They were slaves, or poor people, and the school of Justin
was never so brilliant as that of Epictetus, or the conferences
of Plutarch; it had no such influence as that of Clement of
Alexandria or Origen. Yet it is of great interest to the church
historian; it throws some light on an important subject of
which we know little: the organisation of Christian teaching
in the second century.[4]

---

[4] Cf. Bardy, *L'Eglise et l'enseignement pendant les trois premiers
siècles*, in *Revue des sciences religieuses*, 1932, pp. 1-28: "The
Christian writers of the first three centuries rarely deal with these
problems, and leave us almost completely ignorant of the way in
which the children of Christian families were brought up and instructed," p. 1.

If this organisation was a slow process, this arose in great part from the character of Christian conversion: "Fiunt, non nascuntur christiani," wrote Tertullian. It was men already formed who came to the faith . . . those born in a believing family were rare, and also those who from their tender infancy received the seal of spiritual regeneration." [5] They were certainly rare, but not exceptional. In the interrogation of Justin's companions, Rusticus said to them: "Was it Justin who made you Christians?" Hierax answered: "I was already a Christian, and I will remain one"; Pæon said: "It was from our parents that we received this splendid profession of faith." Evelpistus replied: "I heard with pleasure the teaching of Justin, but it was from my parents that I also learnt to be a Christian."

These disciples were thus not catechumens; neither were they children: they were grown men who had received the Christian faith from their parents, and wanted to know it better. The instruction moreover was not reserved to Christians; it was offered to all: "to whomsoever was willing to come to me I communicated the doctrine of truth" (*Acts*, 3). Close to this house of Martin in which Justin lived, a Cynic philosopher named Crescentius likewise held a school. He was jealous of his neighbour the Christian master, and Justin expected to be denounced by him, as in fact happened.[6] Meanwhile he went on arguing: there was a public discussion between the two masters; the report of this had been kept, and in Justin's view it revealed the complete ignorance of Crescentius. The apologist asks the Emperors, if they have not seen the account of the debate, to have the latter renewed in their presence (*Apol.*, II, iii, 4). The challenge was not taken up, and the only testimony the Roman authorities were to receive from Justin was that of his blood.

The Schools of Rome

These incidents show how Christianity could then be taught, what were its fruits, and also what were its dangers. The latter did not terrify the Christians: in the midst of persecution, Hermas shows us the activity of the teachers in Rome; [7] in the middle of the second century Justin continued

[5] Bardy, *ibid.*
[6] *Apol.*, II, iii, 1; *Tatian*, xix.
[7] These *didascaloi* were mainly teachers of morals, or at least it was that part of their teaching which appealed to Hermas:

their work and extended it. His martyrdom did not destroy the teaching of Christian doctrine; Tatian, a disciple of Justin, continued it.[8] Very soon Tatian fell into heresy and left Rome; Rhodon, his disciple, carried on the teaching. He not only argued with the Marcionites: he also commented on the Hexaemeron and continued the exegetical researches begun by Tatian.[9]

The heretics also taught in Rome: the Marcionites had several schools there, in which divergent teaching was given: Apelles, who acknowledged only one divine principle, was opposed to Syneros who admitted three; [10] then the disciples of Noetus established themselves in Rome, first Epigonus and then his pupil Cleomenes.[11] These schools which sprang up on all sides show the interest aroused in the Church and outside it by theological problems. The bishop of Rome did not fail to interest himself in these matters: some Christians, desirous of following the teaching of Cleomenes, asked permission from Pope Zephyrinus to do so.[12]

It is difficult to determine the subject matter of this second-century teaching, and especially that of Justin. At Alexandria thirty or forty years later, Clement gave to his pupils an encyclopædic formation, and an introduction to all the sciences, sacred and profane. Origen adopted the same method, first at Alexandria and then at Cæsarea. There is no proof that Justin gave such fulness to his teaching, and it seems hardly likely. It is more probable that he directed all his efforts towards demonstrating and defending the Christian religion; apologetics aiming at converting the Pagans and

---

Mand., IV, iii, 1; cf. Vis., III, v, 1; Parables IX, xv, 14; IX, xvi, 5; IX, xxv, 2.

[8] Irenæus, Hær., I, xxviii, 1, quoted by Eusebius, Hist. Eccles., IV, xxix, 3.

[9] Hist. Eccles., V, xiii, 1-8. In this chapter Eusebius quotes some extracts from the polemic of Rhodon against Apelles; he adds (8, cf. 1) that Rhodon admitted that he had been a disciple of Tatian; he mentions a work of his master entitled Problems; it dealt with obscurities in the Scriptures. Rhodon promised to solve these problems. This chapter, in spite of its brevity, reveals the nature of Rhodon's teaching: controversy with heretics, and biblical exegesis. These will also be the chief preoccupations of Origen.

[10] Hist. Eccles., V, xiii.

[11] Hippolytus, Philosoph., IX, 7, ed. Wendland, p. 240.

[12] Hippolytus, loc. cit.

Jews, and controversy refuting the theses of the heretics, and in particular of Marcion. That is at any rate what we gather from the works of Justin, those which are still extant, those the titles of which are mentioned in ancient writers, and a few fragments. We shall examine this literature shortly, but we must stop a moment more at this little school. Justin was its first master, and he had sufficient influence around him to affect a disciple as independent and presumptuous as Tatian.[13] If we bear in mind again the veneration which a great theologian like Irenæus retained for the Roman master, we shall be careful not to despise the apologist-philosopher.

Works of Justin

We possess only three works of Justin of unquestioned authenticity: the two *Apologies* and the *Dialogue with Trypho*. These works have come down to us only in a single manuscript, which is very imperfect, and contains considerable gaps.[14] This very poor manuscript tradition shows the lack of attention paid for a long time to the antenicene apologists. The controversy which they carried on against the pagans and the Jews seemed pointless later on, and attention was turned by preference towards books with an explicit and richer theology.[15]

Fortunately, this single manuscript has conserved what is of greatest value to us,[16] the apologetic work of Justin. Here

[13] Cf. Puech, *Apologistes*, p. 149: "Those who are inclined to despise overmuch the Christian philosopher of Naplouse should not forget that one who was able to attract to himself a disciple like Tatian must certainly have played a fairly prominent part in Rome, and to have exercised a real influence in some circles."

[14] This is the *Parisinus*, gr. 450, completed on September 11th, 1364. The *Dialogue* should be preceded by a dedicatory letter to Marcus Pompeius and probably also by an introduction; both are lacking. In ch. lxxv there is lacking a fairly large portion, containing the end of the first book and the beginning of the second.

[15] On this manuscript tradition of the apologists, cf. A. Harnack, *Die Ueberlieferung der griech. Apologeten. Texte und Untersuchungen*, I, i (1883).

[16] Among the other works of Justin, he himself mentions (*Apol.*, I, xxvi, 8) a "Treatise against all the Heresies." St. Irenæus mentions (*Hær.*, VI, 2) a treatise against Marcion, which was perhaps only a part of the preceding work. The *Sacra Parallela* have conserved for us some fairly large fragments of a *Treatise on the Resurrection* (Migne, *P.G.*, VI, 1572-92). This work seems to be

we can study the most interesting and the most complete examples of the great effort of exposition and defence made by the Church in the second century: the *Dialogue* happily completes the *Apologies,* and shows us another aspect of the Christian demonstration.

In the manuscript, the three works present themselves in the following order: *Second Apology, First Apology, Dialogue.* Dom Maran (Paris, 1742) re-established the original order, and all later editors have followed him: [17] the two *Apologies,* or rather the single *Apology* composed of the book first written and of the appendix called the *Second Apology,* were written between 153 and 155.[18] The *Dialogue* is certainly later than the *Apology;* it seems prior to the death of Antoninus (161).[19] All this work thus belongs to the last years of the life of Justin. We find in it all the fruit of his teaching, and better still, the Christian apologetic as it was set forth in Rome towards the middle of the second century. We will now proceed to study this, without attempting to follow the books of Justin in detail.[20]

attributed to Justin by Methodius; it was probably utilised by Irenæus and Tertullian. Its authenticity appears, if not certain, at least quite probable. Bardenhewer (I, 228) regards it as quite certain; cf. Rauschen-Altaner, *op. cit.,* p. 75; Puech (*Littérature,* Vol. II, pp. 169-70) hesitates.

[17] This order cannot be doubted: the first *Apology* is quoted in the second (IV, 2; VI, 5; VIII, 1). For the rest, this second *Apology* is not a complete and independent work; it forms rather an appendix to the first: as something new became known to Justin, he decided to make use of it without rewriting his work.

[18] Christ was born 150 years previously (I, xlvi, 1); Marcion had already spread his error everywhere (I, xxvi, 5); Felix, the prefect of Egypt (I, xxix 2), was in office in September, 151, probably since 150, and until 154 (Grenfeld-Hunt, *Oxyrhynchus Papyri,* Vol. II, p. 163, cf. p. 175).

[19] The *Dialogue* (xii) mentions the *Apology* (I, xxvi). It seems from this passage that the emperors to whom the *Apology* was addressed were still alive.

[20] Justin's method of composition is rather loose; it is difficult to give an analysis of his books following out all their deviations. We may summarise them thus:

First Apology (cf. Veil, *Justinus des Phil. Rechtfertigung,* Strasburg, 1894):

I-III, Justin explains his object: to enlighten the emperors, to discharge his responsibility, and place it on them.

IV-XII: 1st part of Introduction: the procedure of the perse-

The Knowledge of God

Before his conversion, what Justin sought for everywhere, in all the philosophical sects, was the knowledge of God. When he became a Christian, he found this knowledge there,

cutors is wicked: they persecute a name (IV-V); Christians are neither atheists nor criminals (VI-VII); they allow themselves to be slain rather than deny their God (VIII); they refuse to adore idols (IX, XI); conclusion (XII).

XIII-LXVII: 2nd part: Exposition and Demonstration of Christianity. Christians adore God the Creator and Christ crucified (XIII); Christ is their Master; His moral precepts (XIV-XVII); the future life and the judgment (XVIII-XX); Christ is the Incarnate Word (XXI); comparison with pagan heroes (XXI-XXII); superiority of Christianity; hatred of men and devils (XXIII-XXVI); purity of Christian morals (XXVII-XXIX); Christianity proved by the prophecies (XXX-LIII); two digressions: freedom and the prophecies (XLIII-XLIV); philosophy considered as Christianity before Christ (XLVI); the similarities we notice between Christianity and the philosophies or pagan mysteries coming from the devils (LIV-LX); description of Christian worship: baptism (LXI); the Eucharist (LXV-LXVI); the Sunday liturgy (LXVII).

Second Apology: injustice of the prefect Urbinus (I-III). Why God allows these evils; providence, freedom, judgment (IV-XII).

The *Dialogue* is much longer than the two Apologies (Migne, *P.G.,* VI, 328-469; 472-800).

I-IX: Introduction: History of his philosophical formation and conversion; the knowledge of God; the immortality of the soul.

X-XXX: The Law. Trypho criticises Justin for not observing the Law. Reply: The prophets teach that the Law has been abrogated; it was given to the Jews only because of their hardness of heart; superiority of the Christian circumcision, necessary for the Jews themselves.

XXXI-CVIII: The Law given by Christ. Christ's two comings (XXXI); the Law a figure of Christ (XL-XLV); divinity and pre-existence of Christ proved especially by the theophanies (LVI-LXII); the Incarnation and virginal conception (LXV-); his death foretold (LXXXVI); his resurrection (CVI).

CVIII-end: Christians; the conversion of pagans foretold by the prophets (CIX-); Christians a more holy race than the Jews (CXIX); the subject of promises (CXXI); figured in the Old Testament (CXXXIV). Final exhortation for conversion (CXL).

and strove to possess it more fully and to give it to others. This must be our starting point in our study of his religious thought.

Of the philosophies he had passed through, only one had attracted him: Platonism. This had given him some idea of God, and had promised to reveal Him:

> "Plato said that the eye of the soul is thus made, and has been given us in order that we might, through its own transparency, contemplate that true Being who is the cause of all the intelligible beings, who has neither colour nor form, nor size, nor anything of what the eye perceives, but is a being beyond every essence, ineffable and inexpressible, but the solely beautiful and good, and who appears suddenly in well born souls because of an affinity of nature and a desire to see Him." (*Dial.*, IV).

We note first of all in this text a statement of the divine transcendence. This affirmation will always remain an essential element in Justin's theology. We see there also the bold claim of Platonism to attain to God by the sole powers of nature; this claim will be rejected by Justin as an illusion. He himself once entertained it,[21] but Christianity corrected him. This is the theme of the first chapters of the *Dialogue*.

If we wish to understand the strength and danger of these illusions, we may recall a few statements by contemporaries of Justin. Apuleius, for instance, says:

> "Plato . . . has often repeated that this one Being, by reason of the unbelievable and ineffable greatness of His majesty, cannot be grasped by any speech in any degree, so poor is human language; and that wise men themselves, when they have by great efforts separated themselves from their bodies as far as this is possible, conceive some idea of this God only as a flash of lightning, or the instantaneous bursting forth of a strong light in the midst of the deepest darkness." [22]

[21] "The intelligence of incorporeal things quite enraptured me; the contemplation of the ideas gave wings to my spirit, so that after a little while I thought I had become a wise man; I was even foolish enough to hope that I was going to see God immediately, for such is the aim of the philosophy of Plato" (*Dial.*, ii, 6).

[22] *De deo Socratis.*

"The sovereign Good cannot be explained, but as a result of much intercourse He becomes present to the soul, and suddenly as a spark from a fire, a light shines forth in the soul." [23]

What these philosophers sought for and promised was the vision of God, which was suddenly to shine forth in the soul like a flash of lightning illuminating the night. Such was also the pretension of the mystery religions, but in the mysteries it was the rites of initiation that illumined the initiate; the Platonists thought to arrive at the same result by the desire and energy of the soul. The soul, they said, can attain to this because it has a natural affinity with the Deity (*Dial.*, IV).

It is on this point that Christianity as interpreted by Justin is clearly opposed to Platonism: the human intellect cannot see God unless it is clothed with the Holy Ghost (*ibid.*, IV, 1).

It must be noted, moreover, that what Justin excludes from the natural powers of the soul is the vision of God, not all knowledge of God. The old man who converted Justin to Christianity said to him: "I agree with thee on this point, that souls can know that there is a God, and that justice and virtue are beautiful." (IV, 7).

But this knowledge does not suffice for our religious life: what this requires is to know God as one knows a person, not as one knows a science: "to know a man, or to know God, is not the same as to know music, arithmetic and astronomy"; one attains to these sciences "by study or by exercise"; one knows a person "only by seeing him" (III, 6).

But how can we see God? The Platonist philosophers claimed to lead us to ecstasy by the simple play of our natural powers. That is an illusion. Must we then renounce any personal knowledge of God, and consequently, any religious life?

Divine Revelation

This problem, which seemed insoluble, has been answered by God: He revealed Himself to the prophets, and the prophets have made Him known to us:

[23] *Apud Orig.*, VI, 3. The same hopes are set forth by Maximus of Tyre to whomsoever desires to rise to God: Conference XVII, 9-11; texts quoted in *Histoire du Dogme de la Trinité*, Vol. II, pp. 74-76.

"There were of old, in earlier times than those of these pretended philosophers, men who were happy, just, and dear to God, who spoke by the Holy Spirit, and uttered oracles concerning the future which are being fulfilled now; they are called prophets. . . . They did not speak with logical proofs; above all such proofs they were worthy witnesses of the truth; and past and present events compel belief in their word. Moreover, the wonders they worked gave them the right to be believed, since they glorified the Author of the universe as God and Father, and announced the Christ who comes from Him, His Son. That, the false prophets filled with the spirit of error and impurity have not done, and do not now; they have the audacity to perform wonders to fill men with amazement, and they glorify the spirits of error and the devils. But above all, pray that the gates of light may be opened to thee; for no one can see or understand if God and His Christ do not give him understanding" (*Dial.*, vii).

This important passage sums up the whole apologetic of Justin: it explains the function of prophecy and miracle, and above all of grace. But before studying more closely the preparation for faith, we must consider for a moment this theory of religious knowledge. It is the first time we find in Christian theology so clear an explanation of the difference which separates divine revelation from human speculation; Justin recognises, as he should, that the human mind can arrive by its natural powers at a knowledge of God; but he shows well that our religious life cannot feed on an abstract knowledge; man must enter into personal relations with God, and if he himself has neither seen nor heard Him, at least he must enter into contact with Him through the intermediary of those who are His witnesses, and the depositaries of His revelations.

This divine origin gives to Christian doctrine an authority which no other teaching can claim:

"That which we teach, after learning it from Christ and the prophets who preceded Him, is the only true doctrine, and more ancient than that of all your writers, and if we ask you to accept it, it is not because it resembles the latter, but because it is true." [24]

[24] *Apol.*, I, xxiii, 1. With these texts of the *Dialogue* and the

Christianity and Philosophy

These categorical affirmations express a very definite aspect of Justin's thought: if he himself has accepted Christianity, and if he presses his readers to accept it in their turn, it is not because Christianity can claim the patronage of philosophers, but because it comes from God, and because it is true in consequence. At the same time, he delights, especially in the *Apology,* to show that the philosophers often resemble Christians by their life, by the persecutions they have undergone, and even by the doctrine they have professed:

"Those who have lived according to the logos are Christians, even though they have been regarded as atheists: such were among the Greeks, Socrates, Heraclitus and their like; amongst the barbarians, Abraham, Ananias, Azarias, Misael, and many others whose names and actions we know, but it would take too long to recall here" (*Apol.,* I, xlvi, 3).

To explain this propagation of Christian principles within paganism, Justin points out first of all that the Word of God enlightens all men.[25] All share in the truth which He teaches; but the Christians alone possess it in its fulness; hence the transcendence of their doctrine:

"Our doctrine surpasses every human doctrine, because we have the whole of the logos: Christ, who appeared for us, body, word and soul. For all that the philosophers and legislators have said or managed to discover, they were able

---

Apology we can compare this fragment of the *Treatise on the Resurrection:* "The doctrine of truth is open and free, and does not agree to submit itself to examination. . . . The truth is God Himself, it is from Him that this doctrine comes, and consequently, this freedom is not insolence." Of course, Christian doctrine does not seek to withdraw from examination the proofs of its divine origin, but once this origin has been recognised, the human mind must submit itself to the revelation of God.

[25] "We say that Christ was born a hundred and fifty years ago. . . . It is objected that all those who lived before him were irresponsible; we hasten to resolve this difficulty: Christ is the firstborn of God, His Word, in which all men share" (*ibid.,* xlvi, 1-2; cf. II, viii, 1).

to discover and contemplate it thanks to a partial influence of the logos. But because they have not known the whole of the logos, who is the Christ, they have often contradicted themselves" (*ibid.*, II, x, 1-3).

Thus "all that has ever in the whole human race been well said belongs to us Christians" (II, xiii, 4); the contradictions and errors which disfigure these truths come from human weakness, which apart from Christianity has received from the Word only a partial communication, and has mixed corruptions with it.[26]

These principles explain and justify Justin's attitude of great sympathy and great independence towards Greek philosophy; he delights to see in its most illustrious masters, Heraclitus, Socrates and above all Plato, disciples of the Word; but no one is a master for him; he will repeat with the old man who converted him: "I do not trouble about Plato or Pythagoras" (*Dial.*, vi, 1). He knows that he has received in Christianity the complete revelation of the Word, of whom the greatest among the pagans received only a partial communication; he delights to discover these portions in them; but he will not be envious of them, knowing that he himself possesses the whole.[27]

The explanation which we have just reproduced enables us

[26] "I am a Christian and I confess that all my desire and effort is to be recognised as a Christian. Not that the teachings of Plato are wholly foreign to those of Christ, but they are not wholly like them, any more than are those of the others, Stoics, poets and writers. Each of them, indeed, thanks to a partial participation of the divine seminal logos, well realised what was in conformity with (the partial logos he possessed); but as they contradict one another on very important matters, it is clear that they do not possess infallible science and irrefutable knowledge" (II, xiii, 2-3). The conception of the "seminal logos" to which Justin appeals, especially in the second *Apology*, in order to explain this participation, is of Stoic origin; coming from a materialistic and pantheistic philosophy, it retains its impress; Justin does violence to it in order to adapt it to his Christian faith; but he could not entirely succeed. Cf. *Histoire du Dogme de la Trinité*, Vol. II, pp. 434-9.

[27] Amongst the criticisms which the old man makes of philosophy as Justin represents it before his conversion is this: "Is it then the discourse that thou lovest, and not action or truth? Hast thou not a desire to act rather than to reason?" (*Dial.*, iii, 3).

to understand the origin of the truths scattered in paganism; it also at the same time reveals the deepest thought of Justin. Yet more than once the apologist has recourse to a hypothesis which the Jews had employed and which Christians had often borrowed from them: if we discover more than one similitude between the doctrines and rites of the pagans and those of the Christians, it is because of conscious or unconscious plagiarism on the part of the pagans. Plato said that God fashioned formless matter in order to make the world; it was from Moses that he learnt this (*Apol.*, I, lix, 1-5). The same applies to the final conflagration, affirmed by the Stoics, after Moses (*ibid.*, lx, 8); "it is not we who reproduce what the others have said, but the others who copy what we say" (*ibid.*, x).[28]

This hypothesis of plagiarism was decidedly weak; Justin received it from his predecessors; he reproduced it, but at least he enriched it with a remark which gives it more value: "Amongst ourselves one can hear and learn these things from those who do not know even how to write; these are ignorant people, barbarous in language, but wise and faithful in spirit . . . and we see well that we have here not a work of human wisdom, but of divine power" (*ibid.*, lx, 11).

Whence comes this transcendence of Christian truth, affirmed with such certitude in face of all the philosophies? Justin affirms that "we alone prove what we affirm." What are these proofs?

The Argument from Prophecy

The fundamental proof for Justin, as for the other apologists of this period, is prophecy. We have already noted this in the preface to the *Dialogue;* the *Apology* is no less explicit. Here is the way in which the argument from prophecy is set forth to the pagans:

"There were amongst the Jews prophets of God, by whom the prophetic Spirit announced in advance future events. The kings who reigned over the Jews in the time of the prophets kept the prophecies as they had been pronounced, in books written in Hebrew by the prophets themselves. Now when Ptolemy, King of Egypt, wished to found a library in which he could gather together the

[28] "The evil spirits have imitated the institution of the Eucharist in the mysteries of Mithra" (lxvi, 4).

works of all writers, he became aware of these prophecies. He sent to ask Herod, who reigned then in Judea, to send him these books. King Herod sent them to him written, as I have said, in Hebrew. As the Egyptians did not understand this language, Ptolemy asked him for men capable of translating these books into Greek. The work was carried out; the books are still to-day in the hands of the Egyptians, and everywhere in the hands of the Jews; but the Jews read them without understanding them. They look upon us as their enemies and opponents, and like you they kill and persecute us when they can. And yet, in the books of the prophets, we see it foretold that Jesus, our Christ, is to come, to be born of a virgin, to arrive at man's age, to heal all sickness and all infirmity, to raise the dead, to be hated, misunderstood, crucified, to die, to rise again, to ascend to heaven. We read that He is, and that He is called Son of God, that men sent by him will preach these things to the whole human race, and that it will be above all the gentiles who will believe in him. These prophecies were made long before his coming, some five thousand years before, others three thousand, others again two thousand or a thousand or eight hundred years; for the prophets succeeded one another from generation to generation" (*Apol.*, I, xxv).

We will not dwell on the strange anachronism which makes King Herod the contemporary of Ptolemy Philadelphus,[29] but we note the value attached by Justin, and by all Christian apologists as well, to the Septuagint translation: In relation to the Jews and pagans it is a very effective instrument; being prior to Christianity and established by the Jews, this Greek text gives to Christian reasoning an incontestable starting point. It is still more important to notice how Justin understands prophecy: he seeks it not only in the books which the Jews recognise as having been written by the prophets, Isaias, Jeremias and others; he finds it throughout the Bible, and first of all in the books of Moses, the "first of the prophets," and the one whom in fact he most frequently quotes. The texts he quotes are not only formal predictions, but quite as often stories the symbolical signification of which refers to

[29] On the Septuagint translation and the progressive development of the legend concerning it, see Tramontano, *La Lettera di Aristea a Filocrate*, 1931, pp. 122 *et seq.*

Christ. The prophetic argument understood in this way does not depend on a few passages in the Bible, but on the Bible whole and entire; histories, poems, prayers, all tend towards Christ. This conception, inspired by St. Paul, is legitimate and fruitful; in Justin it will sometimes be weakened by questionable interpretations and by unsatisfactory arguments, but these faults of detail cannot seriously compromise the value of the whole.

The great importance which the apologist attaches to this argument appears first of all in the way in which he develops it. He devotes to it more than a third of the *Apology* (ch. xxx-liii) and almost the whole of the Dialogue. The form of the argument varies from one work to the other, according to the dispositions of the opponent in view. The pagans do not recognise the Bible as a book inspired by God, and so Justin cannot draw from it an argument from authority as he will do in the case of the Jews; he contents himself, as we have seen, with showing them that the books of the prophets are much anterior to Christ, that the authenticity of the text and the correctness of the translation are guaranteed by the Jews, and that these writings contain prophecies concerning the life of Christ and the expansion of his teaching which can be explained only by their divine origin. It must be remembered that most pagans were very susceptible to this kind of argument; many believed in the oracles of the Greek or Latin religions, and thus were not inclined to reject *a priori* all prophecy.[30]

Certainly the distance was great between these pagan oracles and the Biblical prophecies; and the difference was not less profound between the Stoic divination and the Christian theology of inspiration. But both sides agreed in recognising the reality of the predictions, and the action of

[30] For the Stoic philosophers, the effectiveness of divination was one of the best loved theses, and the evidence seemed to them so irresistible on this point that they preferred to prove thereby the existence of a divinity and a Providence (Cicero, *De natura deorum,* II, v, 13; lxv, 162; *De divinatione,* I, v, 9; xxxviii, 82). Marcus Aurelius, the emperor addressed by Justin and later on by Athenagoras, has left us in his *Meditations* (IX, 27) an expression of his belief in dreams and divination. Plutarch equally believed in them (*De defectu oracul.,* IX; *De Pyth. orac.,* XVII, XX), and sought the explanation of phenomena he did not dream of denying in the activity of spirits or emanations from the earth.

God in them. And once the pagans had been led to admit the reality of the prophecies of Israel, it was not difficult to lead them on to acknowledge the doctrine preached by the prophets.

In the *Dialogue,* Justin is arguing with the Jews, and can take for granted the divine origin of the revelation and the sacred character of the Biblical writings. Strong in this belief, and enlightened by the light of Christ, he seems sometimes to regard his arguments as irresistible for those of good faith: "Pay attention to the testimonies I am going to quote: they need no commentary, it suffices to hear them" (*Dialogue,* lv, 3). But often also he shows that this interpretation is difficult to grasp: "Thou sayest, and we also agree, that all the words and actions of the prophets have a symbolical and typical signification, so that most of them are not easily understood by all, because the truth is hidden in them, and those who seek it must make many efforts in order to find and understand it" (*ibid.,* xc, 2).

He even holds that the prophecies as a whole have been understood only since Christ, and thanks to Him, and for this reason he calls Him the interpreter of hidden prophecies (*Apol.,* I, xxxii, 2; cf. *Dial.,* c, 2). The teaching given by the Master does not suffice for this, any more than his example and his life: there are required also in a man moral dispositions, and the grace of God. Those only can understand the prophets who are ready to suffer what the prophets suffered. "Ask above all," says the old man to Justin, "that the gates of light may be opened to thee, for none can see or understand these things if God and His Christ do not give him the grace to do so" (*Dial.,* vii, 3; cf. xxix, 5). And again: "If anyone has not received from God a great grace in order to understand what has been said and done by the prophets, it will be useless to read their words or the accounts of their works, for he will not be able to explain them" (xcii, 1).

The Argument from Miracles

Together with prophecies, Justin presents miracles as a proof of the Christian revelation. We have found this already in the passage quoted above (*Dial.,* vii, 3) concerning the wonders wrought by the prophets in testimony of their doctrine. The mission of Christ was likewise confirmed by His works, and by the marvels which are still being performed in His name (xxxv, 8). Justin returns to this later on with more emphasis:

"Christ healed those who according to the flesh were blind, deaf or lame from birth, making them to see, hear, or walk by His word. Indeed, He even raised some from the dead and brought them back to life; and by His works He confounded His contemporaries and called upon them to recognise Him, but they, seeing all these things, attributed them to a magical power, for they dared to call Him a magician and seducer. He Himself performed these works also in order to show those who were to believe in Him that if anyone has a bodily infirmity, He will make him perfectly whole again at His second coming by raising him up and freeing him from death, corruption and pain" (lxix, 6-7).

It must be recognised that in Justin and the other apologists of that period, the form of the argument is quite different from that of our own time, and supposes different preoccupations.

All our effort nowadays is directed to obtaining the recognition of a fact (a cure, resurrection, or prophecy) as supernatural; in the second century this point was not the most difficult to get recognised; people found no great difficulty in allowing an activity superior to that of natural agents, but the whole problem was to discern the origin of these supernatural activities.

It was the period in which Alexander of Abonouteichos deceived Marcus Aurelius himself by his illusions, and married Rutilianus the consul to a daughter whom he claimed to have had from the moon.[31] It was also the time when the Gnostic Mark was multiplying the feats of magic related by St. Irenæus (I, xiii), and which astonished the faithful.

Moreover, the apologists found no difficulty in recognising the extraordinary power of the evil spirits. Tatian explains thus, according to St. Justin, the marvellous cures they brought about:

"The evil spirits do not cure, they captivate men by cunning, and the excellent Justin has rightly said that they

[31] Lucian, *Alexander*, XLVIII, XXXV.

are comparable to brigands. For as the latter are accustomed to make captives and to give them back afterwards to their relatives in exchange for a ransom, so also these pretended divinities slip into the members of certain men, then by dreams make them believe in their power, command their sick to appear in public in the sight of all, and after enjoying the praises given to them, they fly out of the bodies of their sick, putting an end to the malady which they had themselves caused, and re-establishing the men in the primitive condition" (XVIII).[32]

The superiority of Christ over the evil spirits is shown especially by the exorcisms: the pagans were struck by this, and the apologists recall it with insistence. Thus Justin, in his Second *Apology* (VI, 5-6):

"Christ became man, and was born, by the will of God the Father, for the salvation of believers and the destruction of evil spirits; now you can still convince yourselves of this by what happens beneath your eyes. In the whole

[32] So also St. Irenæus, when combatting the disciples of Simon and Carpocrates, insists on showing that their marvels have not the same character as the miracles of Christ and of Christians: "They cannot give back sight to the blind, or hearing to the deaf; they cannot expel evil spirits, save perhaps those they have themselves introduced; they cannot heal the sick, the lame, the paralytics, the cripples. . . . As for resurrections, they are so far from being able to do it that they do not think it in any way possible. But the Lord did this, as also did the apostles by their prayers, and often, amongst the brethren, in cases of necessity, the whole Church of the place prays, fasts and beseeches, and the spirit of the dead man comes back, and the man is restored at the prayers of the saints" (II, xxxi, 2).
The apologist of the *Clementine Recognitions* (III, lx) stresses still more the beneficial character of true miracles; he makes St. Peter speak thus: "Tell me, what is the use of making statues walk, dogs of bronze or stone bark, mountains leap and fly in the air, or a thousand other marvels of this kind, which you attribute to Simon? But the works of him who is good have for their object the well being of men, like the works which Our Lord did, making the blind to see, the deaf to hear, curing the sick and the lame, putting to flight the maladies and evil spirits, raising the dead, and doing many other things which you see me also doing." Cf. Athenagoras, *Legat.*, xxiii; Tertullian, *Apol.*, xxii; Minucius Felix, *Octav.*, xxvii.

world, and in your own city, there are many demoniacs whom neither adjurations nor enchantments nor philtres have been able to cure: many of our Christians, adjuring them in the name of Jesus Christ crucified under Pontius Pilate, have cured them and still cure them to-day, by mastering and expelling the evil spirits who possess them."

Christian Morals

But of all these miraculous works, that on which Justin dwells for preference, and which is indeed the most clearly divine, is the moral transformation brought about by Christianity. He himself, we recall, had been won to the Christian faith by the heroism of the martyrs (*Apol.*, II, xii, 1). He never tires in his *Apology* of offering to the pagans this decisive proof of the holiness of his religion. He presents Christians to them as men who do not fear death,[33] who prefer truth to life, and who at the same time wait without anticipating the hour when God will call them;[34] they are devoted to their children (*Apol.*, I, xxvii); they are chaste;[35] they are peaceful (I, xxxix, 3); they love their enemies and endeavour to save them (I, lvii, 1; *Dial.*, cxxxiii, 6); in persecution they are patient, they pray, they love all men.[36] Hence it is useless to persecute them unto death; the Church flourishes like a vine that is pruned:

"We are beheaded, we are crucified, we are delivered to wild beasts, to chains, to the fire, and to all torments, and you see that we do not renounce the profession of our faith; on the contrary, the more we are persecuted, the greater becomes the number of those who, through the

[33] *Apol.*, I, ii, 4; xi, 1-2; xlv, 6; II, ii, 14; *Dial.*, xxx, 2.

[34] *Apol.*, II, iv.

[35] *Apol.*, I, xxix: "If we marry, it is to bring up our children; if we renounce marriage, it is in order to keep perfect continence." This exigence and this virtue of Christianity appear in the fact which gave rise to the Second *Apology*: a woman had lived in vice with her husband; she was converted to Christianity, and "considered that it was an impiety to share the couch of a man who sought by all means, pleasures contrary to the natural law and to justice"; she tried in vain to convert her husband; finally she separated from him. She was then denounced by him as a Christian (*Apol.*, II, ii).

[36] *Dial.*, xciii, 3.

name of Jesus, become faithful and pious. When people cut off from a vine the branches that have borne fruit, other shoots appear, flourish, and bear fruits; it is the same with us. The vine planted by Christ, God and Saviour, is his people" (*Dial.*, cx, 4).

This pure morality, this fruitful life, have their source in the teaching and grace of Christ:

"Previously we took pleasure in debauchery, now chastity constitutes our whole delight; once we practised magic, now we are consecrated to the good and unbegotten God. We were greedy for money and possessions; now we put in common what we possess, and share it with whoever is in want. Hatred and murders opposed us to each other; difference in manners prevented us from receiving the stranger in our homes; now, after the appearance of Christ, we live together, we pray for our enemies, we try to win our unjust persecutors, in order that those who live in conformity with the sublime doctrine of Christ may hope for the same rewards as us from God, the Master of the world" (*Apol.*, I, xiv, 2-13).

And he continues, quoting abundantly the moral precepts of Jesus, especially the Sermon on the Mount (*ibid.*, xv-xviii).

Thus is developed this apologetic demonstration, modest and restrained yet strong in a tranquil and irresistible assurance. Justin has not the sarcastic liveliness of Tatian, nor the passionate eloquence of Tertullian. To the odious calumnies spread against Christians he sometimes replies, like the other apologists, by taking the offensive, and reproaching the pagans for their immorality (*Apol.*, I, xxvii; II, xx, 4-5); but he does not dwell on these obscenities; the interlocutor in the *Dialogue* protests that he does not believe in the stories told about the Christians (x, 2); the friends who accompany Justin and who disturb the discussion by their noisy protestations and loud laughter are asked to go away, "so that we may continue our discussion in peace" (ix, 2). In the *Apology* (II, iii, 2) Crescentius is severely recalled to the reserve which befits a philosopher; he forgets it by seeking to please the misguided multitude. Justin, who despises this hostile crowd, has no appetite to oppose it, nor the strength to dominate it; he continues his argumentation before his little circle of chosen hearers, men who are capable of following an argument and of being reached by an idea.

What gives these modest speeches their persuasive force is the assurance of a faith which is based upon God Himself and which is capable of facing death.

This apologetic demonstration is the whole work of Justin, at least all that we possess. It has in addition the advantage of making known to us, as the end to which it leads, the theological doctrine which the apologist professes, and towards which he leads his hearers. We shall not enter here into the details of this theology;[37] it will be sufficient for us to give its main outlines.

Theology

The study of this theology is more difficult than that of the Apostolic Fathers or of Irenæus. The doctrinal teaching is presented, as we have said, as the goal to which the apologist leads his reader; he has not yet arrived there, he ascends towards it, and as much as possible by a path along which his interlocutor can follow him without difficulty. This aim leads him, not indeed to falsify the doctrine he sets forth, but to represent it in a light which will enlighten the neophyte without blinding him. The apologist makes use for this end of analogies, sometimes more apparent than real, which are suggested by the religious conceptions familiar to his reader; if he is trying to convert a Platonist, he will insist on the conception he entertains of the intelligible world and the divine world; if he is addressing a Stoic, he will dwell on the theory of the logos, and in particular of the seminal word, or again on the belief in the final conflagration of the world. Approaching the Christian mystery by this familiar path, the interlocutor will feel more at home.

But this apologetic advantage is not without its disadvantages; by stressing apparent analogies, one runs the risk of imprudently effacing profound doctrinal divergences, or again of disconcerting the reader to whom there suddenly appears, in familiar terms, a quite new and unexpected dogma. This last impression will be obtained by anyone who studies in the second *Apology* the account which Justin gives of the theory of the seminal word as applied to Christ.[38]

[37] We have studied and discussed this in *Hist. du Dogme de la Trinité,* Vol. II, pp. 411-84.
[38] Cf. *ibid.,* p. 436.

On this point, moreover, the silence which Justin maintains in all the rest of his work is a sufficient indication that this conception of the seminal word has not for him the importance which he seems to attribute to it in his *Apology* addressed to the emperor-philosopher. This influence was not very dangerous for Justin, who had in fact little sympathy for Stoicism. But Platonism had once dominated his thought, and continued to attract him; this attraction constituted a danger; he will keep himself from it nevertheless, and will maintain on the essential points the independence of his religious thought.[39] Other apologists will be less prudent and less firm.

The anti-Jewish controversy will also have its dangers. Justin will be able to find arguments he can utilise in defending the Christian religion in the writings of Jews, in the rabbinical literature and above all in the apocalypses, but only too often these arguments defend Christianity only by misrepresenting it.

Of all these arms which apologists derive from their opponents the most effective, but also the most dangerous, is the theory of intermediaries. Between the supremely pure God and the matter which is unworthy of contact with Him, there must be an intermediate agent, without which creation cannot be understood. Similarly the revelation of the supreme God can reach man only by influence of the intermediaries who propagate it. These conceptions, very widespread in Greek philosophy and in Judaism, provided the apologists with an argument, but at the same time constituted a danger for them.

To understand this, we can start with this rule of interpretation put forward by Tertullian when arguing against the Marcionites: "All that you require as being worthy of God you will find in the Father: He is invisible, beyond reach, tranquil, and so to speak, the God of philosophers. All that you single out as unworthy of God, will be attributed to the Son: He is seen, met with, He is the agent of the Father and His Minister, combining in Himself man and God: in His greatness he is God, in His infirmities, man; giving to man all that He takes from God; in a word, all that you regard as unworthy of God, is the mystery of the salvation of humanity" (*Marc.*, II, xxvii).

[39] Cf. *ibid.*, p. 481.

If we consider the supreme God, this exegetical rule might lead to striking out of the Bible all that is thought unworthy of His transcendence, that is to say, all His personal interventions; one will see in Him, as Tertullian says, nothing more than "the God of philosophers." The theology of the Son of God is likewise in great danger: "all that one judges unworthy of the supreme God will be attributed to the Son"; this is a very dangerous rule; one may justify it, as Tertullian does here, by imputing these weaknesses not indeed to the divine nature of the Son, but to His humanity; at the same time there is more than one point in which this interpretation will not work.

The Word in Creation

The first problem which arises is that of the creation. Christian theology taught clearly that God had made all things by His Word; the Greek philosophers were disposed to receive this teaching, but understanding the Word to be an intermediary between the supreme God and matter. The Jews also admitted this conception, which they applied either to Wisdom, or else to the Law.[40]

The apologists made the most of this present offered them by their opponents, but sometimes they allowed themselves to be drawn on to their ground. We read in Justin:

Apol., II, i, 2. "His Son, the only one who is properly called Son, the Word, who before all creatures was with Him and had been generated when in the beginning the Father made and ordered all things by him. . . ."

Dial., lxi, 1. "As a beginning, before all creatures, God generated from himself a Power which was the Word. . . . This can receive all names because He carries out the plans of the Father and is born of the Father by will."

Ibid., lxii, 4: "This Son, really sent forth before all creatures, was with the Father, and with Him the Father converses, as is shown by the sacred text of Solomon: this same being is the beginning before all creatures, and was generated by God as His Son, and it is He whom Solomon calls Wisdom."

[40] Cf. *ibid.*, pp. 456-8.

These texts recall that of St. John:

> "In the beginning was the Word, and the Word was with God, and the Word was God. The same was in the beginning with God. All things were made by Him, and without Him was made nothing that was made."

But the Gospel text has a firm touch which is lacking in the apologist: in St. John the divine life, and the generation of the Word, is wholly independent not only of all the external operations of God, but also of all his plans: from the beginning, eternally, the Word was, and was with God, and was God; when God willed it, He created the world by His Word, but this external and contingent action had no influence on the inner life of God; this was eternally and necessarily what it was, in the simplicity of its essence, and in the Trinity of its persons.

In Justin, on the contrary, at least in the *Apology*, the generation of the Word is closely linked up with the creation of the world; this connection is not without danger: it runs the risk of drawing the eternal and necessary generation of the Word into the temporal and contingent sphere of creation.[41]

The inexact translation given to the classical text in *Proverbs* (viii, 22) led in the same direction: the apologists, like

---

[41] This danger of contamination is still more manifest in other apologists. Thus Tatian says: "By the will of his simplicity, there comes forth from Him the Word, and the Word, which does not go forth into the void, is the first work of the Father. It is he, as we know, who is the beginning of the world" (*Discourse,* v).

Athenagoras: "If, in your high wisdom, you wish to know who is the Son, I will tell you in a few words: He was the offspring of the Father, not that He was made, for God being an eternal intellect from the beginning, had with Him His Word, so that in all the material things, which were like a formless nature or a sterile earth . . . He was amongst them idea and energy, having come from without" (*Leg.* x).

St. Theophilus: "When God willed to make what He had decided, He generated this uttered Word, the first born of the whole creation, not depriving Himself of the Word, but generating the Word, and speaking constantly with His Word" (II, xxii). On all these passages, cf. *Hist. du Dogme de la Trinité,* Vol. II, pp. 453-5. On the theory of the twofold state of the Word, internal and uttered, see *ibid.,* pp. 449 *et seq.*

the Jews of their times, did not translate this text as: "The Lord has formed me at the beginning of His ways, before His works," but "The Lord has formed me as a beginning of His works." Thus one is tempted to regard the Word as the first of the works of God, and that was how the rabbis contemporary with Justin regarded the law.[42] Justin will resist this temptation, safeguarded by his firm belief in the generation of the Word; his unfortunate and unfaithful disciple Tatian will be less vigilant, and while saying that the Word is "generated by the Father," he will also say that he is "the first work of the Father" (*Discourse*, v).

The Divine Appearances

As in the case of the problem of creation, that of the relation between God and the world suggested to the apologists a solution both tempting and dangerous. The Old Testament contains many accounts of theophanies: God appearing to Abraham, Jacob and Moses. The explanation proposed is that it is not God the Father who appears thus, but the Son of God, and thus all these Scriptural texts are so many arguments which enable the apologist to distinguish in God two distinct persons. This is how the argument is presented in the *Dialogue*:

"The ineffable Father and Lord of the universe goes nowhere nor walks, nor sleeps, not gets up, but remains in His own place wherever this may be; He is endowed with a penetrating sight and hearing, not by eyes or ears, but by an unspeakable power; He sees all, He knows all, and not one of us escapes Him; He does not move, and no place can contain Him, not even the whole world, for He was before the world was made. How, then, could this God speak to anyone, or show Himself to anyone, appear in a small corner of the earth, whereas on Sinai the people had not the strength even to see the glory of the one He sent, and Moses himself could not enter into the tent he had made because it was filled with the glory which came forth from God? . . . Thus neither Abraham nor Isaac nor Jacob nor any other amongst men saw the Father and the

[42] Cf. the treatise *Pesachim*, 54 a, Bar.: "Jahveh created me as the beginning of his ways, as the first of his works," and this is understood of the Law. Cf. *Hist. du Dogme de la Trinité*, Vol. II, pp. 457-8.

ineffable Lord of all things absolutely and of Christ Himself, but only Him who according to the will of God is God, His Son and Angel inasmuch as He is the Minister of His plans. It is He whom God willed to be born man of a virgin, He who became fire formerly to speak with Moses from the bush. For if we do not thus understand the Scriptures, it will follow that the Father and Lord of the universe was not then in heaven, whereas it was said through the mouth of Moses: 'The Lord rained on Sodom fire and brimstone from the Lord from the height of heaven' " (*Dial.*, cxxvii).[43]

From the apologetic point of view, this exegesis presented great advantages: the Platonist philosophers could follow it, for they themselves likewise held that the Supreme God is invisible and inaccessible, and manifests Himself to men only by the ministry of secondary gods;[44] the Palestinian Jews, represented by Trypho,[45] thought that in the theophanies it was not God Himself who appeared, but an angel; to refute them it sufficed to prove to them that the personage seen by Abraham or Moses was divine.

While the apologist could feel pleased at this exegesis, the theologian had to suffer from it: not only was he led to represent God as dwelling above the world, and having there His place and His throne,[46] but above all it compromised the consubstantiality of the Father and the Son. At the time of which we speak, the Trinitarian controversies had not yet arisen, and there was less danger in these imprudences, but the Arian crisis would reveal them.[47] To remove them in a

[43] Cf. *Hist. du Dogme de la Trinité,* Vol. II, p. 426; we may consult other similar but less explicit passages in Justin: *Dial.,* lxi, 2; *Apol.,* I, lxiii, 11.

[44] Maximus of Tyre, quoted *ibid.,* p. 665.

[45] It is fairly generally said that Justin is referring to Philo; this is an error (cf. *ibid.,* pp. 667 *et seq.*). The opponents represented by Trypho are the Palestinian Jews; their exegesis and their theology cannot be identified with those of Philo.

[46] Cf. *ibid.,* p. 427.

[47] The Arians, according to St. Phoebadius, will argue as follows: God the Father is invisible, immutable, perfect, eternal; the Son on the contrary is visible, since He was often seen by the patriarchs; He is subject to change, for He appeared under various forms; He is therefore not of the substance of the Father (*De*

decisive manner, St. Augustine will reject the interpretation of the theophanies developed by the apologists: in these appearances it is not the Son alone who is showing Himself to men, but either the Father, or the Son, or the Spirit, or the whole Trinity.[48]

What we have just said will show how far we must recognise Subordinationist tendencies in Justin, and what were their origin. We must recognise a deviation in his theology on two important points: the generation of the Word and His action in the world; His generation is put in too close a relation with the creation of the world, and thereby His necessity and His eternity are compromised;[49] in the manifestations He appears as the envoy or servant of the supreme God rather than the Son of God, equal and consubstantial with His Father.

This deviation is noteworthy, but it does not affect the theology of Justin as a whole, and what is still more important, it did not originate in an earlier tradition which led Christian thought in this direction; we find no trace of it in the Apostolic Fathers, Clement or Ignatius; we shall not find it either in Irenæus. In the apologists it is explained by the preoccupations of controversy: a foreign element has affected the doctrine of Justin, and has made it sometimes go astray.

In any case, we must not exaggerate this inexactitude: when we study carefully the weak points in the theology of the apologists, at least of the greatest amongst them, we realise that they did not give themselves up blindly to the Platonist or Jewish influences which attracted their attention; they resisted them. This resistance was of varying strength, certainly, in the different apologists, and also differed in per-

---

Filii divinitate, viii; Migne, *P.L.,* XX, 45). Cf. Augustine, *De Genesi ad litteram,* VIII, 27, 50; Migne, *P.L.,* XXXIV, 392. Cf. *Saint Augustin théologien de la Trinité,* in *Miscellanea Agostiniana,* Vol. II, pp. 821-36.

[48] St. Irenæus, while reserving these appearances to the Son of God, avoids the danger by presenting these theophanies as preludes to the Incarnation. Cf. *Hist. du Dogme de la Trinité,* Vol. II, pp. 594-8.

[49] We note sometimes a too close bond between the generation of the Word and the creation of the world (*Apol.,* II, vi, 2), but more often Justin affirms emphatically the absolute anteriority of the Word in relation to all creation: *Apol.,* II, vi, 3; *Dial.,* lxi, 1; lxii, 4; c, 2 and 4; cxxxix, 4.

spicacity, but it manifested always the same Christian reaction against the same danger, Jewish or pagan.[50]

Personality of the Word

Having pointed out, as we had to do, these weaknesses in the theology of Justin and the other apologists, we must emphasise the traditional data which Justin maintains firmly and defends with energy.

The Word is really distinct from the Father. This is one of the fundamental theses of the *Dialogue*. Thus we read in chapter lvi, 11:

"I will endeavour to convince you that He who appeared to Abraham, Jacob and Moses and who is described as a God, is other than the God who made all things, I mean other in number, not in thought; for I affirm that He did nothing and said nothing else but what the Creator of the world, He above whom there is no other God, willed Him to do and to say."

Several other texts are invoked in the same sense, in particular, the account of creation. In saying, "Let us make man . . ." the Creator addressed Himself to "someone who was numerically distinct from Him, and who by nature was the Word." The same conclusion is deduced from this other text of *Genesis:* "Behold Adam is become as one of us"; "By saying 'as one of us' he indicates a number of beings together, and who are at least two" (lxii, 2 and 3).

Later on, in commenting on the theophanies, the apologist encounters the exegesis of certain Jewish doctors who saw in the divine Being appearing to the patriarchs a Power which radiated from God but which was inseparable from Him and was reabsorbed into Him. Justin categorically rejects this interpretation:

[50] Cf. *Hist. du Dogme de la Trinité,* Vol. II, p. 459. These apparently opposed elements in the theology of the apologists have provided arguments for the historians who have attacked or defended their orthodoxy. This question has often given rise to keen discussion: in the seventeenth century, by Petavius and Huet; then by Jurieu and Bossuet in France; in England by Bull and S. Clarke; and towards the end of the last century by Duchesne and Newman. Cf. *ibid.,* pp. 499-500.

"It has been proved that this Power which the prophetic text calls God, and angel, is not only nominally distinct (from the Father), as light is distinct from the sun, but that it is something numerically distinct." [51]

The same thesis is defended again by the text of *Proverbs* (viii, 21-25):

"This text shows that He whom the Father thus generated was generated absolutely before all creatures; now that which is generated is numerically distinct from the one who generates, as all will agree" (*Apol.*, cxxix, 4).

Divinity of the Word

That which is thus generated by the Father is "an intelligent being" (*Apol.*, lxii, 2), "an intelligent power" (lxi, 1); in other words, a person. And this person is divine. This essential dogma of Christianity is demonstrated in the *Apology*, but above all in the *Dialogue*. And what gives to these affirmations all their value is the religious faith which animates them. In the *Apology* Justin repeats to the pagans: "We must adore God only" (I, xvi, 6); "we adore only God" (xvii, 3). And yet he also says: "We adore and we love, after God, the Word born of the unbegotten and ineffable God" (II, xiii, 4). And in the *Dialogue*, he thus concludes a long process of reasoning:

"Thus then He is adorable, He is God, He is Christ; He who made all that we see gives testimony of this, and these texts say so clearly" (lxiii, 5).

And again, lower down:

"David has shown that, being Christ, He is a strong and adorable God" (lxxvi, 7).

We thus find ourselves in presence of two series of equally categorical affirmations, to which the martyr's death will give a force of irresistible conviction: We adore only God; we

[51] *Dial.*, cxxviii, 4. By a strange mistake Vacherot attributes to Justin the theory which he refutes (*Hist. de l'Ecole d'Alexandrie*, Vol. I, p. 230).

adore Christ. The great disciple of Justin, Irenæus, has shown the intimate union of these two theses; he quotes first of all from the work of Justin against Marcion this peremptory declaration:

> "I would refuse my faith to the Lord Himself if He preached to us a God other than the Demiurge."

And then he adds:

> "But because it is from the one God who made the world, who created us and who governs all, that the one Son has come to us . . . my belief in Him is assured, and my love towards the Father is unshakeable" (IV, i, 2).

We find here already the answer which the Fathers of the fourth century will develop against the Arians: our faith is given to the Son without disturbing our love for the Father, for the Son was generated by the Father; our homage and our adoration are not scattered over several gods, for the source of the Godhead is one.

The Generation of the Son of God

This dogma of the generation of the Son of God is brought out splendidly by Justin.[52] The apologist does so in contrasting the origin of the Word of God with that of creatures; the world has come from matter, the Word has come from God;[53] the other beings are works of God, $\pi o i \eta \mu a \tau a$, creatures, $\kappa \tau i \sigma \mu a \tau a$;[54] the Word is the bud of God, $\gamma \acute{e} \nu \nu \eta \mu a$, His child, $\tau \acute{e} \kappa \nu o \nu$, His only Son, the only one who is really Son.[55]

The significance of these affirmations is confirmed by the numerous texts in which Justin endeavours to describe, or at

[52] Loofs, who sees in this doctrine a deviation from the primitive faith, writes: "Certainly, as we see from Hermas and Barnabas, it was not the apologists who were first responsible for this deviation; at the same time, so far as we know, no Christian theologian before Justin laid as much stress as he did on the divine sonship" (*Paulus von Samosata*, p. 315).

[53] *Apol.*, I, x, 2; *Dial.*, lxi, 1.

[54] *Apol.*, II, vi, 3; *Dial.*, lxii, 4; lxxxix, 2; *Dial.*, lxi, 1; c, 2; cxxv, 3; cxxix, 4.

[55] *Apol.*, I, xxi, 1; *Dial.*, lxii, 4; cxxix, 4; cxxv, 3; cv, 1; *Apol.*, II, vi, 3. Cf. *Hist. du Dogme de la Trinité*, Vol. II, p. 444.

least to hint at, the origin of the Word: it is like an emission,[56] a going out,[57] a springing forth;[58] it is a fire lit by another fire;[59] a Word which, without amputation or diminution, the Father generates from Himself:

> "Is it not something like what takes place in ourselves? When we utter some word, we generate a word, and we utter it not by an amputation which diminishes the word which is in us. Again it is like a fire lit at another fire: the one at which it is lit is not diminished, but remains the same; and the one which is lit there is seen to be quite real, without diminishing that from which it was lit" (*Dial.*, lxi, 2).

It goes without saying that these are only far-off comparisons—such are the only ones which can be found to throw light on the mystery of God—but at least they turn the mind towards a correct conception of the dogma: the Son of God is not a creature, He is born of the Father. This decisive affirmation opposes beyond any question the theology of Justin and the other apologists to what will later be the Arian heresy. From this fruitful principle bequeathed by the apostolic tradition, the apologists did not know how to draw all the consequences it implied; the Church will find the principle in their works, and will know how to draw all these conclusions which flow from it, even those which had escaped these early apologists.

Martyrdom

"No one believed Socrates so far as to die for what he taught, but for Christ's sake even working people and ignorant folk have despised fear and death" (*Apol.*, II, x, 3). The apologist was to confirm this proud word by his own death. Together with his companions, he was summoned to appear before the prefect of the city, Rusticus the philosopher and master of Marcus Aurelius.[60]

Justin tried to expound his faith; the prefect allowed him to say a few words:

[56] *Dial.*, lxii, 4; lxiv, 1.
[57] *Dial.*, c, 4.
[58] *Dial.*, cxxviii, 3.
[59] *Dial.*, cxxviii, 4.
[60] The *Acts* are in the *Corpus apologetarum* of Otto, III, 2, 262-75 (1879), and in Knopf, pp. 17-20.

"The true doctrine which we Christians follow piously, is belief in only one God, the Creator of all things visible and invisible, and in the Lord Jesus Christ, the Son of God, foretold by the prophets as the messenger of salvation for the human race and the master of good disciples. And I, who am but a man, cannot speak worthily of his infinite divinity; I confess (that this requires) a prophetic power; and the prophets have announced the coming of Him who is as I have said the Son of God. For I know that long ago the prophets foretold his coming amongst men."

We recognise in this brief exposition Justin's apologetic, the argument from prophecy on which he dwelt by preference. Rusticus did not reply: he pressed on the interrogation of Justin first and then of his companions. Lastly, turning once more to the apologist, he tried to shake him:

"Listen, thou who art said to be eloquent and who pretendest to know the true doctrine: if I have thee scourged and then beheaded, dost thou believe that thou shalt then ascend into heaven?" "I hope," replied Justin, "to receive the reward, if I suffer that which thou hast announced to me. For I know that those who have thus lived will keep the divine favour until the end of the world." "Thou fanciest, then," said Rusticus, "that thou wilt ascend to heaven to receive a reward?" "I do not fancy it, I know it, and I am fully persuaded of it." "Let us come back to realities. Come, all of you, and sacrifice together to the gods." "No sensible man abandons piety to fall into impiety." "If you do not obey, you shall be tormented without mercy." "All our desire is to suffer for Jesus Christ our Lord and to be saved. This will be our salvation and our assurance at the fearful and universal judgment of our Master and Saviour." The other martyrs said likewise: "Do what thou wilt. We are Christians, and we do not sacrifice to idols." The prefect Rusticus pronounced the sentence: "Those who have refused to sacrifice to the gods and to obey the order of the emperor will be scourged and taken away to undergo the capital penalty in conformity with the laws."

The holy martyrs, glorifying God, were led to the ordinary place of execution; their heads were cut off, and they consummated their martyrdom in the confession of the Lord.

§3. THE GREEK APOLOGISTS OF THE END OF THE SECOND CENTURY

Tatian [1]

St. Justin deserved an attentive study, the other apologists will not keep us so long. The first we meet with was a disciple of St. Justin; he spoke of his master only with veneration,[2] but he was little like him. Candid and boastful, he wrote at the beginning of his *Discourse:* "We have detached ourselves from your wisdom, and yet I was one of the most eminent of its representatives." Born in the land of the Assyrians (ch. xli) about the year 120, he went to Rome, and there doubtless he was converted, and became a disciple of Justin. As long as his master lived, he was faithful to the Church; "but after the martyrdom of Justin he fell away; he was exalted and puffed up by his title of master, thought himself superior to the others, and founded a new school." St. Irenæus, from whom we take this statement, adds: "He imagined invisible sons, like those we find in the fables of Valentine; like Marcion and Saturninus, he called marriage a corruption and a debauchery; and finally, it was he who conceived the idea that Adam was not saved." [3] This judgment of so eminent a man, who had personally known Justin and doubtless Tatian himself, confirms the impression the *Discourse* gives us: we do not yet find a heretic therein, but we are repelled by the presumptuous assurance of a writer who jeers at and despises his opponents, and who airily settles all the questions he deals with.

Three quarters of the work (ch. i-xxx) are devoted to polemics; the apologist violently attacks the pagan philosophers,

[1] Cf. A. Puech, *Recherches sur le Discours aux Grecs de Tatien;* Paris, 1903; *id., Les Apologistes grecs,* ch. v, pp. 148-71. Edition of the *Discourse* by Schwartz, *Texte und Untersuchungen,* IV, 1.
[2] *Discourse,* xviii and xix. This fidelity to the memory of Justin does honour to Tatian; it also shows the prestige of the master, and all the more because of the very deep differences between the two men, and because the exaggerations of Tatian seem to have made him less likely to be influenced by a balanced mind like that of Justin.
[3] *Hær.,* I, xxviii, 1, quoted by Eusebius, *Hist. Eccles.,* IV, xxix, 3. Eusebius, *ibid.,* 6-7, adds some information concerning Tatian, his *Diatesseron* and his *Discourse.*

pagan wisdom, and pagan religion. In his defence, it has been said that "he borrows from the Greeks the arms with which he combats the Greeks." [4] That is true, but we must add that such arms could only wound;[5] it was not by such arguments that Tatian himself had been converted.[6] A few other apologists, especially Tertullian, imitated him; to excuse them it is recalled that they echoed what they heard proclaimed around them, and that they were glad to reply thus to the calumnies urged against the Christians. But it is to be noted that the most violent polemical writers were two who themselves abandoned the Church, Tatian and Tertullian, and one is glad to register that the best amongst the Christians remained foreign to such methods.[7]

Justin, when giving a reason for the resemblances between the pagan philosophy and Christian doctrine, explains them by preference by the action of the seminal Word, and sometimes also by the theory that the Greeks borrowed from the Jews. In Tatian the former explanation has disappeared save for a slight trace (ch. xiii); all the effort of the apologist is directed to establishing the priority of the prophets over the philosophers, and to infer therefrom that the Greeks are plagiarists (ch. xxxi *et seq.*). This argument was not original,[8] it will often be repeated and it will not enrich Christian apologetic.

[4] Puech, *Recherches*, p. 40.
[5] We may quote, as an example, this series of anecdotes on the philosophers: "Diogenes, who advertised his independence by the bragging of his tub, ate an octopus quite raw, and seized with colic, died from his intemperance. Aristippus, who paraded with his mantle of purple, gave himself up to debauchery with an air of gravity; the philosopher Plato was sold by Dionysius because of his gluttony, and Aristotle was guilty of the extreme folly of flattering Alexander, the wild young fool who, quite in accordance with the Aristotelian principles, put in a cage like a bear or a panther his friend who was not willing to adore him, and had him thus drawn after him. . . ."
[6] He narrates that he was converted by the reading of Holy Scripture (xxix).
[7] It must be put to Tatian's credit that in his attacks on pagan religion, he dwells less than others on mythology, and deals above all with the superstitions, which were in fact most dangerous: astrology (ch. ix-xi), magic (xvii-xx), the Mysteries (xxix). Cf. Puech, *Recherches*, p. 43.
[8] Cf. Puech, *Recherches*, pp. 82-9.

Christian Doctrine

Tatian's exposition of Christian doctrine would be more interesting to a historian than his polemics, but unfortunately his testimony in this matter is difficult to gather: the statement is often obscure,[9] and the thought generally confused. In the theology of the Word, Tatian retains some of the essential points in the Christian dogma, as Justin had set them forth; the Son is born of the very substance of the Father; this is signified by the illustration of the torches, lit one from the other; Justin had given this (*Dial.*, lxi); Tatian repeats it (v), and after him Tertullian, Lactantius,[10] the Nicene Fathers in their Creed. This image is clearly opposed to what the Arians will maintain when they make the Word a creature of God, formed from nothing, and not His Son, born of His substance. We must note again that, for Tatian as for all the apologists, it is not the Incarnation which makes the Word the Son of God, but the divine generation. At the same time it must be recognised that in Tatian the conception of this divine generation is less firm than in Justin;[11] it is moreover obscured by the dangerous distinction between the twofold state of the Word, first latent, and then uttered.[12]

On the subject of the human soul, Tatian confusing eternity and immortality, considered that the soul is by nature mortal,

[9] This obscurity is not always due to Tatian; the most important text (ch. v) has been clearly altered. Already in the tenth century, Archbishop Arethas, to whom we owe the best manuscript of Tatian, added a marginal note in which he accused Tatian of Arianism; the scribe probably had the same impression, and attempted a correction. This text has been studied in *Histoire de Dogme de la Trinité*, Vol. II, p. 450.

[10] Tertullian, *Apol.*, xxi; Lactantius, *Inst. div.*, IV, xxix.

[11] The Word is called "the first born work of God," a contradictory formula combining the idea of creation with that of generation.

[12] "The master of all things, who is himself the substantial support of the universe was alone in this sense that creation had not yet taken place; but in the sense that all the power of things visible and invisible was in him, He included all things in Himself by means of His Word. By the will of his simplicity, the Word came forth from Him, and the Word, who went not out into the void, is the first-born work of the Father. He, as we know, is the beginning of the world. He comes from a distribution, not from a division. . . ." (v).

but that if it has known God, after it has been dissolved for a time it will live again, to die no more.[13] Elsewhere he rather imprudently makes use of Platonist conceptions[14] or Gnostic ones.[15]

All these contaminations show the weakness of a mind which thought itself strong because it was severe, and which allowed itself to be affected by the most unsound elements of the philosophies it despised.

The Defection of Tatian

This *Discourse* was doubtless written very shortly before the defection of Tatian.[16] It was in the twelfth year of Marcus

[13] "The human soul, in itself, is not immortal, O Greeks, it is mortal; but this same soul is capable also of not dying. . . . It does not die, even if it be dissolved for a time, if it has acquired a knowledge of God." We find in Justin (*Dial.*, v) the germ of this confusion: the Platonists commonly held that there was between the human soul and God an affinity of nature; this for them implied immortality. Justin rejects all that, recognising in the soul only an immortality accorded by a grace from God. Tatian goes further, making all souls die, but granting to the souls of the just a kind of resurrection. On these confusions, fairly frequent at this time, cf. Bainvel, art. *Ame aux trois premiers siècles*, in *Dict. de théol. cath.*

[14] "The wing of the soul is the perfect spirit, which she loses by sin; after which she keeps close to the ground like a young chicken, and having fallen from her conversation with heaven, she desires to participate in lower things" (xx).

[15] This above all in his theory of the spirit. Tatian distinguishes between two spirits: an inferior spirit which animates and differentiates the stars, angels, men and animals; and a superior and divine spirit, which he identifies with Light and the Word; if the soul unites itself to this spirit, it forms with it a syzygy or couple, according to the will of God: ch. xiii and xv. Cf. Puech, *Recherches*, pp. 65 and 68.

[16] Harnack, *Literatur*, II, i, 284 *et seq.*, dates the *Discourse* in Justin's lifetime. It would then be a manifesto of the newly converted Tatian; R. C. Kukula, *Tatiens sogenannte Apologie*, Leipzig, 1900, maintains on the contrary that the *Discourse* is an opening lecture in the heretical school founded by Tatian, delivered in Asia Minor about 172 (p. 52). These two extreme theses have found no echo: what Tatian says about Justin is better understood if Justin was already dead; on the other hand, the heresy is not yet declared but it is threatened.

Aurelius, 172-3,[17] that Tatian abandoned the Church. He had, it seems, already left Rome for the East; he lived for a few years more at Antioch, in Cilicia, in Pisidia. The small sect of Encratites which he had founded lasted a long time, but did not spread much; most of his works, which seem to have been fairly numerous, disappeared quickly.[18] Apart from the *Discourse,* only one had a great and wide diffusion: the *Diatessaron.* This is a harmony of the four Gospels, the first, apparently, to be composed. It was long in use in the Syrian Church; it is known to us to-day through Arabic and Armenian translations, and also by Latin and Flemish Gospel harmonies.[19]

[17] This date is given us by Eusebius in his *Chronicle,* an. 2188.
[18] *Hist. Eccles.,* IV, xxix, 7: "He left a great number of works." Eusebius speaks of them, apparently, only from hearsay. Clement of Alexandria (*Strom.,* III, 12) mentions a book by Tatian on *Perfection according to Christ;* Rendel Harris thinks he has re-discovered this in an Armenian translation.
[19] Theodoret, *Hær. fab. comp.,* I, 20 (Migne, *P.G.,* LXXIII, 372) writes: "Tatian also composed the Gospel called *Diatessaron,* suppressing the genealogies and everything which shows the Lord to have been born of David according to the flesh. And this book is in use not only by those of his sect, but also by those who follow the doctrine of the apostles, and who do not perceive the malice of this composition, and who find it more convenient to make use of this summary. I myself found more than two hundred copies of this book in honour in our churches; I collected them all and put them aside, and substituted for them the four gospels of the evangelists." Theodoret was Bishop of Cyr on the borders of the Syrian world; this explains the diffusion of the work in his diocese. For a long time, in fact, the work was in great honour in the Syrian Church Aphraates quotes it, and Ephrem comments on it; at the beginning of the fifth century its use was forbidden. Cf. Zahn, *Forschungen. Gesch. des N. T. Kanons,* Vol. I, Erlangen, 1881, pp. 1-328; Vol. II, 1883, pp. 286-99; *Gesch. d. N. T. Kanons,* II, 2 (1892), pp. 530-56. Latin translation of the Armenian version: G. Moesinger, *Evangelii concordantis expositio in Latinum translata,* Venice, 1876; Arabic: A. S. Marmardji, O.P., *Diatessaron de Tatien,* Beyrouth, 1935.

The Latin text of Victor of Capua is not so much a translation as a revision of the *Diatessaron* (Migne, *P.L.,* LXVIII, 255-358). A Flemish translation has been found and studied by D. Plooij, *A Primitive Text of the Diatessaron,* Leyden, 1923. This publication has led to a great number of articles and studies. Cf. *Recherches,* 1924, pp. 370-1; *Revue Biblique,* 1924, pp. 624-8.

Athenagoras

Four or five years after the *Discourse* of Tatian, there appeared the *Apology* of Athenagoras.[20] The author is quite unknown;[21] but the two books of his which we possess, the *Apology* and the *Treatise on the Resurrection,* are well worth reading; it is a joy for one who has just read the invectives of Tatian to find himself here once more in contact with a truly Christian soul, tranquil and pure.

From the first words, the *Apology* displays a reserve and courtesy in expression. The whole Empire enjoys a profound peace; Christians alone are persecuted: what is the reason? If we are convicted of a crime, we accept the punishment; but if we are persecuted only for a name, we appeal to your justice. Three accusations are discussed: Christians are reproached for being atheists, for eating human flesh, and practising incest; these two last calumnies are refuted briefly; the accusation of atheism is discussed at length (ch. iv-xxx); Athenagoras sets forth Christian dogma and the Christian life in a valuable section from which we can quote here only a few fragments.[22] After expounding the essential features of Christian theology, the apologist continues:

[20] The *Apology* is dedicated to the emperors Marcus Aurelius Antoninus and Lucius Aurelius Commodus. Commodus was associated in the government of the empire on November 27th, 176; Marcus Aurelius died on March 17th, 180; the book was thus written between these two dates. The description of a profound peace in chapter 1 must refer to the time before the war of the Marcomans, which broke out in 178; there is no trace either of the Lyons persecution; note especially what is said about slaves (xxxv): "none of them has been denounced"; the apologist would not have spoken thus after 177. All this takes us back, then, to the end of 176 or the beginning of 177.

[21] The only references we find to Athenagoras in Antiquity are, in Methodius, one explicit citation (*De Resurrect.,* xxxii, quoting *Apol.,* xxix), and two allusions; in addition, a fragment attributed to the lost history of Philip of Sidon (Migne, *P.G.,* VI, 182); this fragment is full of obvious errors: the author says that Athenagoras addressed his apology to Hadrian and Antoninus; he adds that "his disciple was Clement, the author of the *Stromateis,* and Pantænus the disciple of Clement." Nothing can be made of this.

[22] Longer citations and some comments will be found in *Histoire du Dogme de la Trinité,* Vol. II, pp. 494-505.

"Allow me to raise my voice and to speak frankly, as before philosopher-kings: is there one among those who resolve syllogisms, who dissipate amphibologies . . . who has a soul sufficiently pure to love his enemies instead of hating them, to bless those who curse him instead of replying to them at least by insulting words, to pray for those who aim at taking his life? . . . But amongst ourselves you will find poor people, working men, old women, who are doubtless incapable of proving by argument the value of our doctrine, but who prove it by their actions; they do not recite harangues, but they show good actions; when they are struck they do not return the blows; when they are robbed they do not take proceedings; they give to those who ask from them; they love their neighbour as themselves" (*Apol.*, xi).

Here we have the theme, so dear to all the apologists, of the superiority of life over discourse; *Non eloquimur magna, sed vivimus,* as Minucius Felix will shortly say. It is also the argument which Origen will take up powerfully against Celsus: Christianity alone has been able to transform and raise to the highest virtue these working people, these poor folk, whom philosophy had never reached. And the source of all this is the Christian faith, and the goal it sets before us:

"Will those who take as their motto in life, 'Let us eat and drink, for to-morrow we die' . . . be regarded as pious folk? And are we to be regarded as impious, we who know that the present life is short, and worth little, who are animated by the sole desire to know the true God and His Word, (to know) what is the unity of the Son with the Father, what is the communion of the Father with the Son, what is the Spirit, what is the union and distinction of these terms united to each other, the Spirit, the Son, the Father, we who know that the life we await is greater than we can say, provided always we leave the world pure of every stain, we who love mankind so much as to love not only our friends . . . ? Once more, will it be believed that we are impious, we who are such, and who lead such a life to escape the judgment?" (*Apol.*, xii).

Written at this date, on the eve of the massacres at Lyons, this page is very moving; it reveals the profound source of

Christian life; nothing can dry it up or repress it. It also shows what dogma is for the Christian, and in particular, the dogma of the Trinity, which the pagan readers of Athenagoras regarded merely as a speculation like their own; the apologist shows them that it is the term towards which tends the whole life of faith; there is no more expressive commentary on the words of Jesus: "This is eternal life, to know Thee, the only true God, and Him whom Thou hast sent."

Of Athenagoras we possess, besides the *Apology,* a *Treatise on the Resurrection of the Body.* The doctrine defended therein is one of those which the pagans found greatest difficulty in accepting; we see this already in the discourse of St. Paul at Athens (*Acts* xvii, 32); it is also one of those which were most dear to Christians. At this time of persecutions, when the body was constantly menaced with the worst torments and with death, the belief in the glorious resurrection was a great consolation. Also, the pagans took all possible steps to remove the remains of the martyrs, not only to prevent the survivors from getting relics, but also in the vain hope of making the resurrection impossible.[23] It is easy to understand the importance of this doctrine for the apologists: Justin had defended it in a treatise of which we possess only some fragments;[24] and we have a treatise by Athenagoras on the same subject. This little book has the same character as the *Apology;* it is a gentle and lucid discussion; addressed to philosophers, it keeps altogether on their ground; it is thereby deprived of some decisive arguments, namely, those which are based on the positive dispositions of God, the Incarnation and Resurrection of Christ. Here as in the *Apology,* the method to which Athenagoras confines himself made this sacrifice necessary: these two works are impoverished in consequence.

St. Theophilus

Five or six years after the *Apology* of Athenagoras there appeared the three books *To Autolycus.*[25] The author, Theophilus, is known as "the sixth bishop of Antioch after the

[23] E.g., at Lyons, *Hist. Eccles.,* V, i, 63.
[24] The attribution of this treatise to Justin is not certain, but it is likely. Cf. supra, § 2, n. 16.
[25] The death of Marcus Aurelius is mentioned (III, xxvii, xxviii); these three books seem to belong to the first years of Commodus (182-3).

Apostles" (*Hist. Eccles.,* IV, xx); he stands out in the group of apologists because of his pastoral charge, for he was a bishop. He did not address his work to the emperors, nor to pagan opinion in general, but, like the writer of the *Letter to Diognetus,* to a pagan he wished to convert, Autolycus; a real or fictitious personage, we do not know which.

From the beginning (I, ii) he stresses the necessity of a moral preparation:

> "If thou sayest to me, 'Show me thy God,' I answer: 'Show me what sort of man thou art, and I will show thee what sort is my God. Show me if the eyes of thy soul see clearly, and if the ears of thy heart know how to listen. . . . God is seen by those who are capable of seeing him, when they have the eyes of their soul open. All men, indeed, have eyes, but some have eyes that are troubled and blind, insensible to the light of the sun; but from the fact that there are blind people it does not follow that the light of the sun is not shining. Let the blind acknowledge the facts, and let them open their eyes. Similarly, O man, thou hast eyes which are troubled by thy faults and thy bad actions. One must have a soul which is pure like a well-polished mirror. If there is rust on the mirror, it will not reproduce the image of a man; in the same way, when sin is in man, the sinner is not capable of seeing God."

We recognise here one of the theses familiar to the apologists as also to the martyrs. In 177, the aged bishop of Lyons, St. Pothinus was asked by the proconsul: "What is thy God?" "Thou shalt learn this," he replied, "if thou art worthy of it" (*Hist. Eccles.,* V, i, 31). Again under Commodus, the martyr Apollonius said to the prefect Perennius: "The word of the Lord, O Perennius, is perceived only by the heart which sees, just as light by the eyes which see, and it is in vain that a man speaks to fools, or that light shines for the blind" (*Acts,* ed. Knopf, n. 32).

After a long and involved reasoning, in which there is question not only of God but of the resurrection of the body (viii, xiii), and of the evil doings of the gods of Olympus (ix, x), Theophilus ends his first book by saying that he himself once did not believe, and that he was converted by the reading of the prophets. He exhorts his friend to read them in his turn. The second book is for the most part devoted to the exposition of the teaching of the prophets; in the third, the apologist demonstrates the priority of Holy Scripture over pagan literature.

Theophilus has no sympathy for Hellenism; he condemns it wholly and in all its representatives: Homer, Hesiod, Orpheus, Aratus, Euripides, Sophocles, Menander, Aristophanes, Herodotus, Thucydides, Pythagoras, Diogenes, Epicurus, Empedocles, Socrates and Plato. The death of Socrates, which Justin loved to recall as that of a just man persecuted by the wicked, is judged severely: "Why did he decide to die? What recompense did he hope to receive after death?" (III, ii). In this summary condemnation we recognise the moral preoccupation which is so strong in Theophilus; we recognise its sincerity, but regret its narrowness.[26]

Very much on guard against Hellenism, the bishop of Antioch was in contact with Judaism, and sometimes was subject to the influence of its traditions or its legends.[27] Above all he had for the Old Testament a profound veneration; he wrote against Marcion a treatise which has not come down to us;[28] he thus opened the way to those courageous Eastern

[26] The chronology is very weak, but is presented with great assurance: from the Creation down to the day on which he is writing, 5,698 years have elapsed, plus a few months and days; Theophilus is proud of this reckoning: what historian has gone back so far? (III, xxvi). This demonstration might appeal to minds to whom all Antiquity appeared venerable, and Theophilus himself takes it very seriously. Still less importance will be attached to the etymologies in which he delights: the cry Evan (Evoe) is inspired by Satan, who deceived Eve (II, xxviii); Noe was called Deucalion because he said to men: Come, God calls you (δεῦτε, καλεῖ ὑμᾶς ὁ θεός) (III, xix), etc. We find similar fantasies in the Cratylus, but Plato did it for amusement, whereas Theophilus regarded them as proofs.

[27] Whereas he rejects all Greek philosophy, he regards the Sibyls as prophets (II, ix et seq.). He is probably following some haggada when he writes that shed blood coagulates and cannot penetrate the earth, because the earth has a horror for it since the murder of Cain (II, xxix). Similarly, when he affirms that the priests who resided in the Temple cured leprosy and every illness (II, xxi).

[28] This work is mentioned by Eusebius (Hist. Eccles., IV, xxiv), as well as a work against the heresy of Hermogenes. Loofs (Theophilus v. Antiochien adv. Marcionem, Leipzig, 1930) thinks he has found the substance of the treatise against Marcion in the work of Irenæus, Adversus Hæreses, and he has devoted a mass

bishops who down to the fifth century had to defend their churches against the Marcionite propaganda.

§4. MINUCIUS FELIX [1]

The Octavius

Minucius Felix is doubtless the last in date of the apologists known to us,[2] but he is one of the first in charm of style: Theophilus took us to the Eastern world, to the frontiers of the Hellenic and Syrian churches; the reading of the *Octavius* brings us back to the West, and for the first time, puts us in presence of a Latin text.[3]

This little treatise is written in a very attractive style, and all the humanists admired it. "When we read," says Boissier,[4]

---

of learning and ingenuity in order to prove this thesis. But it cannot be upheld. Cf. *Recherches de Sc. Relig.*, 1931, pp. 596-601. On the theology of Theophilus, cf. *Histoire du Dogme de la Trinité*, Vol. II, pp. 508-13.

[1] The *Octavius*, conserved in a manuscript of the ninth century (*Parisius*, 1661) was edited in the Vienna *Corpus* by Halm in 1867, also with a French translation and commentary, by Waltzing (Louvain, 1903). English translation by Freese, published by S.P.C.K. Cf. Boissier, *La fin du paganisme*, Vol. I, pp. 261-89; Monceaux, *Histoire littéraire de l'Afrique chrétienne*, Vol. I, pp. 463-508; P. de Labriolle, *Histoire de la littérature latine chrétienne*, Vol. II, pp. 147-75.

[2] This date is much discussed; between the *Octavius* and Tertullian's *Apologeticus*, which dates from 197, we find striking resemblances; to explain them, the hypothesis of a common source has been given up, and there remain two rival theses: Tertullian is prior (Boissier, Monceaux, De Labriolle); Minucius is prior (Schanz, Ehrhard, Waltzing, Moricca). Fifteen years ago, Dom de Bruyne wrote (*Revue bénédictine*, October, 1924, p. 136): "This question bids fair to take its place amongst the tedious and insoluble problems raised periodically by some courageous seekers." We shall study the *Octavius* briefly without referring again to this discussion.

[3] Pope Victor is said to be the first Christian writer in Latin, but what he wrote has not come down to us. The *Acts* of the Scillitan martyrs begin Latin Christian literature for us; the first work in Latin is Tertullian's *Apologeticus* or else the *Octavius*, according to the side taken in the debate on the relative priority of these two works.

[4] G. Boissier, *op. cit.*, p. 289.

"this charming work, which goes back to the *Phædrus* by way of the Tusculans, and seems illumined by a ray of light from Greece, we see well that the writer imagined a kind of smiling and sympathetic Christianity which ought to penetrate into Rome without making a noise, and renew it without shock." The Church historian, whose curiosity is more exigent, will find something to regret in this charming work, which is after all only a distant introduction to the faith.

Octavius Januarius, the friend of Minucius, meets him in Rome in September; after long conversations, they profit by the fact that the law courts are closed for the holidays and go to Ostia, taking with them a pagan friend, Cæcilius. Perceiving a statue of Serapis, Cæcilius salutes it according to the custom by throwing a kiss to it. Octavius turns to Minucius and says: "Really it is not good, my dear friend, to give up to the vagaries of common ignorance a man who loves you and never leaves you, and to let him address homage one fine day to stones, especially when you know that you are equally responsible with him for his shameful error." Cæcilius is saddened by this incident, and as soon as they arrive at the end of the mole they sit down and the discussion begins.

Cæcilius, who defends paganism, is a philosopher of the Academy; in human things, everything is doubtful and uncertain; we meet with probabilities rather than with truths; hence it is a strange presumption for the ignorant to pretend to know God; we are wiser, we who, in the midst of such incertitude, believe our ancestors and respect our Roman traditions. Those who reject them are intolerable, and Christians more than all others. And here Cæcilius, in his indignation and contempt, echoes all the calumnies uttered against all Christians.[5]

The Apologetics of Minucius Felix

Octavius answers him by stressing in the first place the contradiction between this sceptical philosophy and this intolerant paganism. There is only one God: the spectacle of the world convinces us of this, and popular belief tends to it spontaneously;[6] the poets and philosophers proclaim it; it is

[5] Cf. *supra*, pp. 233-35.
[6] We find here (xviii) the arguments developed by Tertullian in his little book on the *Testimony of the Soul*.

the belief of Christians. By contrast, how silly are the pagan fables, and how shameful are the pagan mysteries! Your calumnies against Christianity can bring a blush only to those who invent them: amongst us everything is simple and pure:

"Is it necessary to raise statues to God, if man is His image? Why should one build temples to Him, seeing that the universe which He formed with His hands is not able to contain Him? How can one enclose this immensity in a small chapel? It is our souls which must serve as a dwelling place for Him, and He wants us to consecrate our hearts to Him. Of what use is it to offer victims to Him, and would it not be an ingratitude, when He has given us all that is born on earth for our use, to give back to Him the presents He has given us? Let us realise that He requires of us only a pure heart and an upright conscience. To conserve one's innocence is to pray to God, to respect justice is to honour Him. We win His favour by abstaining from all fraud, and when one saves a man from danger, one offers Him the sacrifice He prefers. Those are the victims, and that is the worship we offer to Him. Amongst us, he is the most religious who is the most just." [7]

This brilliant page reveals the attractiveness but also the inadequacy of this *Apology:* if Christianity were only that, it would be only a philosophy. Octavius moreover is aware of this, for he promises to return elsewhere to the discussion which he begins here (ch. xxxvi). The only argument he pursues to the end is the spectacle of Christian virtues, especially in martyrdom:

"What a fine spectacle for God is that of a Christian who fights against pain, who vindicates his liberty in face of kings and princes, yielding only to God to whom he belongs, who surmounts, triumphant and victorious, the magistrate who condemns him. . . . This is because the soldier of God is not abandoned in pain, not destroyed by death. A Christian may seem to be unhappy, but he is not. . . . Do you not realise that no one would wish without reason to expose himself to such torments, and could not

[7] Ch. xxxii, 3.

support them without God? . . . Peaceful, modest, certain of the goodness of our God, we uphold the hope of future happiness by faith in His ever present majesty. Thus we rise again to a happy life, and already here below we live in the contemplation of the future. (We despise the disdain of the philosophers) whom we know to be corrupters, adulterers, tyrants, of an inexhaustible loquaciousness against what are their own vices. But we, who make a show of wisdom not by our mantle but by our soul, the greatness of which is not in speech but in our life, we glory because we have grasped what these men have striven to find with such great efforts and have never succeeded. . . . We wish superstition to be driven back, impiety to be expiated, and the true religion to be respected" (ch. xxxvii-xxxviii).

This discourse made a deep impression on the two friends. Finally Cæcilius broke the silence and declared himself converted; he only asked for a further instruction, which was promised him for the next day.

This brilliant *Apology* is then only an introduction to the faith, and this explains its silences: Minucius wished to reach the educated public, and arouse a sympathetic curiosity in favour of Christianity. At the same time we may wonder whether a less reserved exposition would not have been more effective, and thereby wiser. We may well think so; but having said that, we must allow that the *Octavius* has a great charm and a great strength. We do not find in it the vigour or originality of Tertullian; the borrowed elements are numerous, but they are utilised with a very sure and very personal touch; the introduction itself is not a mere addition, but it aims at showing the readers that Christians can be, like them, cultivated people and of good standing, lawyers who profit by the court vacations in order to discuss amongst themselves the most elevated problems. The discussion confirms the impression of the beginning: in Cæcilius's exposition, so vigorous and sometimes so brutal, the pagans would recognise their own objections, in the very form they gave to them or would wish to give them; the defence of Octavius would appeal to them, there is not one objection made against the Christians which is not turned back against the paganism they knew so well and which they excused by habit or by tradition, but which a moment of reflection would lead them to despise. Philosophy would give way in its turn; some of its most elevated theses confirm the Christian doctrines or at least dispose the mind in favour of them; on the other hand, it will acknowledge its inability to uphold life, and this will be done by those who give the most brilliant exposition of it. In face of it, we have Christianity, which it despises, but the moral beauty of which is so simple, so sincere, and so widespread, and which surpasses it in every way. With this description the *Octavius* finishes; it can be understood that its attraction was very great indeed.

Christian Apologetics in the Second Century

If we consider it as a whole, the apologetics of the second century makes known to us in the first place the opposition which Christianity encountered, and which the apologists endeavoured to lessen. At first it was the pagan cults the Apostles found opposing them, as was the case with St. Paul at Athens; their aim was then to combat polytheism and idolatry, and to establish the belief in one only God, in order to pass on to the mission of Christ. Very soon other opponents came on the scene and occupied the first place; these were the philosophers, who gave to Hellenism its consistence; the pagan cults and their mysteries sufficed to deceive and to lull religious needs, but they could not justify themselves before the intellect unless they were transformed and spiritualised by philosophy; the philosophers moreover were not content merely to defend paganism, they attacked the new religion. More and more the combat was taken up by two teams of thinkers, those of the Church, and those of Philosophy.

The issue of this combat could not be doubted; from the time we are considering, it was plain: Hellenism could maintain its empire over men's souls only by deliberate combinations and compromises: philosophy of itself resulted only in a barren speculation and one which was generally uncertain; it had to rest on the pagan cults in order to obtain the force or at least the illusion of a religious energy, but in order to derive from these cults some semblance of life, it had to purify them, elevate them, and transform them; in spite of all these endeavours, it could not give them an objective truth which their whole contents excluded.

Christianity, on the contrary, was everything combined: a belief, a cult, and a moral code; all was in one system, with the same solidity throughout: all that philosophy had anticipated was consecrated by a divine revelation, and this natural theology was continued in mysteries which illumined the present life and prepared for the one to come. All this gave to the apologists a tone of certitude which was calm, sincere and deep, a tone philosophy could not imitate, and which was irresistible; to this must be added the spectacle of the fruits which this religion produced, in its martyrs first of all, and also in the whole mass of its followers, even the most humble; here above all Christianity displayed an evident and decisive superiority over Hellenism.

Such was truly the essence of the debate, and on these questions the affirmations of the apologists of the second century had a lasting value. Besides that, many secondary questions, raised in the course of the discussion, received solutions which were not always the best: Christianity, necessary to mankind, appeared very late; why was this? To this puzzling question the *Letter to Diognetus* replied by affirming the providential plan which will draw salvation from general misery; St. Justin showed the action of the seminal Word which reveals at least some of the indispensable religious truths; Tertullian spoke of the naturally Christian soul; Justin, Tatian and others added that the philosophers have copied from the Bible. Is Christianity a unique revelation, or was it prepared for by a revelation given to all men, or at least to the Jews? This question is closely linked with the preceding one; it was answered only incompletely. The Jewish revelation was imperfectly understood; prophecy was well brought out into the light, but we do not yet find in the apologists the idea of the progressive education of mankind which St. Irenæus will set forth in a masterly way. Whence comes the transcendence of Christian doctrine? Justin saw plainly and said with truth that its source is the divine revelation. There is more incertitude in the exposition of this revealed teaching; the apparent similarities between this theology and the Platonist or Stoic philosophy sometimes hide from the apologists the fundamental opposition between these two systems; hence the dangerous inexactitudes we have pointed out. We must note, moreover, that the apologists undertook their task of their own initiative; the Church was pleased with their zeal, but it did not wish to cover with its authority their sometimes too tolerant philosophy. Very soon, moreover, towards the end of this second century, the struggle against the heretics will force the Church to give to the rule of faith more rigour, to the liturgy more unity, and to the ecclesiastical government a more effective power.

APPENDIX

Chronological Table of Popes and Emperors

Emperors		*Popes*	
Augustus ...... died in	14		
Tiberius	14- 37		
Caligula	37- 41		
Claudius	41- 54	St. Peter	30?-64
Nero	54- 68	St. Linus	64?-76?[1]
Galba, Otho, Vitellius .	68- 69	St. Anacletus ..	76?-88?[1]
Vespasian	69- 79	St. Clement	88?-about 100
Titus	79- 81	St. Evaristus ...	?-?
Domitian	81- 96	St. Alexander ..	?-?
Nerva	96- 98	St. Sixtus	?-?
Trajan	98-117	St. Telesphorus .	?-about 136
		St. Hyginus about 136-about 140	
Hadrian	117-138	St. Pius .. about 140-before 154	
Antoninus the Pious ..	138-161	St. Anicetus from 154-?	
		St. Soter . before 175-175	
Marcus Aurelius	161-180	St. Eleutherus .. 175-189	
Commodus	180-192		
Septimius Severus	193-211	Victor	189-199
Caracalla	211-217	Zephyrinus	199-217
Macrinus	217-218	Callistus	217-222
Elagabalus	218-222		
Alexander Severus	222-235	Urban	222-230
		Pontian	230-235
Maximin the Thracian .	235-238	Anteros	235-236
Pupienus and the		Fabian	236-250
Gordians	238-244		
Philip the Arabian	244-249		
Decius	249-251		
Gallus and Volusianus .	251-253	Cornelius	251-253
Valerian	253-260		
		Lucius	253-254
Gallienus	260-268	Stephen	254-257
Claudius the Goth	268-270	Sixtus II	257-258
Aurelian	270-275	Dionysius	259-268
Tacitus	275-276	Felix	270-275
Probus	276-282		
Carus	282-284	Eutychianus	275-283
Diocletian	284-305		
(with Maximian		Gaius	283-296
Hercules from 285)		Marcellinus	296-304

Constantius Chlorus ..	305-306		
Galerius	305-311	Marcellus	308-309
Constantine	306-	Eusebius	309-
Maximin Daia and			
Licinius	308-	Miltiades	311-

[1] The dates of Linus and Anacletus are unknown. We might attribute to each the twelve years given to them in the tradition enshrined in the *Liber Pontificalis*. Cf. p. 180, *The Post-Apostolic Era to the End of the Second Century*, Book II of *A History of the Early Church*.

General Bibliography

WE HERE indicate a certain number of sources which will be constantly utilised, or collections of ancient texts which should be known.

The first name to be mentioned is that of *Eusebius,* Bishop of Cæsarea in Palestine at the beginning of the fourth century, and author of an *Ecclesiastical History* in ten books, from the beginnings of the Church to 324, and also of a *Chronicle.* St. Jerome translated the second book of the latter work, revised it, and continued it until the year 378. The best edition of the Greek text of the *Ecclesiastical History* is that of E. Schwartz in the Berlin *Corpus: Eusebius Werke,* II *Kirchengeschichte,* Leipzig, 1903, 1908, 1909, 3 vols.

The *Chronicle* is likewise edited in the Berlin *Corpus,* by R. Helm (*Eusebius Werke,* VII: *Die Chronik des Hieronymus,* Leipzig, 1913, 1926, 2 vols.) and by J. Karst (*Eusebius Werke,* V: *Die Chronik des Eusebius aus dem armenischen übersetzt,* Leipzig, 1911).

The *Ecclesiastical History* was translated into Latin by Rufinus, who added two books to it. (Edited by Schwartz and T. Mommsen, 2 vols., in Berlin *Corpus,* Leipzig, 1909. An English translation by Kirsopp Lake and J. Oulton is included in Loeb's Classical Library.)

A Latin historian, the Gallo-Roman Sulpicius Severus, wrote two books of *Chronicles* embracing universal history as far as he knew it, from the creation to the end of the fourth century (edited by Halm in Vienna (*Corpus scriptorum ecclesiasticorum latinorum,* 1866). Another Latin writer, the Spanish priest Paul Orosius, a disciple of St. Augustine, also wrote a universal history which, like that of Sulpicius Severus, was independent of that of Eusebius of Cæsarea: *Adversus paganos historiarum libri VII.* This stopped at the year 416 (edited by Langemeister in Vienna *Corpus,* 1882).

The *Liber Pontificalis* is a chronicle of the Popes begun by an unknown author of the sixth century, and of very unequal value. The best edition is that of Duchesne, Paris, 1886-1892, 2 vols.

In order not to make this bibliography too long, we confine ourselves here to historians properly so called. A list of other Christian writers in Latin and Greek in the first three centuries, who will be referred to on several occasions in the notes to this work, will be found in O. Bardenhewer's *Patrologie,* 3rd edn., Freiburg in Bresgau, 1910 (English translation by Shahan, Herder, 1908), and *Geschichte der altkirchlichen Literatur,* 5 vols., 2nd edn., Freiburg in Bresgau, 1913-1924, with supplement to vol. III, 1923. Their works will be found in Migne's *Patrologia Græca* and *Patrologia*

Latina, and also a great number of them in the two new collections in course of publication, the Berlin *Corpus* for Greek writers (*Die griechischen christlichen Schriftsteller der ersten Jahrhunderte*) and the Vienna *Corpus* for the Latins (*Corpus scriptorum ecclesiasticorum latinorum*).

Christian inscriptions must be looked for in the *Corpus inscriptionum græcarum* and the *Corpus inscriptionum latinarum,* both published by the Berlin Academy, the former from 1856 to 1877, the latter from 1863 and still in course of publication. The Christian inscriptions in Rome have been published by J. B. de Rossi, *Inscriptiones christianæ Urbis Romæ,* I, Rome, 1857-1861; II, Rome, 1888. A third volume with the title *Nova series I* was published by A. Silvagni, Rome, 1922.

On Christian writers in Greek, one should consult A. Puech, *Histoire de la littérature grecque chrétienne depuis les origines jusqu' à la fin du IVe siècle,* Paris, 1928-1930, 3 vols., and on those of Latin language, P. de Labriolle, *Histoire de la littérature latine chrétienne,* 2nd edn., Paris, 1924. See also: P. Batiffol, *Anciennes littératures chrétiennes: I. La littérature grecque,* 2nd edn., Paris, 1898; H. R. Duval, *La littérature syriaque,* Paris, 1899; M. Moricca, *Storia della Letteratura latina cristiana,* Turin, I, 1925; II, 1st part 1928, III, 1st part, 1932.

The *Acts of the Martyrs* are catalogued in the *Bibliotheca hagiographica orientalis,* edited by the Bollandists, Brussels, 1909, the *Bibliotheca hagiographica græca,* edited by the same, Brussels, 1909, and the *Bibliotheca hagiographica latina,* edited by the same, Brussels, 1898-1911, and utilised, with critique and commentaries, in the *Acta Sanctorum,* published likewise by the Bollandists, Antwerp, 1643-Brussels, 1931 (date of the first volume, the work is still in course of publication). The second volume of the month of November of the *Acta Sanctorum,* Brussels, 1894, concludes the systematic edition of J. B. de Rossi and L. Duchesne, of the *Martyrologium Hieronymianum,* the most important martyrological document of antiquity; critical re-edition by Père H. Delehaye and Dom H. Quentin, under the title *Acta Sanctorum novembris tomi II pars posterior qua continetur H. Delehaye commentarius perpetuus in Martyrologium Hieronymianum ad recensionem H. Quentin,* Brussels, 1931.

One of the best known collections of the *Acts of the Martyrs* was made in the seventeenth century by Dom Ruinart: *Acta primorum martyrum sincera,* Paris, 1889. Others are mentioned in the bibliography to Chapter IX.

Numerous texts of Eastern writers are published in the *Patrologia orientalis,* edited by R. Graffin and F. Nau, in course of publication, Paris, 1908—, and in the *Corpus scriptorum christianorum orientalium* of J. B. Chabot, I. Guidi, H. Hyvernat, B. Carra de Vaux, also in course of publication, Paris, 1903.

The *Acts of the Councils* are gathered together in the great collections by Labbe and Cossart (ed. Coleti, Venice, 1728), Mansi

(Conciliorum amplissima collectio, 31 vols. Florence and Venice, 1759—), and general councils only, in E. Schwartz, *Acta Conciliorum œcumenicorum,* in course of publication, Strasburg, Berlin and Leipzig, 1914—. The history of councils has been written by Hefelè, translated and completed and corrected by Dom H. Leclercq: J. Hefelè, *Histoire des Conciles,* in course of publication, Paris, 1907—.

The great juridical collections constitute complementary sources for early ecclesiastical history. *Codex Theodosianus,* ed. J. Godefroy, with commentaries, 6 vols. in 4, Lyons, 1665, republished by J. D. Bitter, 6 vols., Leipzig, 1739-1743; ed. T. Mommsen and P. Meyer, *Theodosiani libri XVI,* Berlin, 1903, and *Corpus Juris civils,* I. *Institutiones et Digesta,* ed. P. Krüger and T. Mommsen, Berlin, 1889; II. *Codex Justinianus,* ed. P. Krüger, Berlin, 1888; III, *Novellæ,* ed. K. Schoell and G. Kroll, Berlin, 1895.

Now we come to a number of general works on the early history of the Church. We must mention in the first place a great monument of erudition, somewhat out of date, especially in the last chapters, but still of the greatest value on the whole because of its fullness, the richness of its documentation, and the soundness of its criticisms: the sixteen volumes of the *Mémoires pour servir à l'histoire ecclésiastique des six premiers siècles,* by the learned and upright Lenain de Tillemont, Paris, 1693-1712.

We must also mention his *Histoire des Empereurs,* Vol. I, 2nd edn., revised by the author, Paris, 1700, Vol. II, Paris, 1691-1738, which contains some valuable material for the early history of the Church.

Here are other works:

Achelis, H. *Das Christentum in den ersten drei Jahrhunderten,* 2 vols. Leipzig, 1912; 2nd edn. of 1st vol., Leipzig, 1924.

Allard. P. *Histoire des persécutions pendant les deux premiers siècles,* 3rd edn., 2 vols. Paris, 1903, 1905.

—*Les persécutions du IIIe siècle,* 2nd edn., Paris, 1898.

—*La persécution de Dioclétien,* 2nd edn., 2 vols., Paris, 1903.

—*Le christianisme et l'Empire romain,* 6th edn., Paris, 1903.

Aube, B. *Histoire des persécutions de l'Eglise,* 2nd edn., 4 vols. Paris, 1875-1886.

Batiffol, P. *Le catholicisme des origines à saint Léon,* I. *L'église naissante et le catholicisme,* 12th edn. Paris, 1927.

Bihlmeyer, K. *Kirchengeschichte, auf Grund des Lehrbuches von F. X. Funk, I: Das christliche Altertum,* 9th edn. Paderborn, 1931. French translation, or rather an adaptation of the 1st edn. of Funk was published by the Abbé H. Hemmer, 2 vols., Paris, 3rd edn., 1891.

Boulanger, A. *Histoire générale de l'Eglise,* I: *L'antiquité chrétienne,* Vol. I: *Les temps apostoliques,* Paris, 1931; Vol. II: *Le temps des persécutions,* Paris, 1931.

Duchesne, L. *Histoire ancienne de l'Eglise,* 3 vols., Paris, 1906, 1907, 1910, English translation: *Early History of the Christian Church,* 1900—.

—*Les origines du culte chrétien,* 5th edn., Paris, 1920. English translation: *Christian Worship,* 5th edn., 1919.

Dufourcq, A. *Histoire ancienne de l'Eglise:*
  I. *Les religions païennes et la religion juive comparée,* 6th edn. Paris, 1924.
  II. *La révolution religieuse, Jésus,* 6th edn. Paris, 1927.
  III. *Le christianisme primitif. Saint Paul, Saint Jean, Saint Irénée,* 6th edn. Paris, 1929.
  IV. *Le christianisme et l'Empire romain,* Paris, 1930.

Ehrhard, A. *Die Kirche der Märtyrer,* Munich, 1932.

Gwatkin, H. M. *Early Church History to A.D. 313,* 2 vols., London, 1909.

Harnack, A. *Geschichte der altchristlichen Literatur:*
  I. *Die Ueberlieferung und der Bestand,* Leipzig, 1893.
  II. *Die Chronologie,* Leipzig, 1897-1904, 2 vols.

—*Die Mission und Ausbreitung des Christentums,* 4th edn., Leipzig, 1924, 2 vols. English translation: *Expansion of Christianity in the first three centuries,* 2 vols., 1904-1905.

Jacquin, A. M. *Histoire de l'Eglise,* I: *L'Antiquité chrétienne,* Paris, 1929.

Kidd, A. *History of the Church to A.D. 461,* Oxford, 1922, 3 vols.

Kirsch, J. P. *Kirchengeschichte,* I: *Kirchengeschichte in der antiken griechisch-römischen Kulturwelt,* Freiburg in Bresgau, 1930.

Krüger, G. *Handbuch der Kirchengeschichte,* I: *Das Altertum,* Tübingen, 1923.

Lietzmann, H. *Geschichte der alten Kirche,* I: *Die Anfänge,* Berlin and Leipzig, 1932.

Mourret, F. *Histoire de l'Eglise,* new edn., Paris, 1921, 9 vols.

Müller, K. *Kirchengeschichte, I Band,* i *Lieferung* 1924, ii *Lieferung* 1927, iii *Lieferung* 1929, Tübingen.

Poulet, C. *Histoire de Christianisme,* fasc. I-VI, Paris, 1932-1934.

Renan, E. *Histoire des origines du christianisme* (Paris, 1861—), 8 vols.

Rosenstock, E. and Wittig, J. *Das Alter der Kirche,* Berlin, 1908, 3 vols.

Zeiller, J. *L'Empire romain et l'Eglise,* Vol. VI of the *Histoire du monde,* published under the direction of E. Cavaignac, Paris, 1928.

We must add to this list the *Dictionnaire d'Archéologie chrétienne et de Liturgie,* by Dom F. Cabrol and Dom H. Leclercq (Dom Cabrol alone for the four first volumes), in course of publication, Paris, 1907—; the *Dictionnaire d'Histoire et de Géographie ecclésiastiques,* published under the direction of A. Baudrillart, A. Vogt and M. Rouzies, continued by A. de Meyer and E. van Cauwenbergh, in course of publication, Paris, 1912—; the *Dictionnaire de théologie catholique,* begun under the direction of

A. Vacant and continued under that of E. Mangenot and E. Amann, in course of publication, Paris, 1909—; the *Dictionnaire apologétique de la foi catholique,* 4th edn., under the direction of A. d'Alès, 4 vols. and Tables, Paris, 1911-1931; the *Lexicon für Theologie und Kirche* under the direction of Buchberger, in course of publication, Freiburg in Bresgau, 1930—; the *Realencyclopädie für protestantische Theologie und Kirche,* 3rd edn., under the direction of A. Hauck, 24 vols., Leipzig, 1896-1913; *Die Religion in Geschichte und Gegenwart,* 2nd edn. by H. Gunkel and L. Zscharnack, 5 vols., Tübingen, 1927-1932; *Encyclopædia of Religion and Ethics,* under the direction of J. Hastings, 13 vols., Edinburgh, 1908-1926.

On the history of dogma, see: J. Tixeront, *Histoire des dogmes,* I, *La théologie antenicéenne,* 11th edn., Paris, 1930; II, *De saint Athanase à saint Augustin,* 9th edn., Paris, 1931; III, *La fin de l'âge patristique,* 8th edn., Paris, 1928; Harnack, A., *Lehrbuch der Dogmengeschichte,* I. *Entstehung des kirchlichen Dogmas,* 4th edn., Tübingen, 1909; English translation: *History of Dogma,* 1894—. Loofs, F. *Leitfaden zum Studium der Dogmengeschichte,* 4th edn., Halle, 1906.

Index